THE NEW
THREAT

Al-Qaeda:
The True Story of Radical Islam

On the Road to Kandahar:
Travels through Conflict in the Islamic World

The 9/11 Wars

THE NEW THREAT

FROM ISLAMIC MILITANCY

JASON BURKE

THE BODLEY HEAD
LONDON

Published by The Bodley Head 2015

2 4 6 8 10 9 7 5 3 1

First published in Great Britain in 2015 by
The Bodley Head
20 Vauxhall Bridge Road,
London SW1V 2SA

A Penguin Random House company

www.penguinrandomhouse.com
www.vintage-books.co.uk

A CIP catalogue record for this book is available from the British Library

ISBN 9781847923479 (Hardback)
ISBN 9781847923486 (Trade Paperback)

Printed and bound in Great Britain by Clays Ltd, St Ives plc
Typeset in Dante MT Std by Palimpsest Book Production Limited, Falkirk, Stirlingshire

Penguin Random House is committed to a sustainable future
for our business, our readers and our planet. This book is made
from Forest Stewardship Council® certified paper.

For Clara,
and her great-grandmothers

CONTENTS

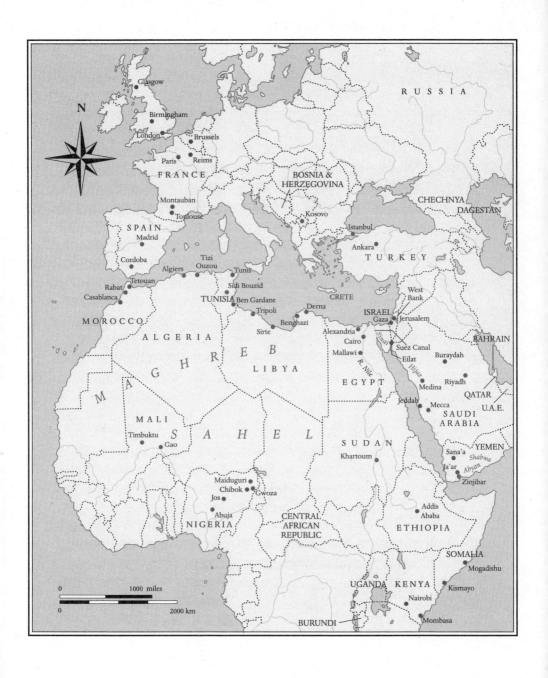

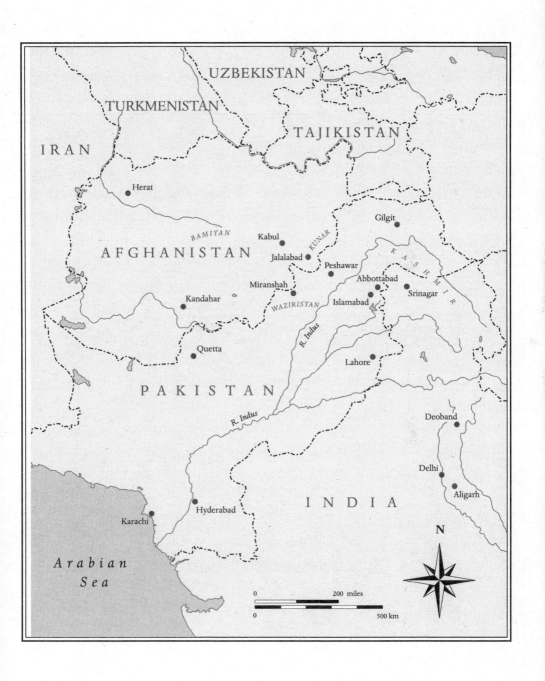

ACKNOWLEDGEMENTS

This book would not exist without the inspiration and enthusiasm of my agent Toby Eady or the commitment, hard work and skill of my editor Will Hammond at Bodley Head. It is, in a very real sense, theirs as much as mine. My thanks to them both.

I am grateful too to all those involved in the scramble to turn a rough manuscript into a handsome book in such record time, to all those involved in its marketing, and to Dan Kirmatzis particularly for his last-minute fact checking. All errors, of course, remain my own.

There are many, many people around the world who have translated for me, passed on contacts, shared their knowledge, made suggestions, kept me safe, told me when to duck, set up meetings, driven me, tolerated my driving, trusted me with their confidential views, or otherwise helped in two decades or so of journalism. I owe them an enormous amount, as I do the many editors at the *Guardian* and the *Observer* who have sent me off to listen, learn, see and write.

Victor and Clara will one day, I hope, understand why I had to forego drawing, hide and seek, cake baking, bike riding, tree climbing, swimming, and even football practice for month after month, and also how their laughter, enthusiasm, curiosity and mischief kept me going.

Above all, nothing would have been possible, or would be possible, without the love, support and encouragement of Anne Sophie.

INTRODUCTION

No one was quite sure who was in charge of Mosul in the early summer of 2014. During the day, government security forces maintained a tenuous hold, but at nightfall they ceded the streets, squares and battered neighbourhoods of Iraq's second city to others.

Mosul, the capital of Nineveh province, had long been a trouble spot, even as far back as the immediate aftermath of the US-led invasion of Iraq in 2003. As a bastion of Iraq's Sunni Muslim minority, it maintained a tradition of support for Saddam Hussein's Sunni-dominated regime. The deposed dictator's two sons had taken refuge there, and Sunni militants had briefly seized control of it in 2004. The presence of many tightly knit military families and a long history of exposure to extremist religious ideologies combined with ethnic tensions and a complex tribal tapestry made the city of one million inhabitants a problem.

So when on the morning of 8 June Atheel Nujaifi, the governor of Nineveh, had a meeting with US officials, it took place in Erbil, a city dominated by Iraq's Kurdish minority sixty miles away. Mosul was deemed much too dangerous for Americans to visit. Indeed, it was increasingly dangerous even for the governor.

Nujaifi, appointed five years earlier, had alarming news.[1] Over the previous three days hundreds of armed pickup trucks carrying Islamic extremist fighters had crossed the nearby border from Syria, which had been embroiled for more than three years in a brutal civil war. Having driven through the lawless tracts of scrubby desert to the west of Mosul, this sizeable force of Sunni militants was now assembled on the outskirts of the city. The Iraqi Army, controlled directly by Prime Minister Nouri al-Maliki and almost exclusively Shia, had agreed to provide assistance, but no one in Baghdad, the Iraqi capital 270 miles to the south, seemed to appreciate the urgency of the situation and reinforcements might not arrive for a week.

As the Americans scrambled to assemble some kind of response, it became clear that events had overtaken them. Extremists had begun moving into Mosul more than forty-eight hours before.[2] There had been no mass assault and only a few hundred fighters were engaged at any one time but clashes had taken place across much of the sprawling city.[3] A massacre of policemen had prompted mass desertions, and a bid by government forces to clear outlying suburbs had failed. Tribal militias and local groups once loyal to Saddam had also joined the fighting, and a series of carefully targeted raids on jails freed hundreds who immediately swelled the militants' ranks. In Baghdad, though, senior government officials had rejected an offer from Kurdish leaders to send their own forces into the city and reassured the US officials that Mosul was not under serious threat.

The full weight of the militant offensive came to bear, however, three days after the initial assault began. The few hundred fighters who had first infiltrated the city had by now become a force of between 1,500 and 2,000 as sympathisers rallied to their black flags in increasing numbers. A massive car bomb broke resistance at a crucial defensive position around an old hotel, almost entirely eliminating any organised resistance to the militants in the parts of Mosul west of the river Tigris. On 9 June, Nujaifi made a televised appeal to the people of the city, calling on them to form self-defence groups, stand their ground and fight. Hours later he fled, narrowly escaping from the provincial headquarters as police held off hundreds of militants armed with rocket-propelled grenades, sniper rifles and heavy-vehicle-mounted machine guns. Most of the senior military commanders had already deserted, and the two divisions of underequipped, undertrained Iraqi troops supposedly defending the city, totalling around 15,000 men on paper but perhaps only a half or a third of that in reality, disintegrated.

A small group of militants had routed a force of regular soldiers that was between three and ten times more numerous, itself part of an army of 350,000 on which somewhere between $24 billion and $41.6 billion, mainly US aid, had been spent over the previous three years.[4] In scenes reminiscent of the US-led invasion of 2003, thousands of army soldiers dumped their weapons, stripped off their uniforms and ran. Several hundred were captured, and some were made to lie down in hastily dug trenches on the outskirts of the city and were shot. Soon Mosul's airport, its military airfield, banks, TV station, a major army base equipped with enormous quantities of weapons, munitions and US-supplied equipment were all in militant hands. By the afternoon, the battle for the city was over.

'We can't beat them,' one Iraqi Army officer said as he fled. 'They're like ghosts: they appear, strike and disappear in seconds.'[5]

There was worse to come. After securing Mosul, the militants pushed on south, through the dry farmland either side of Highway One, seizing the oil refineries at Baiji and Tikrit, the home town of the late Saddam Hussein, on 11 June. They had moved so fast that government forces had no time to flee. At Camp Speicher, a former US base on the outskirts of Tikrit, over a thousand men, mostly soldiers and air force cadets, surrendered without a fight after being promised safe passage. Mobile phone footage shows a column of hundreds being marched out of the city. Others were forced into trucks and driven to the banks of the Tigris. There, at least 150 were executed. First they were forced into lines, blindfolded and wrists bound, each man taking the shirt of the man in front between his teeth. Then, in threes, they were forced to kneel. Further footage, filmed by the militants themselves, shows men killing with appalling nonchalance, one holding an assault rifle to victims' heads one-handed before squeezing the trigger, walking slowly from one to the next, another shooting a succession of men in the head with a handgun, sending their bodies toppling into the river in a scene reminiscent of an abattoir. The executions continued for three days. Between five hundred and eight hundred deaths were confirmed by human rights organisations, with the overall toll reaching possibly twice that figure. Designed to terrorise local opponents and the international community, the killings, like the decapitation of Western hostages a few weeks later, sent a very simple message: We are not like any other group before. We will do what no others have been prepared to do. We will go further than all others have gone. Fear us. Respect us. We are al-Dawlah al-Islamiyah fil 'Iraq wa al-Sham, the Islamic State in Iraq and Syria.[6]

The four-day campaign in June 2014 was unprecedented in the annals of violent Islamic extremism. Militants had seized cities before. Some, such as the Taliban in Afghanistan and al-Shabaab in Somalia, had even managed to bring significant swathes of territory under their control. But none had taken on a state's army in this way, nor acted with such speed or astonishing efficacy. Hasty appraisals of the attack on Mosul as 'opportunistic' were rapidly revised as intelligence analysts and experts recognised a reality that had escaped them over previous months: that the campaign had been meticulously prepared over two years or more. First, raids had been mounted to break militant leaders out of prisons, simultaneously undermining faith in the ability of local authorities to keep order. These culminated in an assault which freed several hundred veteran militants from the notorious Abu Ghraib prison on the outskirts of Baghdad. Then carefully targeted violence, ranging from mass-casualty suicide bombing to individual assassin-ation, was combined with widespread use of social media in a bid to degrade the morale of government forces. Senior government officials in Mosul itself were assassinated or forced into exile, allowing the militants to establish a shadow administration in the city and its surroundings. An offensive was launched to secure rear areas in Syria, give new fighters combat experience and to hone tactics. Raids were stepped up on the outskirts of the city to degrade any remaining defences. Finally, a combination of military operations at a tactical level and strategic alliances with local communities or other insurgent groups prepared the ground for the actual assault. If their initial successes took the attackers by surprise, they were ready and able to exploit them ruthlessly.

The militants pushed some way beyond Tikrit but by midsummer a front had stabilised, broadly along the divide between majority Sunni and majority Shia zones in Iraq. The Islamic State in Iraq and Syria now controlled a major city, two or three smaller ones, dozens of towns, oilfields, banks, courts and stocks of conventional weaponry including tanks and artillery, all in the heart of one of the most stra-tegically important bits of real estate on the planet. Around seven million people spread over an area the size of England stretching across eastern Syria and north-western Iraq lay under their putative authority.[7] Carefully produced propaganda videos portrayed a proto-state of an extent, apparent organisation and, above all, audacity not seen for generations. Shortly after taking control of Mosul, the leader of the militants, Ibrahim Awwad al-Badri al-Hussein al-Samarrai, better known by his nom de guerre of Abu Bakr al-Baghdadi, declared the foundation of an entirely new entity: al-Dawla al-Islamiya, the Islamic State.

He then went even further, announcing in an audio recording, released in five languages, that he had assumed the role of caliph, leader of the world's 1.6 billion Muslims, with Mosul as the re-established caliphate's seat. There had been no caliph since 1924 when the institution had been abolished in the wake of the collapse of the Ottoman Empire. This was a stunning statement of ambition and intent, an apparently concrete step to realising the ultimate dream of three generations of Islamic extremists. And, for its supporters, it was a prelude to a new golden age that would unite the world's Muslims under a single authority and restore the community to the position of dominance it had lost over the previous five centuries. To make sure the message was fully understood, IS uploaded a video entitled 'Breaking the Borders' which showed a bulldozer breaching the sand barrier demarcating the Syria–Iraq border, drawn by former colonial powers in 1916. The dominance of the West had been broken, the images announced. The Islamic State's motto was 'baqiyah wa-tatam-madad', meaning remain and expand. As summer turned to autumn, there was little to indicate it would not do both.

The seizure of Mosul, the second largest city in Iraq, in June 2014 by the Islamic State was the most significant single event involving Muslim militants anywhere in the world since the attacks on New York and Washington thirteen years before. The strikes of 9/11 brought a new type of terrorism to the world's attention, one that had in fact been emerging, largely unremarked outside of specialist circles, during the 1990s. The fall of Mosul revealed that an equally dramatic transformation of Islamic extremism had been taking place since 2001. The Islamic State's success, broadcast by social and mainstream media, galvanised aspirant extremists in a way not seen since the immediate aftermath of the US-led invasion of Iraq in 2003, or even the Soviet invasion of Afghanistan in 1979. It prompted thousands of young men and women from around the Islamic world and the West to leave their homes and travel to Syria. Leaders from Algeria to Pakistan pledged allegiance to the Islamic State, declaring pockets of territory 'liberated land'.

Simultaneously, other groups, including al-Qaeda, appeared to be intensifying their activities. In one month alone, November 2014, around 5,000 people died in violence linked to Islamic militants world-wide.[8] In December, a group killed 132 children aged between eight and eighteen in an attack on a military school in Pakistan. A month later in Paris, three gunmen shot dead seventeen people, including eight members of the editorial staff of a satirical magazine that had printed cartoons of the Prophet Mohammed. The killers claimed allegiance to an al-Qaeda affiliate in Yemen and the Islamic State. That same week several hundred died in a raid on a village in north-eastern Nigeria by the movement known as Boko Haram, a name which roughly translates as 'No to Western Education'.

Every incident underlined that, despite the death of Osama bin Laden, despite huge expenditure of blood and treasure, and despite new laws and enhanced powers for security services, Islamic militancy has not been beaten. Instead, a threat faced by the West for more than twenty years has entered an alarming new phase. If anything it appears more frightening than ever. Why? Why does Islamic extremism not only endure but seem to be spreading? Why does its violence and utopian message appeal to so many? How real is the danger it poses? Why is the phenomenon so extraordinarily resilient? How will it evolve in the decades to come?

This book suggests some answers to these questions. It describes the nature of Islamic militancy today and the threat it poses now and is likely to pose in the future. Its scope is broad, in the belief that it is impossible to counter a threat without fully understanding its history and the environment that produced it. This means that in the pages that follow I try to explain the long-term roots of Islamic militancy in the Muslim world and, crucially, the Muslim world's sometimes troubled relationship with the West. I will also attempt to describe the situation on the ground – the lived reality of violence – for communities and nations worldwide, for extremists and those who resist them. In doing so, I hope to reveal the economic, social, cultural and political factors that can feed, or indeed starve, extremism.

I first travelled to the Middle East in 1991 while still at university, for an ill-advised if adventurous spell alongside the Kurdish peshmerga fighters who had just begun to carve out their autonomous enclave in the north of Iraq under the protection of Western air power. My weeks among these extraordinary men at such a momentous time was the beginning of a deep fascination. It led to a journey which has taken me through the offices of Taliban administrators, the homes of the bereaved families of suicide bombers in Gaza, Kashmir and Afghanistan, through interviews with militants in cells and in training camps, in cafes on sunlit squares and grubby safe houses down dark alleys, conversations with spies of varying seniority and reliability, and discussions with ideologues of many extremist organisations, some violent, some less so. It has taken me through the heart of several major conflicts and many minor ones. In writing this book, I have drawn on the experience, personal and professional, of reporting on Islamic militancy over a twenty-year period, during which I have lived in or visited almost every country affected by the phenomenon, from Morocco's Atlantic seaboard to Indonesia's islands, from the East End of London to China's western provinces.

This work focuses on those organisations and processes which pose the greatest threat to London, New York and Paris today – this is what concerns most readers, understandably – but one of its recurring themes is how impossible it is to distinguish between Islamic militancy that affects us domestically and the phenomenon as it manifests itself worldwide. We should be aware, though, that the number of those in the West who have died in international acts of terrorism, including the nearly 3,000 killed in the 9/11 attacks, is only a fraction of the total of those who have died in the Islamic world from violence related to extremism. From 2001 to 2011 around 250,000 people were killed in what, in my last book, I called the '9/11 wars', that series of interlinked conflicts exacerbated, catalysed or provoked by the strikes on New York and Washington.[9] Though the vast majority of casualties were Muslims, all faith communities suffered. Few in Europe or the US are aware of the second most murderous terrorist attack in the last several decades: multiple suicide bombings directed by a previous incarnation of the Islamic State against the Yazidi minority in northern Iraq in 2007, which killed more than eight hundred and injured twice as many.[10]

From 2011 to 2015, the total was even greater. A study released in May 2015 by the London-based International Institute for Strategic Studies estimated that while fifty-five armed conflicts had led to 49,000 fatalities across the world in 2010, 180,000 people had died in forty-two conflicts in 2014. The vast proportion of the deaths were in conflicts involving Islamic extremists though not all, clearly, were killed by the militants themselves. Only a tiny fraction of the total casualties were in developed countries. James Clapper, US director of National Intelligence, said, with 13,000 attacks killing more than 30,000 people, 2014 was likely to be 'the most lethal year for global terrorism' in the forty-five years the statistics have been kept.[11]

Yet, investigating the specific danger to the West, however parochial or self-centred that may seem, is still important, not least because the reaction of the West in terms of policy and intervention in the Islamic world is so crucial to the evolution of Islamic militancy. In the aftermath of the 9/11 attacks, a series of misconceptions about those responsible – bin Laden and al-Qaeda – became widely accepted. Some focused on the person of bin Laden himself – his wealth, health, history. Others contributed to a warped understanding of the organisation that he led. Al-Qaeda, until then a relatively marginal group with no real support base and only a few hundred members, was portrayed as a sprawling global terrorist organisation, with obedient 'operatives' and 'sleeper cells' on every continent, and an ability to mobilise, radicalise and attack far beyond its real capacities. Historic incidents with no connection to the group or its leader were suddenly recast as 'al-Qaeda operations'. Any incident anywhere in the world could become an al-Qaeda attack. The threat posed by the group was described in apocalyptic terms. Its ideological motivations were systematically ignored while the individual agency of its leaders was emphasised. If they were killed, the logic went, the problem would disappear. Al-Qaeda's links with other terrorist or extremist organisations were distorted, often by political leaders who hoped for domestic gain and international support. So too were supposed links – all imaginary – to the governments of several states. One result was the 'global war on terror', a monumentally misconceived strategy which is in part to blame for the spread of radical Islamic militancy over the last decade.

Despite the lessons learned over the years, and the very different approach of political leaders in the US and Europe, there is a new danger that at least some of those mistakes will be repeated.[12] The emergence of the Islamic State (IS) prompted popular reactions that resemble those in the aftermath of the 9/11 attacks, and which, despite the generally sensible analysis of the administration of Barack Obama, risk influencing policy. 'They will open the gates of hell to spill out on the world,' said one right-wing US politician of IS after the fall of Mosul.[13] The atmosphere in Europe following the attacks in Paris of January 2015 also recalled that of a decade earlier, with the same hysterical claims of 'no-go zones' in European cities where Islamic law had supposedly been imposed.[14] IS, despite no real evidence, was linked to plans to acquire weapons of mass destruction as well as, ludicrously, to send Ebola-infected 'operatives' against its enemies. Media in the US reported a network of IS 'sleeper cells' in the 'homeland', and 'sleeper agents' in Europe, exactly as they had with al-Qaeda in 2002. These claims were, at best, a gross misrepresentation of how either organisation operates and how individuals are radicalised.[15]

IS has also been linked, and sometimes deliberately conflated, with an extraordinary range of global 'bad guys', ranging from Hamas, the Palestinian Islamic extremist organisation, to Mexican drug cartels.[16] If early analysis ignored the importance of ideology for al-Qaeda in the Islamic world, current analysis of IS misses the centrality of its bid to restore the lost power and glory of Islamic empires and the resonance of that project with many in the Middle East and beyond. Obama, explaining how his administration would 'degrade and ultimately destroy' IS, described the enemy as 'a terrorist organization, pure and simple'.[17] This is just not true. IS in particular is a hybrid of insurgency, separatism, terrorism and criminality with deep roots in its immediate local environment, in broader regional conflicts and in geopolitical battles that link what happens in Raqqa or Mosul to chancelleries in capitals across much of Asia and the West.

In 2015, governments rushed to stiffen counter-terrorist legislation and increase police powers, just as they had in 2002. Then and now, the efforts to reinforce legal powers of security agencies and curtail the freedoms of citizens were accompanied by statements from policy-makers describing the threat in blood-curdling terms. Theresa May, the British home secretary, said in November 2014 that 'the threat we face is now more dangerous *than at any time before or since 9/11*'. This was an extraordinary and misleading statement.[18] As with al-Qaeda, successive leaders around the world have systematically exaggerated the involvement of IS in local violence in their own countries to obscure their own failings, or those of their forebears, and to obtain material, diplomatic and moral support in Washington.

There is another problem, also tenacious, which is resurfacing. My first book, which specifically focused on al-Qaeda, was largely devoted to showing that there was more to Islamic militancy than just bin Laden and his group, however devastating the strikes in New York and Washington might have been. There is now a danger that IS begins to be seen as encompassing all of Islamic militancy today, as al-Qaeda was once thought to do. IS is not 'the new al-Qaeda', even if the older group has declined substantially and lost its dominant position among extremist organisations. IS may have inspired other groups, re-energised the global militant movement and pioneered new strategies and tactics that have so far been extremely effective, but there are still many other important players we should be taking into account. In the eighteen months or so before the summer of 2014, when IS captured the world's attention, extremists had raided a Western-run gas refinery in Algeria, captured and briefly held Timbuktu, bombed the Boston Marathon, beheaded an off-duty soldier on the streets of London, killed scores in an upmarket shopping mall in Kenya and kidnapped two hundred schoolgirls in Nigeria. Each of these attacks was dramatically different. If two involved so-called 'lone wolves', three were the work of a major organisation; if some were clearly aimed at capturing global attention, others were driven primarily by a local agenda; the group behind the Kenya attack was under huge pressure; those behind the Nigeria kidnapping and the seizure of Timbuktu were surging to prominence. And these were just the most spectacular operations. Many others received little global attention. A significant number of these took place in Afghanistan and Pakistan, two theatres of violent activism which were being rapidly consigned to the margins of world affairs as international troops moved out of one and policymakers' attention moved away from the other.[19] In Syria itself, of course, IS has no monopoly on Islamic extremist violence, though it would like to establish one. The point is a basic one. Islamic militancy remains a very diverse phenomenon which will not be destroyed by the elimination of a single group, still less an individual. The idea that some kind of silver bullet exists is attractive, and deeply reassuring, but sadly without foundation.

One reason we are so tempted to aggregate, and to simplify, is that the complex reality of Islamic militancy often appears mystifying. It is easier to blame fanaticism, or decide that a particular religion is inherently violent or belligerent, than to carefully unpick the multiple causes, the many strands, the constant evolution of a major ideological and social movement. During the Cold War, communism was similarly reduced to a simplistic caricature, often underpinned by certainties about the essential nature of the Russians. For some in the 1970s and 80s, all terrorism – left-wing and right-wing, ethnic or nationalist – around the world was the work of the KGB. Of course analysis depends on generalisation, but there is a danger that in ignoring complexity the overall picture becomes deeply misleading.

In the pages that follow I try to be selective rather than simplistic. I describe a number of more recent acts of violence in detail, but mention many others in passing. Similarly, I focus on those groups I feel are most significant, leaving aside, with some regret, numerous fascinating features of the current landscape of Islamic militancy. The main concern of the book is on extremism from within the Sunni majority tradition, as the direct threat to Europe or the US from groups within Islam's minority Shia strand is currently negligible. Palestinian groups based in the West Bank or Gaza are also marginal to the primary thrust of this narrative as their focus remains almost exclusively local and their extremism has very different historical and cultural roots. Local groups in South Asia and those in the Far East receive less space than they deserve simply because they too currently pose much less of a direct threat to the West.

One guiding principle has been to choose examples that demonstrate the fallacy of one particular misconception – the one that is perhaps the biggest obstacle to a genuine understanding of the problem. Many believe that Islamic militancy represents some kind of regressive historical riptide that is in opposition to the onward march of human progress. This is wrong-headed, complacent and dangerous. Extremism is not 'medieval', as politicians often say, echoing the dismissive, uncomprehending ignorance of their nineteenth-century predecessors when confronted with a similar wave of violence.[20] Nor are its leaders 'temporally perverse', as one commentator memorably described Osama bin Laden.[21] They may be distant in terms of morality or values but they are not distant in time or place. They do not exist in some kind of other world. Rather, Islamic militancy is fundamentally, profoundly contemporary, a product of the same global interaction of politics, economics, culture, technology and social organisation that affects us all. It is of its time, which is now, created and shaped by its environment, which is here. When Islamic militant groups do not keep pace, they fade from the scene. Those that manage the challenges and exploit the opportunities of our fast-changing world thrive. Islamic militants use social media because we all use social media; they seek resources, from money and territory to hydrocarbons and weaponry, in the way that many actors do across the world today, whether formally recognised within the international system of states and multilateral institutions or not; they multi-task as terrorists, insurgents and administrators because we all now play roles which are increasingly ill-defined; they exploit and are formed by the dramatic disruption that digital technology and the Internet has brought; they 'swarm' people and resources rapidly and efficiently because they can now in a way that was never possible before; for many of them, financing is effectively crowd-sourced from donors, often via the Internet in a way that would be recognisable to any entrepreneurial start-up anywhere in the world. The phenomenon of Islamic militancy is diverse, dynamic, fragmented and chaotic – like so many other forces which shape our lives today. The shift within the phenomenon from hierarchical structures to flatter ones, from vertical to interconnected, from top-down to 'peer to peer', does not simply reflect that of the wider world: it is an integral part of it. Indeed, violent extremists are not just a product of broader trends, they often anticipate them. The Islamic State's new vision of 'pop-up caliphates' scattered across continents but all loyal to a single leader and a single political entity appears much more 'modern' than the increasingly outdated idea that states are defined by the possession of contiguous territory. As successive generations of terrorists have shown, extremists are frequently ahead of the curve, not behind it.[22] Through looking at them, we can learn something of ourselves and, for good or bad, of our future.

In the end, though, this book is primarily about individuals, about their stories, and how they, directly or indirectly, come to inflict great pain and suffering on other individuals. Islamic militants do extra-ordinary, immoral, appalling things but often remain very ordinary themselves. To counter the threat such people pose we need to compre-hend them: their motivations, their objectives and their twisted world view. Trying to understand does not imply any sympathy. It simply means we need to set aside our very natural anger, disgust and fear in order, as dispassionately as possible, to learn. We need, above all, to avoid the trap that the extremists have fallen into: that of shutting ourselves off, of closing our minds, of succumbing to the temptation of wilful ignorance. In the aftermath of terrorist attacks, victims, the maimed and the bereaved, always ask a very fundamental, very human question: 'Why did this happen?' We owe it to them to make the effort it takes to find the answer.

1

THE RISE OF ISLAMIC MILITANCY

Survey the new landscape of violent Islamic militancy and the immediate impression is of an impenetrable chaos. There are scores of groups who all apparently subscribe to the same basic principles of Islamic extremism but who have different names, are based in different places, and have apparently different priorities, tactics and strategies. By one count there are thirty-three individual militant groups in Pakistan alone.[1]

In the appalling violence in Syria, there are hundreds of 'brigades' of fighters who are Islamic militants by most definitions.[2] There are two Talibans, each of which is split into a multitude of different factions. There is al-Qaeda, of course, and then a bewildering array of its supposed affiliates, most of which operate with varying degrees of autonomy and most of which are, predictably, fractured themselves. Then there is the Islamic State, with a whole new range of connections. There are freelancers, lone wolves, stray dogs, self-starters, clean-skins, leaderless networks, cells and even 'groupuscules', all of which apparently have the power to cause harm, though whether greater or lesser is sometimes unclear. There is virtual militancy online, real militancy offline. None of this is static and the evolution of Islamic militancy is neither linear nor uniform. All is in constant flux.

But we can still make sense of this apparent chaos and confusion. Actors within contemporary Islamic militancy can still be divided into three broad categories.[3] The first is that of the major groups, of which there are only two.

Al-Qaeda was founded more than twenty-five years ago by Osama bin Laden, the Saudi-born propagandist and organiser, in Pakistan, where most of its remaining senior leadership is probably still based. Emerging from the chaos of the last years of the war in Afghanistan against the Soviet occupiers and their local auxiliaries, the group's goal was to unite and focus the disparate elements of the fractious, parochial, squabbling extremist movement in order to bring radical reform of society, states and religious practice in the Middle East, primarily, and beyond. During the early 1990s, bin Laden, the son of a wealthy construction tycoon, had little idea of how to reach that goal but by the end of the decade, from a base in Afghanistan, had decided that attacks on the US would be the most effective strategy. Strikes against the 'Far Enemy', the US and its allies, would take the place of campaigns against the 'Near Enemy', the local regimes in the Islamic world, including in bin Laden's native land, which he regarded as primarily responsible for the myriad problems facing Muslims everywhere. Bin Laden and a small group of close associates went on to orchestrate several of the most important terrorist operations in recent decades, including the one which is arguably the most spectacular in centuries, which on 11 September 2001 killed 3,000 people and destroyed the iconic twin towers of the World Trade Center, one of New York's most distinctive land-marks, as well as badly damaging the Pentagon, the home of the US Defense Department. Though al-Qaeda is now undoubtedly very much diminished compared to a decade ago, it has nonetheless repeatedly proved itself tenacious and resilient, with significant powers of regeneration. Its current leader, the veteran Egyptian militant Ayman al-Zawahiri, is a pragmatist who lacks bin Laden's talent for or interest in public relations and has adjusted the strategy of targeting the 'Far Enemy' to have a greater focus on the 'Near Enemy'. He has, however, frequently reaffirmed his and his organisation's desire to kill large numbers of Westerners, in Europe, the US and around the world, and continues to make considerable efforts to do so. Al-Zawahiri, with a small number of remaining veteran militants and a large number of newer recruits, heads 'al-Qaeda central' – also known as 'old al-Qaeda' or 'al-Qaeda senior leadership', AQSL in the acronym-ridden world of counter-terrorism.

The challenger for pre-eminence in the world of Islamic militancy is of course the Islamic State. There are, naturally, many similarities between the two groups. The rivalry between them can usefully be compared with that between top football teams who have different styles, visions and cultures but play the same sport. Both clearly share much in terms of world view and values. Both are led by individuals who demand absolute obedience, though they rarely get it. Both have resources to distribute – money, expertise, opportunity for combat experience or training, safe havens, communications capabilities – and can provide access to further streams of funding or recruitment. Both have established and respected names, or 'brands'. Both provide a psychological focus for anyone who is drawn towards extremist violence, even many thousands of miles away, who needs and wants to feel part of something bigger. They are the two largest nodes in the vast network of networks which constitutes modern Islamic militancy.

But when looked at more closely, IS and al-Qaeda differ enormously. There is a deep personal animosity between their leaders – al-Baghdadi has repeatedly made a point of explicitly repudiating the authority of al-Zawahiri and claiming to be the true inheritor of the legacy of bin Laden. The Islamic State has explicitly rejected the 'Far Enemy' strategy and has prioritised the struggle against the 'Near Enemy'. It has shown itself most interested in the immediate seizure of territory and local resources, limiting its involvement in international terrorism against the West to attacks on tourists in Muslim-majority countries while calling for local actors in Europe or the US to mount individual attacks themselves. There are other significant differences too. The leadership of al-Qaeda went to significant lengths to minimise violence between Muslims, seeing fitna, meaning 'division' and referring to the differences between Muslims (rather than between Muslims and non-Muslims), as one of the fundamental reasons for the problems facing the Islamic world as a whole. By contrast, sectarian violence against co-religionists is fundamental to IS, arguably its *raison d'être*. IS has accused al-Qaeda of being more interested in publicity than anything else. Al-Qaeda has accused IS of indiscriminate violence.[4] The older group has always seen the creation of a new caliphate as a long-term aspiration; the Islamic State went ahead and declared its existence in June 2014. Another difference, exposing an important distinction in the intellectual approach and backgrounds of the leadership of each group, is their respective attitudes to the apocalyptic prophecies which have emerged as a major component of Islamic militant thinking in recent years. The final confrontation with the forces of unbelief was, for al-Qaeda, a distant prospect and part of a popular tradition that educated men like bin Laden and his immediate associates largely disdained; for IS it was not just imminent but actually taking place.[5] These two groups are the major players, the market leaders, in today's militant world and so it is natural that they compete, but the reasons for that competition go well beyond a simply desire to win or retain the top position among extremist groups. The battle between al-Qaeda and IS is over the future direction of the entire Islamic militant movement. As we shall see in chapters 3 and 4, their differences illustrate some of the most important debates and dilemmas facing extremists over recent decades, and the rivalry between them is thus a key factor in determining the nature of the current threat facing the West and its evolution in the future. It is too early to call a winner.

The second category within contemporary Islamic militancy (and the subject of chapters 5 and 6) includes all those other active groups with some degree of organised structure. A number of these have a formal connection to one of the major groups. These relationships vary from loose support to genuine allegiance implying total obedience to orders from above. There are four current official affiliates of al-Qaeda: in Yemen (al-Qaeda in the Arabian Peninsula, AQAP), in Somalia (al-Shabaab), in North Africa and the Sahel (al-Qaeda in the Maghreb, AQIM) and in Syria (Jabhat al-Nusra). All of these groups can and do act independently of the central leadership of al-Qaeda, particularly in the local campaigns which occupy the vast majority of their time and energy. They nonetheless broadly recognise al-Zawahiri's leadership. All exist in places with a history of violent Islamic militancy often going back decades. Three of them – AQAP, al-Shabaab and AQIM – have been constructed out of older groups that include elements which long pre-date any involvement with 'al-Qaeda central'.[6]

The Islamic State has evolved a different outreach model, relying on the simple example of the new religious and political entity it has created, its apparent military success and propaganda to win support among Muslim communities worldwide. Many of the group's advantages have come from its ability to integrate a large number of diverse Sunni militant networks within Iraq and, to a lesser extent, Syria. Some of these 'internal affiliates' had existed independently for a long time. All were crucial to the group's early successes. It would have been odd if IS had not sought to replicate this model externally too. Between November 2014 and March 2015, IS announced the foundation a series of 'governorates', or 'territories', in Libya, Afghanistan and Pakistan, Egypt, Yemen, Saudi Arabia and West Africa. These too integrated a series of pre-existing networks, while creating new ones. Yet this overarching network is still very much a work in progress and it is still too early to judge how successful this project will be.

Of all these groups, only one has so far shown any systematic interest in striking in the West. This is al-Qaeda in the Arabian Peninsula, which has been linked to a series of technologically advanced bids to bring down passenger planes in the US and claimed responsibility for the attack on *Charlie Hebdo*, the satirical magazine in Paris, in January 2015.

Within this second category there are also many independent groups. A large number of these are based in South Asia and include the Afghan and Pakistani Taliban, as well as a range of other groups in both countries and in India and Bangladesh. Some are purely sectarian outfits; others have a regional if not international reach. There are also independent Islamic militant groups in Syria, Mali, Algeria, Jordan, Lebanon, small factions in Gaza, in Malaysia and Indonesia, the Philippines, the Caucasus, western China and elsewhere. All subscribe to the same broad world view as al-Qaeda and IS but are much smaller, concentrating almost exclusively on local, parochial struggles. Again, as with the affiliates, some are simply the latest protagonists in conflicts that have been going on for decades. Their relations with each other and with the bigger players are dynamic, reacting to circumstance and, particularly, to internal power struggles or the efforts of local authorities and security forces, both civilian and military. Some of these independent actors have cooperated with major groups on occasion, a few have even done so more or less systematically. For example, individuals within the Pakistani Taliban, the fractious coalition of groups responsible for the Peshawar school massacre of December 2014, in which 132 children were killed, have collaborated with al-Qaeda repeatedly. But this does not make it an al-Qaeda affiliate. As we will see, one trend currently emerging is an increasing degree of contact and coordination between these independent outfits, without involving the senior leadership of either al-Qaeda or IS. Many of the groups in this second category – both affiliates and independents – are really more coalitions of fragmented factions than coherent hierarchical organisations. Several have successfully attacked Western or international interests locally but few currently appear capable or willing to launch attacks in capitals in Europe or the US. Although for this reason they receive less attention than they perhaps deserve in the pages that follow, they are still dangerous in a variety of ways. They channel volunteers to groups more committed to an international agenda, provide opportunities for combat experience and training for new recruits, experiment with new tactics which can later be adopted elsewhere, destabilise areas of the world which are of critical strategic importance to the West, and create chaos and anarchy in zones which in turn open opportunities for other groups seeking to target Europe or the US.

It is the third category that currently most worries counterterrorism officials. These are the 'inspired warriors', the volunteers, the radicalised individuals in the West who, with or without the assistance of groups in any of the above categories, commit violent acts 'in the name of God' in their home countries or elsewhere. Most form small networks, a few act almost entirely alone. The three men who killed seventeen in Paris fall into this category, so too do the Tsarnaev brothers, who bombed the Boston Marathon in 2013, and the two Nigerian-born converts who killed a soldier in east London in May of that year. Many such networks are driven by group dynamics, as much as ideology. In their structure and often language too, they resemble gangs or other equivalent communities. Some are described by sociologists as 'fictive kin' or imagined families. It is no coincidence that British militants refer to each other as 'brother'. The vast proportion of the thousands of young Europeans who have made their way to Syria to fight would be included in this category, though only a fraction of those who return have so far attempted to execute violent acts in their native countries. So too would the substantially more numerous volunteers from cities and towns along the North African shoreline, from Jordan, Turkey and Saudi Arabia, from the Caucasus and particularly central Asia. This new form of low-level extremist activity is also seen in the Asian subcontinent where hundreds of young men from India, Bangladesh and the Maldives have all made their way to Syria and Iraq to join IS or have become active at home, and in the Far East. In Indonesia, the world's most populous Muslim majority country, the numbers involved remain small but are important nonetheless.

Collectively, this third category is living proof that terrorism is a social activity like many others, albeit a repugnant one. As we will see in chapters 7 and 8, the lone wolves are not really lone but embedded within a much wider and deeper culture of Islamic militancy. Mohamed Merah, a 23-year-old of Algerian origins living in south-western France who went on a shooting spree which left seven dead in 2012, had spent years mixing with people whose views could accurately be described as extremist, even if they never directly took part in any violence themselves. Those who struck in Paris in January 2015 had years of involvement in a series of interlinked militant networks, some committed to attacks in France, others to violence overseas. Bigger conspiracies do not evolve in some kind of social vacuum either. Police investigating bombings in Istanbul in 2003 estimated that several hundred people had some kind of idea of what was being planned, but none had informed the authorities.[7] Britons turning up in Pakistan in 2006, East Africa in 2010 and Syria in 2014 were tangentially connected to networks involved in the 7/7 bombings of 2005. These webs of personal relations involved scores if not hundreds of different people, few of whom were directly involved in acts of violence.

Indeed, few extremists commit acts of violence. In fact, many may explicitly oppose them, certainly 'at home' and, less often, abroad. This raises important questions. The killers of the soldier in London had spent years among people who, if aggressive in rhetoric, certainly did not call for attacks on British servicemen in the UK and would almost certainly have attempted to stop the planned murder had they known of it. However, what such people share with the bombers, or stabbers, or shooters is a conviction, based on selectively sampled holy texts, mythologised historical

examples, legends, conspiracy theories, prejudice and circular argument, that good and evil, belief and unbelief, the West and the world
of Islam are engaged in a cosmic struggle ongoing for 1,300 years
(at least). Such views are not restricted to the offline world either.
An online community of the sympathisers, fellow travellers,
preachers, retweeters, Facebook posters and others exists too. This
also propagates and shares the anti-Western sentiments, the anti-
Semitism and homophobia, the prejudices and the aspirations that
are fundamental to Islamic extremism today.

But the relationship between ideas and actual violence is complex.
Extremist views are a necessary, but not sufficient, condition for Islamic
militant violence. There are many today who strive for revolutionary
change of a type the vast majority of Britons or Americans or Europeans
would abhor, but who do not believe that violence is the right strategy
to attain their ends. Rightly, we continue to debate what protest and
argument we collectively believe is acceptable in our societies, what is
fair opinion or hate speech, what is legitimate criticism of, say, US foreign
policy in the Middle East, and what is unfounded and inflammatory.
Our third category – which I call the 'movement' of Islamic militancy
– therefore only includes all those men (and increasingly women) across
the West and the Islamic world, who exist outside the organised groups
and who believe not only in the cosmic conflict outlined above but that
victory in that struggle will only come through violence, and who
furthermore either seek to commit terrorist acts themselves or actively
help or encourage others to do so. The movement is thus the tangible
manifestation of a violent ideology and worldview. It is described
primarily in the last third of this book though is present, in one form
or another, throughout. It is perhaps the most significant development
of the last decade and may well be the most durable. Without it, none
included in the other categories can thrive, or, possibly, exist.

These, then, are the three categories which can help us make sense
of the threat we face today: two major groups or nodes of activism;
a range of other networked organisations, of which some are formally
linked to bigger ones, as well a large number of independent groups;
and finally a broader community whose members, if disorganised,
still adhere to the same, surprisingly well-defined, ideology and methodology as other militants.

Many of the elements of today's militancy have been present for decades. Foreign fighters were travelling from the UK to fight in extremist groups in Kashmir, the disputed Himalayan former princedom, in the late 1990s. In 1994 Algerian militants hijacked an Air France passenger jet and may have planned to crash it into Paris. Suicide bombing dates back to the early 1980s and suicide attacks go back much further. But as the world changes, new circumstances produce very different results. Changes may not be immediately evident, however. Often, a new kind of militancy emerges only gradually, complementing rather than supplanting what went before. Towards the end of the last decade, some analysts thought they detected an overall decline in modern Sunni militancy. I was one of them. This was in part real but it was also a result of a transformation taking place within the movement, one that would turn out to leave it perfectly poised to exploit the chaos of the Arab Spring.

Tracking such trends is difficult. Officials at MI6 ruefully spoke to me of how, as the impact of the Syrian conflict became clear, they had to build an entire new 'grid' of intelligence material, effectively setting aside a decade of work.[8] In May 2014, President Barack Obama told cadets at West Point that the main threat to the US was no longer from 'al-Qaida central' but from 'decentralized al-Qaida affiliates and extremists, many with agendas focused on countries where they operate'.[9] Even at this late stage, weeks before the fall of Mosul, Obama failed to mention what was then the Islamic State in Iraq and Syria.[10] His statement was not inaccurate, but was incomplete. During their wars in Iraq and Afghanistan, the better US senior officers frequently reminded their juniors that if they thought they had understood a threat, it meant it was time to reassess everything they believed they knew. The threat from Islamic militancy is a work in progress. However familiar it may seem, it is always 'new'.

For this reason, any attempt to describe the threat at its current state of evolution requires us to know something of the origins of Islamic militancy as a whole. This means knowing something of the demographic changes that destabilised the Muslim world in the 1960s and 70s, the rise of three particularly influential ideologues, and the revolutionary and religious models of thought that inspired them, and the Soviet war in Afghanistan that provided the testing ground, networks and inspiration for action.

In the second decade of the twenty-first century it is easy to forget that the link between terrorism and religious fanaticism is, in fact, a relatively recent one. Of course there have always been religiously inspired violent extremists. The Jewish zealots who stabbed eminent Romans to death on the streets of first-century Jerusalem, the Thugs in what became today's India who killed in the name of the Hindu goddess Kali, or the Shia Muslim sect which became known as the Assassins have all been cited as forerunners of today's religious terrorists.[11] But terrorism as a concept is far more recent than any of them. Its origins are to be found in late-eighteenth-century, post-Enlightenment, revolutionary Europe, and specifically in the reign known as 'the Terror' of the French revolutionaries. For most of its history, it has been dominated by actors motivated by ethnic, nationalist, separatist or secular revolutionary agendas. Attacks by groups with a primarily religious agenda occurred only rarely. Until the early 1980s, the most famous terrorists with Middle Eastern groups were Leila Khaled, a hijacker still seen as a feminist icon today, and Carlos the Jackal, a promiscuous, hard-drinking Venezuelan playboy.[12]

The terrorist act that changed all this was the assassination of President Anwar Sadat of Egypt in Cairo in October 1981. Sadat's killers were very different from most of the terrorists of the decade before. As he fired on Sadat amid a crowd of dignitaries attending a military parade, Khaled al-Islambouli, the young officer who led the assassins, shouted: 'I have killed Pharaoh and I do not fear death.' The reference to the ancient rulers of Egypt was a deliberate framing of Sadat's regime as pagan and un-Islamic. The killing was to be understood as a first step towards replacing it with a new religious rule. In fact, al-Islambouli and his co-conspirators were far from alone in their hatred of Sadat and what they believed he stood for, nor in their desire to see a revolutionary transformation of society along religious lines. The small group responsible for the president's death was one of scores of such cells that had formed in Egypt over the previous decade. And there were similar groups in virtually every other country in the Islamic world. These in turn were on the outer fringe of what was in fact an ideological movement that had taken hold throughout the Middle East and the broader Muslim world at the time: a generalised rediscovery of religious observance and identity, coupled with a distrust of Western powers and culture.

In the century between 1830 and 1930 almost the entire Islamic world, from Morocco's Atlantic seaboard to the easternmost tip of Java, from the central Asian steppes to sub-Saharan Africa, was invaded or subjugated or both by non-Muslim powers. These included Russians and Han Chinese (in south-west China or Turkestan), but primarily they were European. The technological, economic and military superiority of the invaders inevitably prompted much interrogation in the Muslim world as to the failings that had led to this debacle. Often the appearance of Western soldiers, sailors, scientists and, eventually, administrators simply revealed the essential weaknesses of local institutions – a sclerotic clerical establishment, corrupt or incompetent rulers, archaic administrations, antiquated financial systems which discouraged investment, or rigid educational systems that failed to stimulate innovation or critical thinking. Fierce debates pitting reformists against traditionalists had been taking place long before European armies and fleets arrived, but when they did the effect was dramatic and traumatic.

Almost all the invasions provoked a violent reaction among many local people. Resistance took many forms but, naturally enough in a deeply devout age, religion played a central role. Islam provided a rallying point for local communities more used to internecine struggle than campaigns against external enemies. From Western Africa to the Far East, European troops and their local auxiliaries battled men whose motivations might be wildly different but who all shared a profound belief that they were acting in defence not only of their livelihoods, traditions and homes but of their faith.[13] All were eventually crushed. The technological and other advantages of the invaders were simply too great and the divisions among their enemies too deep. But to the believer, even these failures reinforced their faith: if victory was a sign of the favour of God, defeat was evidence the true path had been abandoned.

Most of these movements had faded by the beginning of the twentieth century and the great upheaval of the First World War, but not all of them. Violence continued into the 1930s in places such as British India's 'North-West Frontier', in Italian Libya and in Palestine. Even where there were no foreign rulers, some local 'tyrants' faced the same kind of resistance. In 1929, for example, Afghans rose up against their king, who had decided to 'modernise' his country with a series of radical reforms.

But violence was not the only response. In India, in the aftermath of the failed revolt against British rule in 1857, the Deobandi school chose to isolate themselves and their community in order to insulate their Islamic culture from Western influence (even if they adopted a Western-style syllabus system in their religious schools). Others favoured wholesale adoption of Western ideas and values, on the grounds that their superiority had been all too brutally proven. This was the approach of the founders of the Islamic University at Aligarh, who believed that elite young South Asian Muslims should and could rival their Western counterparts in the arts, sciences and sports. But there was also a middle road. In India, a political organisation called Jamaat Islami was founded in 1926. It sought religious and cultural renewal through non-violent social activism to mobilise the subcontinent's Muslims to gain power. This approach involved embracing Western technology and selectively borrowing from Western political ideologies, while rejecting anything seen as inappropriate or immoral. In the Middle East in 1928, an Egyptian schoolteacher called Hassan al-Banna founded an equivalent group: the Muslim Brotherhood. Like the South Asian Jamaat Islami, it combined a conservative, religious social vision with a contemporary political one. For its followers, the state was to be appropriated, not dismantled, in order to create a perfect Islamic society. This approach was later dubbed Islam*ism*. Across the Islamic world there remained those who rejected any compromise at all. It was only through violence, such men maintained, that the rule of the West could be brought to an end, and their own societies reformed and redeemed. In contrast to them, the Brotherhood, like Jamaat Islami, prioritised – purely pragmatically – peaceful activism.

By the early 1960s, European powers had withdrawn from much of the Islamic world, but the challenges that they and the societies they represented remained. Many newly independent regimes adopted nationalist, quasi-socialist and broadly secular ideologies seen by many of their citizens, not unjustifiably, as Western imports. Again, this was accepted, even welcomed, by some, ignored by others, and deeply resented by many. The establishment of the state of Israel, now recognised by the international community after a bloody war and the flight of hundreds of thousands of Palestinians from lands they had worked or owned for generations, acted as a new focus for diverse grievances among Arab and Muslim communities. Anti-Semitism had long existed in the Islamic world but, fused with anti-Zionism, gained a new and poisonous intensity. Defeat in the Arab–Israeli war of 1967 deepened a sense of hurt, loss and humiliation.

More importantly, these regimes now also faced the challenge of immense demographic change. In Egypt, for example, the population had doubled between 1800 and 1900 and doubled again by 1950; by 1978 it had doubled once more to reach 40 million. The urban population grew disproportionately as land shortages and economic opportunities drew people to the cities. Around 2.5 million people lived in Cairo in 1950. Six million lived there in 1970. By 1980 the sprawling, seething metropolis covered around 140 square miles and was home to 10 million people. Most of the migrants from the countryside ended up in cramped tenements, squatter camps, even cemeteries, without proper water or electricity, sanitation, schools, health care or policing. Food was in short supply, and expensive. At the same time, a vast expansion of university tuition over previous decades meant that many of those who were unemployed had the expectations that go with literacy and education. Less tangible was a crisis of values. In the new shanty towns and low-rise apartment blocks, tribal bonds that had structured communities in the countryside counted for little, traditional leaders lost their authority, villagers who married, worked and played together were scattered, extended families broken up. For the older people there was loss. For those young enough not to know anything of the former rural life, there was disorientation.

The vision of the country's ruler did not provide much help. Sadat had wanted to turn his country into a prosperous, pro-Western nation. This required, he believed, the replacement of the socialist-style economic policies of previous decades with a new capitalism and so he launched a programme of reforms designed to encourage private enterprise and attract foreign investment. Over the course of a decade, the top 5 per cent of the population saw its share of national income grow from 15 to 24 per cent, while the share of the lowest 20 per cent dropped by four points to 13 per cent. Perhaps most importantly, the critical middle 30 per cent in Egypt saw their share of GDP halved.[14] The new private health clinics were too expensive for all but the very wealthy. New roads were built but there was almost no investment in public transport. Prices soared as inflation raged unchecked, officially hitting 35 per cent by 1979.

Worse still, a growing economic gap between rich and poor was accompanied by a growing cultural gap. During bread riots in Cairo in 1977, favourite targets for arson and vandalism were nightclubs – of which more than three hundred opened during the decade – and luxury US-made cars – of which imports had gone up fourteen times.[15] Both were symbols of the lifestyle of an elite that was enjoying greater connection with the rest of the world, and particularly the West, but which was increasingly detached from the majority of the Egyptian population. By the end of the decade, more than 30 per cent of prime-time television programming was from the US, with episodes of *Dallas* repeated ad infinitum. Inequality was combined with a sense of cultural invasion. It was an explosive mix.[16]

Of course, decades of Western-influenced nationalism and socialism had not dispelled the deep religiosity of many believers. In this time of crisis, some turned inwards, to mystic, personal strands of their faith. Others went in the opposite direction, into their communities, seeking change. One obvious alternative to the apparently bankrupt ideologies of leaders across the Muslim world was Islamism, of the type promoted by the Muslim Brotherhood in the Middle East and Jamaat Islami in South Asia. For a start, it appeared authentically local. It was also well organised, with a strong presence on university campuses and in professional bodies. Islamism promised to re-establish confidence and pride and to provide a solution to the many pressing challenges now faced by tens of millions of people. If the roots of modern Islamic militancy lie anywhere it is here: in the resurgence of Muslim faith identities and the activism of the 1970s. Throughout this crucial decade, Islamists gained support. Alongside them was the minority who called for violence to bring about revolutionary change and usher in a new, just order.

In Egypt, those advocating violence were young, twenty-seven years old on average, and mainly from rural or small-town backgrounds. Al-Islambouli, the man who shot the president, was twenty-six and from the upcountry town of Mallawi. Most had come to Cairo or Alexandria for further education, and were living with other students or by themselves. Almost all were the first in their families to study for a degree. Two-thirds of their fathers were middle-ranking government employees. They were upwardly mobile. Those who were working had done well: they included pharmacists, doctors, teachers, engineers, army officers. Most had achieved very high grades in public exams. Most came from stable families. That they saw Zionists, Jews, the US and Communists as eternal enemies of Muslims, Arabs and Egyptians was hardly exceptional. They were definitively not 'abnormal'.[17]

However, if the multiple crises of Egypt in the 1970s could have been mapped, these men lay at their intersection. If they were insulated from the worst of the soaring prices, or had marginally better homes than those in the slums, they had much greater ambitions, both personally and for their country, and a keen sense of injustice. Recent immigrants, living far from their families, they also suffered acutely the loss of community and solidarity of the village or small town. In the phrase of Saad Eddin Ibrahim, the Egyptian sociologist who studied them in depth at the time, they represented the 'raw nerve of Egyptian society'.[18]

Of course Egypt was not the only country in the Islamic world to have developed a 'raw nerve' in the mid- to late 1970s. Nowhere from Morocco to Malaysia remained untouched by the religious revival, nor by strains of Islamism and extremism. These varied hugely, but the profile of those involved in violent activism was strikingly similar everywhere.

In Iran, for all of its differences – a Shia rather than a Sunni tradition; a Persian rather than an Arab heritage – the parallels with Egypt were clear. Improved living conditions meant that by the mid-1970s two-thirds of the population was under thirty. There were eight times as many students at new universities and colleges in 1977 as there had been fourteen years earlier. Year-on-year growth rates averaged 8 per cent as agriculture was mechanised, factories built and infrastructure extended. The urban population exploded: in the space of a decade, Tehran's population grew from 3.3 million to an astonishing 5.1 million. Settled on the southern edge of the city, the new migrants experienced the same dislocation and uncertainty as their counterparts in Cairo.[19] Inflation led to soaring prices. A wealthy elite, with foreign-educated children and holidays in Paris, was increasingly distant from the rest of the population. Bitter memories of a CIA-backed coup that had overthrown a popular prime minister in 1953 and decades of clerical and popular anti-US sentiment made the reigning Shah's pro-Western tilt even less sustainable. Violent repression bred more violence, and eventually revolution.

Saudi Arabia too was suffering traumatic transformation. This was largely owing to the discovery of huge quantities of oil a year or so after the kingdom was founded in 1932. Saudi Arabia's revenues went from less than a million dollars before the Second World War to more than $50 million in 1950. It is difficult to think of any historic parallel to this sudden deluge of wealth on what was a poor, conservative, isolated nation. By the late 1960s, the average Saudi income was approaching that of the US. The real spike came in 1974. In response to Western support for Israel during the 1973 war, Middle Eastern producers imposed an oil embargo that sent the price per barrel from about $3 to more than $12. Saudi state expenditure went from around $2 billion in 1972 to an incredible $35 billion in 1976.[20] Vast construction projects were launched – of roads, mosques, palaces and shopping malls. Old neighbourhoods were bulldozed. Entire cities appeared out of nowhere. Foreigners poured in, with new hotels and office blocks built to accommodate them. There were even moves by the relatively reformist King Faisal to open the proliferating new educational establishments to women, who were now appearing on television (itself a relatively recent introduction) for the first time. Once again, there was violence. In 1979, hundreds of extremists led by Juhaiman al-Utaiba, a former national guardsman of Bedouin origin, stormed the main mosque at Mecca and then proceeded to hold off security forces for days, inflicting heavy casualties. Utaiba and his followers were from a variety of backgrounds, and, other than in their youth, do not fit the same profile as militants in Iran and Egypt and elsewhere at the time who were largely newly educated members of the urban middle class, but their vision was similar.

Change is continuous, but the stresses it generates tend to accumulate, lying below the surface until eventually the earthquake comes. The broad-ranging religious revival was an expression of social and economic tensions building up over decades. The catalyst for the explosion was a series of events: military defeats, oil-price hikes, political choices by men like President Sadat of Egypt and Mohammed Reza Pahlavi, the Shah of Iran. Equally important, though, were the ideologues who formulated and promoted the new extremist thinking. Two thinkers in particular were hugely influential, and remain so today.

When police and intelligence officers raided the homes of those involved in the conspiracy to kill Sadat in the days after the assassination, they came across an unpublished booklet written by the leader and theorist of the cell, a 27-year-old engineer called Abdel Salam Farraj Attiya. The police did not know the work, nor the man who had written it. It was entitled 'The Neglected Obligation'. Farraj had hoped the book's incendiary content would be widely read, and hundreds of copies had been printed in an underground workshop in the slum neighbourhood of Embaba, but his immediate superiors feared the attention it would attract from the authorities and ordered its destruction. Only sixty copies survived.

But if Farraj and his work were new to them, the police also found writings by a man they had known very well indeed. This was Syed Qutb, a fastidious, celibate, misogynist school inspector, part-time literary critic and Muslim Brotherhood member. Qutb's book *Milestones* has been repeatedly cited as the foundational text for the entire movement of contemporary Islamic militancy.[21] Indeed, almost half a century later, works by both Farraj, who would be hanged alongside Sadat's killers in April 1982, and Qutb, who had been hanged in 1966, still circulate widely: in mosque bookshops in London, as PDF files on the Internet, in the libraries of religious schools in Pakistan, passed from hand to hand in militants' dormitories in Syria and, of course, still read in their authors' homeland.[22]

The influence of left-wing ideologies in Farraj's 'Neglected Obligation' or Qutb's *Milestones* is striking. 'After annihilating the tyrannical force, whether political or a racial tyranny, or domination of one class over the other within the same race, Islam establishes a new social and economic political system, in which all men enjoy real freedom,' says Qutb, echoing *The Communist Manifesto*.[23] They also both contain ideas of practical utility. But anyone tempted to think that these documents, and others like them, are esoteric literature dealing with abstruse theological debates is badly mistaken. They are revolutionary tracts, ideological handbooks for a new wave of militants. Both Qutb and Farraj saw a world divided between belief and unbelief, light and darkness, peace and war, justice and tyranny, virtue and vice, corruption and purity. These divisions were stark. There was no middle ground and no room for compromise. The imperative for men on earth was to work towards the triumph of righteousness over evil and wrongdoing.

Similarly, what inspired these men to act 'in the path of God' and guided their ideas on how to do so was not a spiritual calling. It was not a deep attraction to the principles of the Muslim faith, nor even a deep understanding of the injunctions contained within the holy texts of Islam. Instead it was a historical example: the achievements of the Prophet Mohammed and of the first generations of his followers, the so-called Salaf. This is as true for today's militants as it was for Qutb, Farraj and their associates in the 1960s and 70s.

Muslims believe that the Prophet Mohammed was picked by God or Allah to be His messenger and to bring to Earth His final instructions on how human beings should conduct themselves individually and socially for eternity. But His message had immediate and specific relevance too. Arabia in the seventh century was fragmented and divided. Tribes fought tribes, sects battled sects. All worshipped their own local gods, whose effigies were placed in the main shrine, the Ka'aba, in the temple town of Mecca. This was an era of anarchy and iniquity. Mecca had benefited from a shift in trading routes and the city's rulers had, over the course of a few generations, grown rich, in part from the pilgrimage trade. Such rapid transformation led to social tensions. Mohammed, who lived from 570 to 632 CE in the west of what is today Saudi Arabia, was a social reformer and dissident political activist as well as a spiritual guide. He offered reassurance and a vision of a better future. Following revelations received during a summer meditative retreat in a cave, he called for an end to crass consumerism and the implementation of social justice – as well, of course, as devotion to the one true authority that was God. His first converts were among his immediate family and associates.

Though initially the authorities in Mecca ignored him, it became increasingly clear to them that this new preacher and his message posed a threat. In 622 CE Mohammed was forced out of his home town and travelled to the city of Yathrib, now known as Medina, 220 miles away. This event, known as the Hegira, is considered so significant that it is the year zero of the Muslim calendar. In Medina, Mohammed grew his community of believers, known as the *umma*, through his own example, charisma, military abilities, judgement and capacity to unify, or destroy, warring tribes. He eventually defeated the Meccan forces and returned to his home town after eight years of exile, whereupon he swept away the idols and the corrupt rulers, and brought the people of the city together under his leadership.[24]

In the Middle East of the 1960s and 70s, this story, told and retold in the mosque, home and school, was familiar to all Muslims, whether practising, politicised or neither. Its echoes in the present were hardly lost on the new wave of extremist thinkers who drew on it heavily, secure in the knowledge that it could be cited as incontrovertible historical evidence of the righteousness of their cause, particularly when contrasted with the abject failures of their current leaders. Qutb, writing in lucid, accessible language quite unlike the register used by clerics, explicitly invoked the example of seventh-century Arabia when describing the Egypt of his day as plunged in *jahiliyya*, the chaotic, violent, tyrannical 'ignorance' that prevailed before the time of Mohammed. 'Mankind today is on the brink of a precipice,' he argued in *Milestones*. 'The Muslim community must be restored to its original form . . . [It is] now crushed under the weight of . . . false laws and customs.'[25] In the absence of a new prophet, he argued, Muslims had to act themselves to ensure the implementation of the law revealed to Mohammed, the sharia, in their own contemporary community. 'A vanguard must set out . . . marching through the vast ocean of jahillyya which encompasses the whole world,' Qutb argued.[26] Farraj too maintained that it was because Muslims had ignored their duty to violently extirpate wrong-doing and combat the forces of unbelief that their community had lost the power of the first believers. It was this, he said, that had led to the divided, humiliated, weakened state of the Muslim world of the twentieth century.

While citing the example of the first believers, Qutb and Farraj
rejected the authority of contemporary clerics. Islam has no formal
priesthood with powers of intercession but has instead a body of
scholars whose rigorous training prepares them to interpret the texts
of the past in the changed circumstances of the present. Qutb and
Farraj explicitly rejected the argument, long maintained by official
clergy throughout the Islamic world, that only those with the correct
religious qualifications could decide when and where opposition to
an established ruler was legitimate. They could hardly have argued
otherwise as neither Qutb nor Farraj had any formal religious qualification themselves. They were not the first people to do so – the
immensely influential Indian-born journalist Abd Ala'a Maududi,
the founder of the Islamist Jamaat Islami organisation, had done so
decades earlier – but in the ferment of the time their ideas resonated
with a generation in the Islamic world impatient for change.[27]

This rejection of the authority of scholars, so many of whom had
been carefully co-opted by state authorities, was genuinely revolutionary. If an individual had no responsibility to obey those who
traditionally held power over a community, activism of a very new
kind became legitimate. But it also prompted a more practical question. The extremists might be obliged to act. They might even now
do so without the consent of parents, sovereigns or scholars. But they
still did not have any power. So how was this transformation to be
achieved? Once again, the life of Mohammed provided useful examples. Some attempted to reproduce the Prophet's flight from Mecca
to Medina and his establishment of the first truly Muslim community.
Hundreds of young men and a handful of young women followed
Shukri Mustafa, a charismatic agricultural science graduate turned
Islamist preacher, to desert caves where they tried to live as the first
Muslims had done. Neither the physical nor political environment in
Egypt was particularly conducive to such a venture. When the group
kidnapped a well-liked former minister to force the release of some
of its members who had been arrested, a violent confrontation with
the authorities ensued. Mustafa was hanged for sedition, more than
five hundred of his followers were imprisoned, and the experiment
ended. Nonetheless, the movement had numbered between 3,000 and
5,000 active members at its height.[28]

Others chose to follow the example of the Prophet in his later years and to bring an end to the corrupting rule of those in power directly. In April 1974, a group of extremists attempted to take over the Technical Military Academy in Cairo, seize weapons stored there, and march on a meeting hall where many of the ruling elite were scheduled to hear the president speak. After eliminating the nation's political leadership, they hoped to declare the Islamic Republic of Egypt, and implement their literalist, rigorous vision. The operation was a fiasco but, as the group's members knew it would, its failure encouraged others.[29] Seven years later Farraj and his group killed Sadat.

In the 1970s, the West might have been reviled but it was not a target for Islamic militants, even if their nationalist counterparts were causing mayhem in airports, at the Olympics and on the streets of Western capitals. Even Qutb, who loathed the US and all it stood for, had not actually wanted to use violence against the West. 'I do not ever recall [Qutb] saying that we should wage war against America or Britain; rather he wanted us to be vigilant against the West's cultural penetration of our societies,' one of the theorist's close associates later remembered.[30] Sadat's killers did not for a moment contemplate attacking European or American targets, even in Egypt, let alone further afield. So how, in the space of less than two decades, did the West become not just a target, but the primary focus of the most effective Islamic extremist group yet established?

One cause was the enduring influence of the Iranian revolution. Though left-wing ideologies also commanded significant support in Iran in the 1970s, it was the cleric Ayatollah Khomeini who most successfully mobilised the restive masses in the new urban shanty towns and slums. He did this partly by articulating many Iranians' fear of Western cultural invasion with a savage brilliance. His success in instigating revolution in 1979 lent powerful credibility to his arguments, and rapidly the stock phrases of his newly triumphant Iranian Islamists – terms like the 'Great Satan', 'Westoxification' and the 'Crusader–Zionist alliance' – entered everyday vocabulary across the Islamic world. But Iran was rapidly plunged into its bloody war with Iraq and its global rhetoric was not backed by action. In consequence it was not in Tehran that the critical steps towards targeting the West were taken but further east, in what had hitherto been a geopolitical backwater: Afghanistan. Here, in the fertile chaos of a war between the Soviet-backed Afghan government and the insurgent mujahideen, emerged the principal axis of modern Muslim extremism: a new, updated, idea of jihad.[31]

2

THE ORIGINS OF GLOBAL JIHAD

Islamic scholars have long argued over the exact definition of jihad.

The root of the word jihad is the Arabic *jhd*, meaning strain, effort, struggle, endeavour or striving, against something, or sometimes someone, undesirable. It does not necessarily mean 'holy war'. On the crucial issue of when jihad in the sense of holy war is justified, or even obligatory, the Koran appears to offer contradictory guidance. Some argue that this is because of the existence of different factions among the early Muslims, all of whose positions on this crucial question needed to be represented somehow.[1]

Others point to the fact that God's revelation to Mohammed was not delivered in one single instant but over many decades. The Koran is a compilation of these various revelations, arranged roughly according to length, not by chronology or subject matter.[2]

But by returning each revelation to its historical context in the life of the Prophet, possible reasons for the variation become apparent. Early Koranic verses, delivered to Mohammed while his community was small and weak, urge patience and spreading the word of Islam through non-violent means alone. 'There is no compulsion in religion, for the right way is clear from the wrong way,' the Koran says (2:256). But later verses, received by Mohammed when approaching the height of his power, enjoined an offensive against unbelievers. 'Fight and slay the pagans wherever ye find them and seize them, beleaguer them and lie in wait for them' (9:5).

In the centuries that followed the death of the Prophet, these later verses, known collectively as the 'Sword verses', were held by the official clerics of the powerful and expansionist imperial Muslim dynasties to abrogate the earlier, more pacifistic ones. These rulers' often controversial campaigns were thus conveniently sanctioned as God's will.[3] Militant ideologues of the nineteenth and twentieth centuries, fighting against occupiers and invaders from Turkestan to the Rif Mountains of Morocco, stressed this later interpretation too. The same understanding was adopted by the Islamist groups founded in the 1920s, whatever their commitment to non-violent activism. The Muslim Brotherhood's slogan ran: 'Allah is our objective; the Prophet is our leader; the Koran is our law; jihad is our way; dying in the way of Allah is our highest hope.' The militants of the 1960s and 70s had adapted the idea of jihad once more, shifting away from the pragmatism of the Muslim Brotherhood.

Syed Qutb argued that true Muslims were few, but all believers were obliged to take up arms against their corrupt rulers in a righteous effort to establish a perfect, just Islamic society. These rulers were designated as apostates, worse than unbelievers, and should be put to death. Farraj agreed, writing that a jihad to reform oneself and one's society constituted a sixth obligation in addition to the five that, for many, define a Muslim: profession of faith, prayer, giving alms, the pilgrimage to Mecca and fasting during the holy month of Ramadan. Hence the title of his pamphlet: 'The Neglected Obligation'.[4]

Then, at the end of 1979, a decade-long war broke out between insurgents in Afghanistan and the Soviet Union. This violent conflict, pitting Muslim fighters against the troops of an avowedly atheist power, prompted further calls for violent jihad. During that decade, the most prominent jihadist ideologue to emerge was a man named Abdullah Azzam.

Azzam, a Palestinian who had fought in the 1967 war against Israel and had studied at Cairo's famous Al-Azhar University, had earned both practical and theological credentials. Though based in Pakistan from the early 1980s, Azzam travelled widely across the Islamic world and the West. Charismatic and energetic, he spoke frequently and published at a ferocious pace, convincing his audiences to contribute however they could to the struggle of the mujahideen in Afghanistan. Azzam's works were not careful arguments but fiery polemics, their many logical inconsistencies obscured by an impassioned rush of angry prose, and his fantastical, flowery language established a style of writing which is still the norm for extremists today.

Azzam's most famous work had the unequivocal if less than catchy title of 'Defending the lands of the Muslims is each man's most important duty'. In this pamphlet, still much quoted, Azzam distinguished between two kinds of jihad (although both were interpreted purely as violent struggle). Offensive jihad occurs where there is no immediate threat from unbelievers. It entails 'appointing believers to guard borders, and the sending of an army at least once a year to terrorise the enemies of Allah'. This is a job for the state and should be organised by a community's legitimately appointed leader. However, when an invasion of Muslim lands has already occurred, and the jihad is thus defensive, the effort to expel the unbelievers is 'compulsory for all believers', whether or not it has been organised, or even sanctioned, by someone in authority. This in itself was not an innovation, but Azzam then went further than anyone else, arguing that the defensive jihad was incumbent on Muslims *irrespective of which part of the Islamic world had been invaded*.[5]

Farraj and Qutb had advocated prioritising efforts against the closest enemy to hand – in their homelands – and had barely dealt in practical terms with any broader conflict. For Azzam, the petty borders of nation states must be ignored and every Muslim should be mobilised for the struggle wherever it was necessary. The availability of modern transportation made the obligation all the greater. It meant, he said, that 'the war in Afghanistan was only a beginning' as 'jihad will remain an individual obligation until all the other lands that were Muslim will be returned to us so Islam will reign again'. Azzam's argument at the time of the Afghan war would transform the entire extremist movement. The global community of Muslims he envisaged would be one where all fought for each other, across the planet. It was a call to arms that resonated throughout the Muslim world.

Thousands made the journey to fight the war against the Soviets and the Afghan governments they backed. They came from villages on islands in the South China Sea, and from port towns on the North African Atlantic coast. Some came from the West. Most came from the Middle East, particularly Egypt, Libya and Saudi Arabia. The consequences for the Islamic militant movement were huge. Some were simply practical. At a critical moment in the emergence of a new wave of violent activism, the conflict provided an invaluable haven for those facing repression, torture and long prison terms in their homelands. They did not travel to Afghanistan, which was far too dangerous to provide a base, but to Pakistan, and particularly to Peshawar, the frontier city where for an entire decade they had space to develop their ideas, hold debates, publish books, give lectures and plan strategies in almost total security. Personal relationships built during the years of the conflict would be of crucial importance in later years, as, for a few, would the simple experience of combat. Only a minority of those volunteers who travelled to Pakistan to help the Afghans actually fought. Most were involved in humanitarian assistance to the millions of people displaced by the war. Of those that did fight, some were traumatised, others were hardened; some were repulsed, but many were emboldened. One was Osama bin Laden, who first travelled to Pakistan to help those battling the Soviets in the neighbouring state in 1981. At that time he was a softly spoken, devout young man who impressed associates with his modesty. Almost a decade later, after several brief but intense forays into the combat zone, he was a confident publicity-hungry leader.

Outside of Afghanistan itself, the war mobilised support from governments, official clerics, dissident religious networks, the Muslim Brotherhood, neighbourhood mosques and many tens of millions of ordinary worshippers, creating a vast international network of donors, supporters and activists. The collective effort to support the mujahideen in their battle against the Communists provided a sense of common purpose and solidarity.

But it was the myth rather than the reality of the conflict that was the greatest legacy of the war in Afghanistan. The reality is that the foreign volunteers never constituted more than a tiny minority, certainly no more than 20,000 and probably fewer, of the hundreds of thousands, possibly millions, of fighters who took part. Ill-equipped, ill-trained and unused to the tough conditions, these 'Afghan Arabs', as they were known, were seen more as a nuisance than an aid by the local men who constituted 95 per cent or more of the fighters. Indeed, most were reviled for their puritanism, desire for martyrdom and contemptuous attitude to local communities. The foreign 'mujahideen' – the word means those who pursue jihad – were barely mentioned in contemporaneous accounts of the war, whether penned by Afghan, Pakistani, US or Russian authors. The idea that they played a significant role in the defeat of the Soviet Union's project in Afghanistan is nonsense. In fact, most of the overseas volunteers arrived towards the end of the war, years after Soviet policymakers had already decided to withdraw their troops. Nonetheless, for Islamic militants, the defeat of the Soviets became a much-cited example of how, as in the earliest days of the Muslim faith, a tiny group of believers armed with the truth triumphed over an overwhelming army of unbelievers. It was a legacy that would have an enormous impact in the decade that followed.

Through the mid- and late 1990s I interviewed scores of Islamic militants. Some were active, some had recently given up arms. All had fought, either with the gun or the pen, in one or other of the many campaigns that followed the Soviet withdrawal from Afghanistan in 1989. Some of these men were veterans of that conflict, still known simply as 'The Jihad' in much of the Islamic world. Having defeated a superpower in Afghanistan, these men had returned to their home-lands confident of winning another, easier, victory over the regime in their own land, in order to install a pure Islamic one.

One group of fighters – interviewed one evening in a dingy office down an alley in the Pakistani city of Lahore – had fought in Kashmir, where separatists and Islamists battled Indian security forces in the late 1980s and 90s. Around 30,000 people were to die before the brutal insurgency began to fade a decade later. Others I spoke to had been active in the factional fighting that ravaged Afghanistan between 1989 and the coming of the Taliban to power in 1996. In Algeria, where the most brutal of all the conflicts of the period raged, I interviewed former fighters who had been amnestied. They recounted how they had taken up arms with one of the early militant groups after an election that looked set to be won by Islamist parties had been cancelled in 1992. They had believed their campaign would last a few weeks or months. Instead, they had finally given up many years later. In London, I sat with Egyptian activists who spoke of Sadat's assassins, and who were hoping for a breakthrough against his successor, Hosni Mubarak. These men had sought asylum in Britain, as had several senior members of the Libyan Fighting Group, dedicated to the overthrow of Muammar Gaddafi's rule. Also in London were equivalent campaigners from Saudi Arabia, Kuwait, Jordan, Tunisia and Morocco. There was violence too in Somalia, the Caucasus and in the Far East, which caused tens of thousands of deaths. In the middle of it all was the war in Bosnia, seen by some veterans and many aspiring militants, with astonishing blindness to the facts, as the new Afghanistan.

These disparate struggles shared many causes, not the least of which being that many of the challenges faced by Muslim states in the 1970s were as acute if not worse in the late 1980s and early 1990s as they had been twenty years before. The same regimes were still in power and a huge 'youth bulge' was compounding already severe overcrowding of educational facilities and accommodation. A crash in the price of oil had ruined many states' finances – Saudi Arabia and Algeria were particularly badly hit – forcing drastic cuts in the generous welfare payments that had staved off serious dissent through the 1980s. The Saudi royalty's desperate appeal to the US for military protection during the Gulf War with Saddam Hussein had exposed their weakness. The countries to which the hardened, motivated, angry and confident men who had fought in Afghanistan often returned were already, to quote Syed Qutb, 'on the brink of a precipice'.

But the violence of these years remained almost exclusively focused on what bin Laden was later to call 'the Near Enemy': their local regimes. By the end of the 1980s, though anti-US sentiment was certainly strong in much of the Islamic world, actual attacks on Western interests by Islamic militants had been infrequent. Those that had occurred had specific local causes, such as the Western intervention in the civil war in Lebanon. Though the campaigns of the early and mid-1990s may have killed as many as 200,000 people, Western casualties remained negligible. This explains why, despite appalling savagery that presaged what we see today in Syria and elsewhere, these conflicts have, slightly astonishingly given the death toll, been almost entirely forgotten in the Western world. Another reason, of course, is that they were overshadowed in a very dramatic way by what followed. The interviews I conducted with the former militants, over tea and dates in a safe house on the outskirts of Algiers, took place about two weeks before the 9/11 attacks.

So why did militants turn to attack the West? One important reason is to be found in Saudi Arabia.

As a state, Saudi Arabia owed its foundation to the alliance of the battle-hardened latter-day followers of Mohammed ibn Abd al-Wahhab, who had preached an austere, puritanical interpretation of Islam in the Arabian peninsula since the late eighteenth century, and an ambitious, capable tribal leader called Abdulaziz ibn Saud. In 1979 came three events that shook the Saudi monarchy: the seizure of the grand mosque in Mecca by a group of local extremists, the invasion of Afghanistan by the Soviets and the Iranian revolution. Each involved a different enemy – violent local militants who branded their rulers apostates, atheist Communists and Shia Islamists – but each revealed a new and potentially deadly threat to the reign of the house of Saud. One response of the kingdom's rulers was to use a substantial amount of the vast wealth generated by their oil revenues to expand the proselytisation of the Wahhabi creed, one of the most rigorous, intolerant and conservative existing in Islam, throughout the Sunni Muslim world.[6] This had been a policy for some time but now the effort was massively expanded in an updated though much more far-reaching version of the original strategy that had brought them to power sixty years before. The aim was to reinforce their own religious credentials at home while increasing their influence overseas, allowing them to reassert their claim to both religious and political leadership in the Islamic world.

Over the ensuing decades, tens of thousands of religious schools, mosques, Islamic universities and religious centres were built world-wide. Hundreds of thousands of scholarships to Saudi universities were offered and stipends paid to preachers. Tens of millions of copies of holy texts and, more importantly, deeply conservative interpretations of them, were published and distributed. This strategic choice was to have a huge impact on the Muslim world, fundamentally altering faith, observance and religious identity for hundreds of millions of people. It also contributed, as intended, to a shift of cultural influence from Egypt, once the unchallenged intellectual centre of the Arab world, to Saudi Arabia, its religious centre.

The effects of this campaign were reinforced by the connection made by many around the Islamic world between the immense wealth and level of development of the Gulf States and their apparent piety. More practically, life and faith in these countries were experienced at first hand by millions of temporary workers from poorer, troubled Muslim-majority countries, most with very different traditions of Islamic practice, who were drafted in over the decades to perform menial jobs. Despite the hardships they encountered, many went home profoundly impressed by what they had seen and heard, not least in local mosques, and would act as individual propagandists, both practising and spreading the harder-edged faith traditions of the Gulf themselves.

Efforts were redoubled after 1991 and the public relations disaster of having to ask US troops to defend the kingdom against potential invasion by Saddam Hussein. By the mid-1990s, rigorous, literalist strands of Islam, previously absent or seen as alien, had established a powerful presence across the entire Islamic world and in communities in the West.[7]

These doctrines rarely encouraged violence directly, but their inherent intolerance would greatly facilitate it. At the centre of the creed spread so industriously by the Saudis through the 1980s and 90s was the most rigorous possible understanding of *tauheed*.

The concept of *tauheed* is fundamental to the Islamic faith and is encapsulated by the first line of the call to prayer: 'There is no God but Allah, and Mohammed is His prophet.' This uncompromising principle is not merely the prime article of the faith, though. It was the founding principle of Islam's worldly power too. As successive tribes accepted Islam – the word means submission – and the authority of Mohammed, the tribes of the Arabian peninsula had been united in a single, unique, righteous community.[8] The many gods had been replaced by one; the many tribal armies by a single victorious force; the many tribal rulers by a single authority. The religious concept of *tauheed* was thus given physical substance; the oneness of God was reflected in the oneness of the community of believers.

The Gulf-trained and Gulf-sponsored preachers holding forth around so much of the Islamic world in the early 1990s repeated this message: the strict principle of *tauheed* needed to be applied in every domain – spiritual, temporal, personal, public, political, social and cultural. There was little room, therefore, for diversity among the community of believers. Pluralism was polytheism, polytheism was apostasy. Difference was more than just a threat, it was a deliberate rejection of the teachings of God. Not all adherents of this austere interpretation subscribed to the idea that those Muslims who did not meet this severe standard were to be excommunicated, but many came close.

One marker of this new intolerance was its attitude to local shrines, often vestiges of pre-Islamic practices or associated with the Sufi mystic strand of Islam and an integral part of traditional worship for many Muslims. Early Wahhabis had demolished thousands of such sites in the Arabian peninsula. In the 1990s, this destruction was seen much more widely. One of the most spectacular examples of this iconoclasm was seen in 2001 when the Afghan Taliban destroyed the 1,200-year-old statues of the Buddha in Bamiyan.[9]

Another was the attitude to the Shia, who, as apostates, could theoretically face death. Funds flowed from private donors in the Gulf into militant organisations in Pakistan primarily committed to a sectarian agenda of violence against Shias as well as in Taliban-run Afghanistan. The worst massacres of Shia in Afghanistan occurred between 1999 and 2001 as the Taliban tried to consolidate power, not in their earlier campaigns. In Pakistan, revealingly, the increasing violence against Shia was accompanied by a rise in attacks on Christians. Elsewhere there was a notable intensification in the already fairly ubiquitous anti-Semitic rhetoric, and of course that against the West. Both were linked to the insistence on *tauheed* in an increasingly globalised environment. In a world without borders the West's baleful influence was almost impossible to escape. One possible strategy would be to purge territory of all that might be seen as Western – the preferred option of the Taliban. A second option would be to force the West itself to cease its interventions in the Muslim world. This would be the strategy adopted by Osama bin Laden.

The new 'global' approach to Islamic militancy was inspired also by the conspicuous failure of the mainstream Islamist movement to fulfil its early promise. Governments across the Muslim world had been forced to make significant concessions to the Islamist agenda, but by the mid-1990s had begun to gain the upper hand. Many Islamist parties or organisations were co-opted or simply crushed, and in the rare instances where Islamists had gained some degree of power, their record was unimpressive.[10] Nearly twenty years after the slogans of the Islamists had replaced the broadly discredited verbiage of the national-ists, their own promises were looking less and less convincing.

Nor had the returning veterans of the Afghan war delivered much either. Their campaigns had won early victories in Algeria, Egypt and Somalia, and they appeared to be playing an increasingly important role in the wars in Bosnia and Chechnya, two new 'theatres of jihad', but none of these early advances were sustainable. In Algeria, extremists turned on each other, and the local population, with an indiscriminate savagery that swiftly destroyed the entire movement. Militants in Egypt, weakened by collapsing public support, an ill-judged attack on foreign tourists and effective security operations, declared a truce in 1997. The Taliban, which had maintained nominal authority over around three-quarters of Afghanistan, had been unable to bring much improvement to the lives of everyday people. They were forced instead to rely on spectacular public violence such as the executions I witnessed in Kabul in 1998 and 1999 to maintain law and order. A slogan painted on the wall of the Ministry of Justice – 'Throw reason to the dogs, it stinks of corruption' – suggested one possible reason for this lack of success. Few of the Taliban's senior leaders, many of whom had grown up as refugees in Pakistan, had received anything but a religious education, and the teachings of the rigorously conservative Deobandi tradition were of little use in trying to run, or rebuild, a modern economy. Almost everywhere, violent Islamic extremism focused on local objectives had failed. To some, this indicated that it was time to implement a new approach.

Meanwhile, with the end of the Cold War, the US had established itself as the sole superpower, and within two years of the fall of the Berlin Wall it was intervening militarily in the Islamic world in a way that would have been inconceivable only a few years earlier. The Gulf War of 1990 to 1991, the imposition by the United Nations of sanctions on Iraq and the arrival of US troops in Somalia in 1993 all reinforced fears of a new age of Western expansionism. The fact that the US suffered casualties in Mogadishu, some inflicted by Islamic militant veterans from Afghanistan, before their hasty departure strengthened confidence that, for all their state-of-the-art weaponry, Western soldiers could never overcome opponents armed with the true faith. More broadly, the liberal humanitarian interventionism supported by Bill Clinton and Tony Blair was often seen rather differently in the Islamic world. Indeed, the whole process of 'globalisation' was perceived as distinctly less benign than either of these two leaders maintained. In Israel–Palestine, the first Intifada, with its powerful images of stone-throwing teenagers taking on Israeli tanks, had contributed to the sense that the West had 'double standards', as did the widespread belief that peacekeepers had failed to protect Muslims in the Balkans. The West's continued support for repressive and undemocratic regimes in Egypt and Algeria hardly helped. Nor did Al Jazeera, the cable and satellite channel launched from the gas-rich emirate of Qatar in 1996. Al Jazeera's aim was to represent the views of ordinary people and its journalism often seemed to reinforce prejudices as much as challenge them.

And so, as militants looked for a new direction and a new target, there was only one obvious contender: the West. From the early 1990s, attacks on Western interests, including on US or European soil, became more and more frequent. In 1992, a hotel in Yemen was attacked with a bomb in an apparent bid to kill US troops. In 1993, a young Kuwaiti-Pakistani tried to bring down the World Trade Center in New York with a giant bomb. On a rather less ambitious scale, an immigrant courier from Pakistan shot dead two CIA employees outside the agency's headquarters in Virginia. In 1994, there was the incident involving the hijack of a French plane by Algerian extremists. There were bombings of US troops in Saudi Arabia. Around the same time, an Egyptian radical cleric known as the Blind Sheikh issued a fatwa from his jail cell in the US calling on 'Muslims everywhere . . . to cut off all relations [with] the Americans, the Christians and Jews, tear them to pieces, destroy their economies, sink their ships, shoot down their planes and kill them wherever you may find them'.[11] In 1995, one veteran of the war against the Soviets, a highly educated, well-travelled former engineer called Khaled Sheikh Mohammed, launched an impossibly ambitious bid to bring down a dozen US-bound planes over the Pacific simultaneously and assassinate the Pope. There was a plot detected in the US itself to bomb the New York subway. In all, terrorist attacks involving US targets went from sixty-six in 1994 to two hundred in the year 2000. Of all international attacks around the world, those against US targets or US citizens rose from about 20 per cent in 1993–95 to almost 50 per cent in 2000.

Not all of these attacks were by Islamic militants, and only a handful were the work of al-Qaeda.[12] But looking back, it seems fairly clear that, when it came to targeting the West in general and the US in particular, bin Laden and Ayman al-Zawahiri, the Egyptian medical doctor turned Islamic militant who had become bin Laden's close associate by the end of the decade, were following broader trends as much as leading them.

What bin Laden did provide, however, was a coherent argument for prioritising the US as a target over local regimes. Deploying his undoubted talents as a propagandist, he wove together all the major strands of violent Islamic activism and made them intelligible as well as relevant. He mixed the legacy of men like Wahhab with that of Qutb and Azzam. His communications and arguments would typically begin with reference to a local conflict but would soon merge into a global narrative: of the cosmic struggle between good and evil, belief and unbelief, the mujahideen and the Crusader–Zionist Alliance. A complaint about the presence of the US troops in Saudi Arabia would be followed by a reference to UN sanctions on Iraq, which would both then be framed as part of the broader battle between the West and Islam. One major theme was the plight of Palestine. Familiar arguments – such as the obligation of the individual to wage violent jihad anywhere in the world – were given a new twist. The emphasis on the US as an enemy and target was conscious, careful and deliberate. The al-Qaeda leaders were convinced it would resonate. 'The nation in this decade is geared against the US,' explained al-Zawahiri in 2001.[13] And it was very much a product of its time.

The international nature of bin Laden's version of jihad – which further underlines quite how of its time it was – becomes especially apparent from the particular, practical circumstances that allowed it to flourish: the sprawling network of training facilities established in Afghanistan over the previous two decades. Without these, it is difficult to see how bin Laden could have put together the 9/11 attacks, or created the networks which would enable al-Qaeda to survive the US-led assault on Afghanistan that followed them.

None was particularly impressive. Most of the dozens of training facilities functioning in Afghanistan by 2001 were little more than a couple of lines of rough canvas tents, some basic cement buildings and a makeshift assault course. Even the most elaborate were comprised of scruffy barrack blocks where scores of young men from all over the Islamic world, though largely Saudi Arabia, Egypt, Libya, Syria and Jordan, learned basic light infantry skills, did calisthenics, read the Koran and watched motivational videos.

The average age of these young men was around twenty-five. Almost all had been born in the 1970s. The majority were, if not wealthy, then far from poor. Though some were of below-average education, particularly in terms of their knowledge of their own faith, most appear to have been of normal intellectual ability. Many were the sons of migrants, either from the countryside to the city or internationally. Many had degrees, though few had good jobs or the prospect of useful and satisfying employment. All would have faced the standard challenges of finding a home in hugely over-crowded cities, raising the money for marriage, dealing with a hugely incompetent bureaucracy and the petty, daily tyranny of bribe-taking officials from traffic cops to hospital administrators. Many came from very large families; few would have had much opportunity for the risk-taking adventures, or even sport or music, which divert young men elsewhere from more destructive activity. They were, twenty years later, the contemporary version of the 'raw nerve' identified by Saad Eddin Ibrahim, the Egyptian sociologist, in his homeland around the time of Sadat's assassination.

But there was one significant difference between them and that generation. Much of the extremist narrative of the global battle between good and bad, belief and unbelief, was already well integrated into their view of the world well before they reached Afghanistan. This had not been the case for their counterparts in the Middle East of the 1970s, for whom the new thinking of the jihadis came as a revelation. The earliest years of the young men finding their way to the training camps in Afghanistan had been spent in societies where the religious revival was fully entrenched. At school, in the home, in the street, often in the mosque, they would have been steeped in anti-Semitism and anti-Americanism. Many would have been exposed to the Gulf-backed religious propaganda. They would have closely followed the successes and failures of militant groups in their own countries, or in Bosnia, or elsewhere. The new televisions in their homes would have broadcast images of the renewed conflict in Chechnya and, from 2000, the second Intifada, as well as Hollywood films and local or Western soap operas.

In Afghanistan, that narrative was made real. The word and the deed matched. Here was a territory where rigorous monotheism was imposed, where no pluralism was tolerated, where the authorities were committed to jihad. Here, the theological concept of *tauheed* was a concrete physical reality, an example to the *umma*. Shias or giant

statues of Buddhas or even international NGOs had no place in it.
Nor did the West or Western influences. The whole of Afghanistan
had become sacralised space, with the camps themselves offering
enclaves of Islamic purity in a country being purged of wrongdoing.

It was in these camps that bin Laden sought volunteers to strike
the West in the West.

One source was a camp called al-Farouq, where those who had
performed well with the Taliban front lines were sent and where the
more competent English speakers ended up too. Instructors linked to
al-Qaeda spotted talent among the trainees. Suitably prepared, the
selected volunteers were brought to bin Laden, who suggested to
them that, admirable though their efforts on the Afghan battlefield
might be, they could make a greater contribution to the jihad with a
special operation against the 'Far Enemy'. Some declined, some were
rejected as insufficiently motivated, others were simply inept. But
sufficient numbers of them accepted the summons to allow bin Laden
to deploy several dozen individuals over a three-year period in the
unprecedented campaign of attacks that culminated in 9/11. The ease
with which these young men were convinced that it was 'time to kill
the Americans on their own ground', as one of the 9/11 hijackers said
in a will videoed six months before his death, is striking.

In the wake of that atrocity, many were astounded that New York
and Washington, both at the very centre of global networks of power,
technology and culture, could have been attacked from a place as
'backward' and 'medieval' as Afghanistan, as distant in time as it was
in space. But this stark opposition lacks the nuance of reality. No one
could pretend any equivalence in terms of connectivity, infrastructure,
human or financial capital between a war-battered, landlocked, arid
failed state in southern central Asia and the most powerful cities in
the most powerful nation ever known. But in its own way Afghanistan
was an extraordinarily globalised place, just not in the sense recognised by most commentators. Though excluded from the formal
transnational systems constructed and dominated by the West,
Afghanistan was nonetheless connected by a wide range of extensive
networks, albeit of a different kind. There was the web of relationships between conservative Muslims scholars, donors, schools,
foundations, NGOs and governments – all very present in the country
– which stretched across much of the globe. There was the informal

banking system which allowed huge sums to be transferred all over the world – from a small shop in Kabul's money market, or indeed simply someone's front room – in total security for a pittance. (I used it on several occasions, and marvelled at the efficacy, and non-traceability, of the transaction.) There were the drug-smuggling and people-trafficking routes, some of the most successful anywhere in the world. Pakistan, Saudi Arabia and the United Arab Emirates had recognised the Taliban as legitimate rulers of Afghanistan and assisted the movement greatly, if in different ways. This international axis of conservative Sunni states was aligned against an equally international axis of Iran, India and Tajikistan, which all helped the opposition forces. Workers from Afghanistan, or at least the refugee camps full of Afghans in Pakistan, sent home remittances from across the Islamic world. The porous eastern border allowed Karachi to act as a de facto warm-water port, plugging Afghanistan into some legal and many very illegal trade networks. All these connections were features of a globalised landscape, just one that most observers in the West could not even visualise, let alone see.

Then of course there were the militant organisations themselves. Dozens of different groups from a score of different states ran camps in Afghanistan. Delegations from other militant outfits, operating in Malaysia, Iraqi Kurdistan or Morocco, passed through, seeking funds, advice and technological assistance with attacks even further afield. The Millennium Plot of 1999, targeting Los Angeles airport, a US warship and sites in Jordan and which was planned largely in Afghanistan, connected Los Angeles with Montreal with Dubai with Amman with Jalalabad. Claims of responsibility for attacks were faxed from Afghanistan to north London groceries to appear in Arabic-language newspapers read worldwide. When a religious opinion, a fatwa, was needed to decide a dispute between groups, a radical cleric in Europe was consulted and his judgement, a sixty-page document, made its way to Afghanistan within days and was circulated widely.

Finally, of course, there were the volunteers themselves. All of the young men who took part in the 9/11 attacks in one way or another – and the total number was around thirty – had grown up in an age of 'globalisation', and their lives and references were dramatically different from their counterparts even ten, let alone twenty years before. Nineteen of them were able to live apparently routine lives in the US for months on end without prompting suspicion. One came from cosmopolitan Beirut. Another had spent many years in Arizona. A third was a fan of Formula One. Fourteen came from Saudi Arabia, mostly from respectable lower-middle-class urban families. Even these passed their time in the US shopping, eating pizza, working out in gyms, reading flight manuals, without attracting particular untoward attention.[14] In the final months before the attack, the participants used all the means of modern communication, from SMS messages to satellite phones to email, and took scores of flights around the US, across the Atlantic, around Europe, through the Middle East. For all those involved, from bin Laden down, the step from a local focus to a much broader one, from the Near Enemy to the Far Enemy, from fighting a local regime to attacking a US embassy in the Islamic world and killing US civilians 4,000 miles away across a continent and an ocean, was no longer a particularly large one. Indeed, in a world where distance meant less and less, it was not really a step at all.

One final factor made the transition to global jihad almost inevitable: the media.

Scholars have long recognised the symbiotic relationship between terrorism and the development of mass media. The first major waves of terrorism in the modern age coincided with the spread of mass printing techniques and the mass consumption of news in the 1860s and 70s. There was never any doubt about the connection. In 1880, a German anarchist called Johannes Most wrote a pamphlet called 'Philosophy of the Bomb'. 'Outrageous violence', he said, 'will seize the imagination of the public and awaken its audience to political issues.' In the same period, the phrase 'propaganda by deed' began to be widely used. Nearly a century later, as televisions began to make their appearance in US and European homes, those fighting colonial regimes immediately recognised the implications of the screen now appearing in front rooms across the developed world. In 1956, Ramdane Abane, the strategist credited with turning round the independence struggle in Algeria, asked rhetorically if it was better to kill ten enemies in a remote gully 'when no one will talk of it' or 'a single man in Algiers which will be noted the next day' by the new media.[15] The extraordinary attention focused on terrorists during the 1970s coincided with, and was partly due to, a series of technological innovations which allowed American TV networks to broadcast their acts cheaply and quickly all over the world.[16] One of the reasons the assassination of Sadat was so memorable was that it had been filmed and so millions could eventually watch the grainy, colour images of Khaled al-Islambouli and the others running across the Cairo parade ground to fire into the viewing stand where the Egyptian premier stood.

However, for most of the 1980s and 90s, the means of mass communication were still dominated by states and large corporations. Only they could afford the infrastructure required to produce material and broadcast it to millions of people. Islamic extremists had to make do with pamphlets, audio cassettes and, eventually, videos. These were passed from hand to hand, circulated in mosques or sold in specialist bookshops. Though they could have a potent mobilising effect on those already disposed to participation, or help solicit donations from reluctant supporters, they reached few in comparison to the television or even newspapers. There was still no effective way for militants to reach a bigger audience in the US, let alone the Middle East, where the media was tightly controlled by governments, without somehow convincing news organisation executives or officials to broadcast their statements or news of their violent acts. The former was inconceivable. The latter, though fraught with difficulty, at least allowed them to get some kind of message across to millions.

But this began to change in the middle of the 1990s, at exactly the time the various local struggles around the Islamic world sank into bloody stalemate or outright failure. The biggest single development was the arrival of local-language satellite television channels, along with the spread of dishes that allowed unprecedented numbers of people across the Islamic world to watch them. These new channels were prepared to screen material that regimes would never show and swiftly became hugely popular. Al Jazeera led the way, but was only part of a broader phenomenon. As well as contributing to the sense of a common 'globalised' Muslim identity and broadcasting images of violence towards Muslims in places like Kosovo or Gaza into tens of millions of homes and cafes, these new channels also offered a new outlet to extremist strategists like bin Laden.

Bin Laden had long recognised the importance of the media. During the war against the Soviets in Afghanistan he had helped with propaganda efforts, while also carefully constructing his own image by inviting carefully selected film-makers to spend time with him during his rare trips to the front lines. While based in Sudan from 1991 to 1996, bin Laden had used sympathisers in London as a conduit for tedious and verbose written statements. But the limitations of this were clear. Immediately after returning to Afghanistan he tried (but failed) to use defunct out-of-date broadcast equipment that had been left behind by the Soviets and found by followers in Jalalabad. Over the next five years, he gave a string of carefully choreographed press conferences to invited local and international press despite a specific prohibition by the Taliban. A series of videoed statements were carefully couriered to Al Jazeera's offices in the Pakistani capital. 'We seek to instigate the [Islamic] nation to get up and liberate its land, to fight for the sake of God and to make Islamic law the highest law and the word of God the highest word of all,' bin Laden explained in one.[17]

But this too was unsatisfactory. The coverage of these often rambling communiqués was, as it always had been, determined by editors, whether in Qatar or in Western capitals, and bin Laden expressed his frustration at this to associates.[18] One tape sat unopened on a secretary's desk for days before being broadcast, others were heavily edited, some were simply not deemed newsworthy at all.[19] The escalating series of operations bin Laden launched from 1998 onwards must be seen in the context of this desperate desire to grab the attention of the planet's mass media. The East Africa bombings of 1998 received massive but fleeting coverage before being overtaken by events elsewhere. The attack in 2000 on the USS *Cole* attracted some attention but no substantial reaction. Bin Laden invited an Al Jazeera reporter and cameraman to a celebration at which he read out a poem praising the suicide bombers who had hit the vessel off Yemen but the footage was cut.[20]

In the months before the 9/11 attack, al-Qaeda's leader had a follower equip a 'media van' with satellite television receivers and radio antennae to monitor broadcasts.[21] His aim was to follow coverage of the operation in the US as it happened. In the event, at the remote location where the al-Qaeda leader heard the news on 11 September 2001, reception was so poor that the only option was the BBC World Service.

But this time bin Laden had succeeded, unequivocally, where so many other terrorists had failed, to capture the undivided attention of the entire planet – and in real time. For several years to come, every utterance he made would be broadcast, often in its entirety, by the world's media, then picked over, discussed, analysed and repeated. The images of the spectacular attacks themselves would be played and replayed too. No terrorist before or since has attained such power to communicate with so many people.

Bin Laden did not initially accept responsibility for the operation on the US east coast, though he publicly underlined the reaction he hoped to see. 'Every Muslim has [now] to rush to make his religion victorious,' he said in his first message after the attacks, a videotaped speech broadcast by Al Jazeera on 3 November 2001. 'Those young men said in deeds . . . speeches that overshadowed all other speeches made everywhere else in the world.' A few weeks later he told an interviewer that his own 'life or death does not matter' because 'the awakening has started'.[22]

3

AL-QAEDA AND THE ORIGINS OF ISIS

In the late 1990s, there was little to indicate that Baghdad was one of the oldest and most fabled centres of cultural, political and commercial activity of the Islamic world. The city was bleak and depressing. In the summer, the heat shimmered above the sprawling poor neighbourhoods, and if children swam between the rushes on the embankments of the Tigris few others braved the foul-smelling water. In winter, fog shrouded the broad, empty thoroughfares and clung to the grim, concrete ministries. There was scant evidence of the city's former glory, nor its fabulous and fertile intellectual activity, beyond some of the street names. One morning's 'thought for the day' printed in the *Baghdad Observer* in early 2000 adequately summed up the general atmosphere: 'Keep your eyes on your enemy. Be ahead of him but do not let him be far behind your back.'

In the centre of the city, on Mutanabbi Street, named after a brilliant tenth-century Iraqi poet, was the famous book market.[1] Literature, technical manuals and writing materials had been sold on the site for a thousand years or more – a part of the city's history as a site of constructive exchange between cultures and communities in Asia, Europe and the Middle East over centuries. Baghdad was where the only remaining copies of the most important works of Greek philosophy were translated into Arabic, thus preserving them for posterity. A local saying paid tribute to the locals' literary appetite: 'Cairo writes, Beirut prints and Baghdad reads.' Here on Mutanabbi Street works from all over the world lay piled on shelves in tiny shops or simply on the pavement.

Even in the early 1990s, Mutanabbi Street had been popular among middle-class Iraqis seeking original or translated copies of Western classics. But by the end of the decade, there was little demand for such works.[2] One stallholder showed me a volume of French Romantic poetry, a Hemingway and some dog-eared Shakespeare. 'No one wants these any longer,' he said. 'Now they are just thinking about their chances on judgement day.'

The origins of Islamic extremism in Iraq do not lie in the creation of the Islamic State, or even in the US invasion of 2003, but in events that took place many decades before. Iraq was formed by the British in the aftermath of the First World War out of three provinces of the defeated and defunct Ottoman Empire, eventually becoming independent in 1932. In 1958, its monarchy was overthrown in a military coup and it was declared a republic. In Iraq, as in neighbouring Syria, it was Ba'athism, a modernising quasi-socialist ideology developed in the pre-war period, that became dominant. Religion was pushed into the background. By 1968, after a series of bloody coups and counter-coups, a group of Ba'athists had definitively seized power. Saddam Hussein, a young thuggish cadre from Tikrit who had risen up the ranks of the Ba'ath Party by acting as an enforcer to successive leaders, became president in 1979 and proceeded to eliminate any potential threat to his power with methodical and extreme violence.

Yet there were some things that Saddam and his multiple security services could not contain. One was the religious revival seen throughout the region. Iraq too was passing through a period of massive and traumatic change, with soaring rates of literacy, huge migration from the countryside to overcrowded cities, and oil revenues which were fifteen times greater in 1974 than they had been in 1972. There was a new inequality too, as well as a new exposure to Western values and ideas. Saddam, for all his brutal authority, was unable to insulate the population from either the political Islamism of the Muslim Brotherhood and its offshoots or the surge in personal piety and observance that was also part of the broader religious resurgence being seen across the Islamic world.[3]

This revival was further fuelled by the first Gulf War of 1990 to 1991, in which US-led forces fought Iraq after its invasion of Kuwait, and particularly by the sanctions imposed on the country in the aftermath of the war by the United Nations.[4] The conflict destroyed much of the country's infrastructure, and completed a process of economic evisceration which had seen the country's per capita GDP slide from $1,674 in 1980 to $926 ten years later and just $546 in 1991.[5] The sanctions then ruined what remained of the middle classes and plunged the working classes into misery. They also provided ample opportunity for the corrupt and powerful to get very rich indeed. For everyone else, life was a daily struggle to get fresh food, power, medicine. A controversial United Nations study claimed that around a third of all Iraqi children were malnourished. Saddam's security sources intensified their campaign of intimidation and violence. One former torturer, who I interviewed in prison shortly before the war of 2003, described holding babies over boiling water to get parents to speak, and how women had been raped in front of their fathers. Videos that were later found of executions and torture showed much worse. In such conditions, many turned to faith.

In fact, there had always been a deep piety among the poor, but as religious networks filled the void left by the weakened central state this took on a more organised, politicised aspect. In both the Sunni and Shia communities, traditional faith or tribal leaders found their authority and influence reinforced after years of decline. The weakening of the state allowed others to build, quietly and carefully, a presence as well: clandestine preachers, funded by major institutions in Saudi Arabia and other conservative Gulf States, went from village to village and house to house. They concentrated their efforts particularly on the tough outlying zones to the west of Baghdad. The Muslim Brotherhood was also active and Shia Islamists attracted growing followings.

Recognising the trend, Saddam himself trimmed his secular sails to the increasingly devout prevailing wind, launching an Enhancement of Islamic Belief campaign in the early 1990s. Drinking and gambling were restricted, religious education expanded in schools and work started on one of the world's largest mosques – to be known as the Saddam Hussein Mosque – in Baghdad. Officials announced the president's recently discovered blood links to the Prophet Mohammed. For decades, Saddam's state propaganda machine had reinforced a powerful anti-Western, anti-Israeli and anti-Semitic world view. Now an explicitly religious element was added. The state-controlled media was packed with religious programming, a radio station entirely devoted to readings from the Koran was launched, and even the youth channel run by Uday, Saddam's depraved son, started to carry hours of lectures by clerics. 'The Prophet Mohammed waged the Muslims' first war against unbelievers during Ramadan and now we face the same circumstances. We must unite to fight,' I heard a state-appointed cleric say in 1999 as he delivered a sermon in a mosque in Baghdad. Hundreds of US and British air strikes every year, which usually did little damage but were carefully publicised by Baghdad, reinforced the propaganda.[6] In a school a teacher explained to me how her pupils were taught that 'Iraq . . . is a rich country, an oil country, but that the Zionists and the Americans . . . don't want any other countries to be advanced . . . The [US] government are causing the problem because they are run by the Jews.' On a wall was a poster showing a pencil and an AK-47 and the slogan 'The pen and the rifle have only one purpose. Even a student can be a warrior.'

Crucially, in addition to the perceived conflict with the West there was also a very real conflict among the Muslims of Iraq. This schism between Sunni and Shia Muslims originates in a disagreement over who should succeed the Prophet on his death in Mecca in 632 CE. Mohammed had left no clear instructions and a debate took place between his closest associates who eventually chose Abu Bakr, a close adviser, early convert and friend of Mohammed with a deep knowledge of the tribes of the Arabian peninsula and their allegiances. But the Prophet's son-in-law Ali had long been seen as a strong candidate. Ali gracefully accepted the decision but many others didn't. Support for his candidature united a variety of disaffected factions who were collectively known as the Shi'atu Ali, the party of Ali, or, eventually, the Shia. And it was in Iraq that their disagreement was seared into the cultural memory: fifty years after Abu Bakr's succession, Ali's son Hussein launched a bid to claim his birthright. Promised support failed to materialise, and Hussein's small band of followers, including old people and small children, was annihilated by a much larger force. Hussein was killed, and his body mutilated. Over the next centuries, the split between the partisans of Ali, the Shia, and those of customary law, the Sunni, would come to encompass and articulate all sorts of ethnic, cultural and political differences.

When the British drew the boundaries of modern-day Iraq, they broadly ignored these sectarian divisions. They implemented their usual strategy of cultivating a local elite to do most of the governing for them, and echoing the example of the Ottomans before them this elite was largely drawn from the Sunni Arab community, despite the fact that mass conversion of rural tribes to Shia Islam in the late nineteenth century had left it very much in the minority.[7] Though the Ba'athists had included some Shia early on, Saddam Hussein's political, military and commercial support base had been almost entirely composed of fellow Sunnis. When the US invaded in 2003, Sunni Arabs comprised perhaps only around 25 per cent of the 26 million population.[8] This meant that when US occupiers declared that they would create a liberal, free-market, Westernised and, above all, democratic Iraq, it was very clear who would be the winners and who stood to lose a dominant position that they had enjoyed for five hundred years.

With the toppling of Saddam, the eclipse of Sunni power was rapid and brutal. The US administrators appeared largely unaware of the history, demographics and sectarian competition in the country, and blithely reinforced the fears of the Sunnis by implementing a broad campaign of 'de-Ba'athification'. Tens of thousands of Sunni civil servants and army officers found themselves unemployed. Millions just felt humiliated. 'They cross the oceans to plunder our wealth. They don't respect old people. I can't sleep because of their heli-copters. Even if the kids throw stones they shoot. They have taken my Kalashnikov, they have taken money from my house, they have taken my pride,' one sixty-year-old shopkeeper in Ramadi, in the Sunni-dominated and strategically crucial Anbar province, told me in the summer of 2004 as US soldiers blew in the doors of neighbours' homes with explosives and led men away, their heads covered in sacks. The massive public celebrations of a resurgent faith among the Shia majority, and the mobilisation of Shia Islamist militias, reinforced the Sunni community's sense of existential threat.

Over the coming years, though there was much violence from the Shia community, it was groups of Sunnis who were responsible for the most effective and widespread attacks against the occupying forces. These were largely spontaneous, not primarily organised by 'regime remnants' as officials in Washington and London insisted, and involved groups of friends, colleagues, worshippers at the same mosque, even men whose children attended the same school, coming together, procuring weapons, learning new skills and finally launching opportunistic insurgent operations. An active fighter, who called himself Abu Mujahed, described to me how he had been a fan of American popular culture, particularly Aerosmith, the stadium rock band, and had welcomed the invasion. However, he had begun to doubt the intentions of the US and their allies when, watching Al Jazeera on a clandestine satellite dish during the initial campaign, he had seen images of civilian casualties. He had been deeply shocked by the generalised chaos which followed the deposition of Saddam and then angered by the continuing economic problems. By the summer of 2004, Abu Mujahed had decided that the US had invaded simply to stop Iraq exploiting its own oil and developing as a strong Muslim nation. Every morning he went out to execute mortar attacks on US positions before going to work in a ministry.[9] Others laid ambushes before opening their shops.

Much of the essentially informal insurgency that erupted in the year that followed the 2003 invasion was organised along tribal lines, though religious networks also played a role. US troops trained in conventional tactics struggled with an elusive enemy. The western and north-western provinces of Anbar, Salahuddin and Nineveh rapidly became the epicentre of the violence. One man emerged as the most notorious among those taking up arms against the occupiers and their local allies. He was Ahmad Fadil Nazal al-Khalayleh, better known as Abu Musab al-Zarqawi, and was to become one of the most important and influential figures in the recent history of Islamic militancy and of critical importance in the formation of the militant groups that would eventually evolve into the Islamic State.

Al-Zarqawi was born in 1966 in the tough western Jordanian industrial city of Zarqa, and grew up in an unremarkable modest working-class family.[10] A high school dropout, he had turned to petty crime by his early teens and was jailed for violence and sexual assault. On his release, influenced by Abdullah Azzam's propaganda and a local conservative cleric, he travelled to Afghanistan.[11] Al-Zarqawi was too late to take part in the conflict against the Soviets but stayed for several years nonetheless, living on the margins of the extremist community in Peshawar and possibly fighting with the more militant of the Islamist groups during the civil war which followed the departure of Moscow's troops.[12] He returned to Jordan in 1993 but was swiftly arrested on charges of plotting to launch bomb attacks in the kingdom and sentenced to fifteen years in prison. Released in 1999 in a royal amnesty on the accession of King Abdullah, Al-Zarqawi returned to Afghanistan, where he was introduced to bin Laden by an intermediary.

The two men shared little, in either background or views. Bin Laden had grown up in luxury, and was quiet, devout and highly educated. Al-Zarqawi was semi-literate, brash and had a superficial understanding of Islamic texts picked up from conversations with extremist clerics. Neither appears to have been particularly impressed by the other. But bin Laden was persuaded by an associate who felt that the younger man's connections in Jordan could be useful and grudgingly agreed to provide a small amount of money to allow al-Zarqawi to set up a rudimentary training camp near the western Afghan city of Herat.[13] This provided a home for a handful of followers, as well as their families, which in turn allowed al-Zarqawi to announce the formation of a group which he called Jamaat al-Tauheed wal-Jihad, the Union for Tauheed and Jihad.

Al-Zarqawi continued to keep his distance from bin Laden's al-Qaeda. He had no involvement in, or knowledge of, the 9/11 attacks and was forced to abandon his Afghan base in their aftermath. He used contacts among Afghan Islamists made a decade before to cross Iran and reach a small enclave carved out by three militant groups in a corner of Kurdish-controlled northern Iraq.[14] Ejected from the enclave by local forces and air strikes during the war of 2003, al-Zarqawi, now thirty-five, made his way to Iraq's Sunni-dominated west, where he found support among members of his Bani Hasan tribe, the extent of which stretches across the border from Jordan into Iraq, and was able to attract many of the volunteers coming from across the Middle East to join the new conflict.[15] He was also able to integrate several existing extremist insurgent networks into a functioning coalition under his leadership. A series of high-profile suicide bombings and attacks on US as well as local Iraqi forces raised his profile significantly, as did his role in the kidnap and killing of Western civilians. It was at this point that bin Laden got back in touch.

One of the original purposes of al-Qaeda was to build a coalition of groups around the world and overcome the disunity that bin Laden saw as one of the principal causes of the failure of the militant movement. He had made desultory attempts to organise a network under his overall leadership during the early 1990s while based in Sudan but had lacked the resources or the prestige. The deal he had been proposing to other factions was relatively simple: funding or other logistical assistance in return for nominal loyalty. This was not a particularly attractive offer from a young, little-known activist, whatever cash might be forthcoming to sweeten what would otherwise have been a fairly humiliating arrangement. Algerian groups peremptorily rebuffed bin Laden's ambassador in around 1993, as did an Indonesian organisation approached at the same time. It was only after his return to Afghanistan in 1996 that such efforts began to meet some success. Here, as al-Qaeda's profile rose, a series of groups travelled to obtain much-needed resources, particularly training. Not all swore allegiance, but some did, providing al-Qaeda with the skeleton of a network around the Islamic world and sometimes beyond. The attacks the group successfully executed between 1998 and 2001 brought a flood of donations, primarily from devout and wealthy individuals in the Gulf, and global notoriety. Unable to engage directly in the unexpected conflict in Iraq that erupted in 2003, bin Laden needed a proxy. So his motives for contacting al-Zarqawi were fairly transparent: al-Qaeda would gain a powerful presence on the ground in the most urgent and important theatre of extremist violence anywhere in the world since the 1980s, and maintain its recently acquired pre-eminence among militant groups too. 'A strike against the United States in Iraq . . . would be a golden opportunity,' he explained later.[16]

The benefits for al-Zarqawi were less clear, though potentially substantial. The former street thug, who carefully covered his prison tattoos when filmed or photographed, would gain a degree of respectability within extremist circles that he could never have obtained alone. He also, potentially, had access to logistic assistance, should he need it, and strategic guidance, should he want to take it. Yet al-Zarqawi had his own view of how to prosecute his campaign and appeared unwilling to listen to anyone else. One letter he sent to the al-Qaeda senior leadership in January 2004 made this very clear. After laying out his vision for the campaign to come, al-Zarqawi issued a blunt ultimatum. If the letter was couched in flattering terms, addressed to 'the dwellers on the mountaintops, the hawks of glory, the lions of the mountains, the dear and courageous sheikhs, the two honourable brothers', it was brutally honest. Al-Zarqawi was ready to 'rally, obey and even pledge allegiance' to bin Laden if his strategic vision was accepted. But if the leader of al-Qaeda 'gauged things differently', then that was fine too. Al-Zarqawi would go it alone.[17]

In the end, it was bin Laden who gave way. In October 2004, al-Zarqawi announced that his group had become the 'Tanzim Qaeda al-Jihad fi Bilad al Rafidayn', or 'al-Qaeda Jihad Organisation in the Land of the Two Rivers', a reference to the Tigris and the Euphrates and a deliberate rejection of colonially imposed frontiers and states. After a theatrical pause which must have enraged the Jordanian, al-Qaeda's senior leadership publicly acknowledged the group as an affiliate.

The first component of al-Zarqawi's strategy was simple: to seize and hold real ground – to endure and expand, as the Islamic State's motto later put it. Much of al-Zarqawi's time and energy over the previous decade had been spent looking for a secure base. Unlike bin Laden, who had always lived in relative security, al-Zarqawi had spent most of his life looking over his shoulder. In Jordan in the early 1990s, he had been jailed because he had nowhere to hide when the Jordanian security services came looking for him. In 2001 he had been forced to leave Afghanistan, and then, in 2003, his temporary haven in northern Iraq. He knew, from bitter experience, the value of having a secure base from which operations could be launched, and to which the mujahideen could retreat when in trouble. The creation of an enclave for his militants was also inspired by the historical example of Mohammed (rather than by the texts or principles of the faith). Al-Zarqawi described the group he led in Iraq as 'the spearhead and vanguard' of the Muslim nation. 'This battlefield is unlike any other,' he had explained in his letter to bin Laden. 'This is jihad in the Arab heartland, a stone's throw from [Saudi Arabia] and Al-Aqsa [mosque in Jerusalem] . . . We must spare no effort in establishing a foothold in this land.'[18]

This was not easy, however, as al-Zarqawi was well aware. There were 'no mountains in which to seek refuge and no forests in which to hide' in Iraq. Worse, local people would show hospitality but would not allow their homes to be used 'for launching operations'. The result was that 'the noose around the mujahideen's throats [was] growing tighter'. One of his closest comrades, Abu Anas al-Shami, an extremist cleric who joined al-Zarqawi's group and acted as its in-house religious adviser, described their plight in emotive terms. 'We realised that after a year of jihad we still had achieved nothing on the ground,' he wrote in early 2004. 'None of us had even a lot the size of a palm tree on the whole of the earth, no place to find a refuge at home in peace among his own.' Over the next two years, this would remain the case. Al-Zarqawi's fighters took partial and temporary control of major population centres – such as Fallujah, the city in Anbar province – and smaller towns and villages across western and north-western Iraq but were not able to establish the safe base they sought. Even the small enclaves they were able to carve out were only ever tenuously held.

The principal challenge they faced was not the occupying forces of the US, and certainly not the weak Iraqi Army, but relations with local communities. There had been indications very early in the conflict in Iraq that the apparent welcome given to the Muslim volunteer fighters arriving in Iraq to join the battle against the US might not last indefinitely. Tensions had soon emerged, which became more acute as the militants imposed stricter and stricter rules on the communities they sought to control. These included bans on smoking, on watching (hugely popular) Egyptian soap operas and on worshipping at ancestors' graves. Women were ordered to wear the full head-to-toe covering traditional in the Gulf but alien even in conservative parts of Iraq. The foreign fighter's habit of taking local women as temporary wives led to further local resentment. Nor did the militants seem capable of bringing anything resembling security, which was about the only thing which could have made submitting to their authority worthwhile.

Though it was clear that anger was growing everywhere, with increasing clashes between foreign extremists and local communities, al-Zarqawi persisted. The energy he and his men devoted to 'promoting virtue and prohibiting vice' through preaching, public executions, torture and repeated edicts in Fallujah in the autumn of 2004, for example, was at least as great as that dedicated to constructing bunkers to resist the anticipated assault of US troops. Other factors also contributed to the growing backlash. When al-Zarqawi's fighters appropriated lucrative smuggling networks they denied powerful tribal sheikhs the revenue on which their patronage networks depended, threatening the very basis of their status and power. The newcomers were also unwitting social revolutionaries. Senior appointments were made according to moral zeal rather than military achievements or position in a deeply hierarchical society. One of their senior commanders was, to the disgust of local sheikhs, a former electrician.

The problems with the first part of al-Zarqawi's strategy to establish

a base made its second main component all the more urgent. This
was to attack Iraq's Shias. These, al-Zarqawi had told bin Laden, were
'an insurmountable obstacle, a crafty and malicious scorpion, a spying
enemy and a mortal venom'. Among the many crimes of this 'treacherous and disloyal sect' were 'patent polytheism, tomb worship and
circumambulating shrines'. In post-Saddam Iraq, they were 'creeping
in like snakes to seize the army and police apparatus . . . while dom-
inating the economy like their Jewish masters'. Their growing power
needed to be destroyed.

The Jordanian's animosity towards his co-religionists, though he
would not have accepted them as such, was in part simple prejudice,
common in a region riddled with sectarian strife. But there was cold
calculation too.[19] The 'heretics' were the 'key to change' because 'if
we manage to drag them into a religious war, we will be able to rouse
the Sunnis' who have 'the sharpest blades' and, 'bolder and more
courageous than the Shia', would triumph amid the 'clashing of
swords', al-Zarqawi wrote. The chaos and violence would also, by
way of a bonus, 'enrage the people against the Americans'.

Right from the beginning, 'al-Qaeda in Iraq', as al-Zarqawi's group
was erroneously known to most Western officials and analysts, had
dispatched suicide bombers against Shia targets. Such attacks intensified through 2004 and 2005. Some targeted the police and the army,
both largely staffed by Shias, but the majority did not. A double
bombing killed sixty pilgrims and shoppers in the holy cities of Najaf
and Karbala. More than 150 construction workers died in another
in Baghdad. This, al-Qaeda in the Land of the Two Rivers said, was in
retaliation for the operation which had forced them out of the border
town of Tal Afar. Ninety-five died when three car bombs exploded in
a vegetable market in the city of Balad. Nearly a hundred more died
in a day of mosque bombings in the eastern town of Khanaqin.

The third component of his strategy involved the media. This had
evolved dramatically in the half-decade since bin Laden planned his
major, news-seeking strikes at the end of the 1990s. Digital technology
now allowed extremists to control the production and dissemination
of images themselves, one of the most significant developments in
the history of terrorism. Violent extremists faced the same disadvan-
tages as anyone else broadcasting online – the competition for any
individual's attention was much greater – but they reaped the rewards

too. Unlike bin Laden, al-Zarqawi had no need to create content deemed newsworthy by media professionals if he wanted to communicate with 'the masses'. He could create his own bulletins, carefully designed to speak directly to exactly the people he wanted to speak to, and disseminate them himself. He did not need, or indeed want, a plane flying into a Western building to get his message across, and so had no need, or desire, to make the massive investments such an operation required.

Nor did he have to worry about what might be considered too gruesome to broadcast, as soon became horrifically evident. The group set up makeshift studios-cum-torture chambers and filmed videos of decapitations. These were laden with symbolism: the orange overalls worn by the Western hostages and victims were identical to those worn by prisoners in the US prison camp at Guantánamo Bay, Cuba. They were also horribly, unflinchingly graphic. The video which brought al-Zarqawi global notoriety was that of the execution of a young American contractor. This was downloaded around half a million times within twenty-four hours of its release. Many more videos followed.

The al-Qaeda senior leadership had been watching developments in Iraq with increasing anxiety. Despite its early promise, the whole project of developing the group's presence in Iraq risked going very badly wrong, potentially inflicting irreparable damage on an image carefully cultivated over a decade or more.

There appeared little that the senior leaders could do about it, though. Bin Laden had fled Afghanistan under US bombs, reaching Pakistan in early 2002. By the time al-Zarqawi was reaching the height of his power in western Iraq in early 2005, the leader of al-Qaeda central was already installed in the house in the northern garrison town of Abbottabad where he would remain, cut off from telephones and the Internet, for the next six years until his death. Bin Laden's deputy, al-Zawahiri, and others within the organisation repeatedly wrote to the leader of their Iraqi affiliate to remind him of the importance of maintaining good relations with local communities and encourage him, for the moment at least, to put any battle with the Shia on hold. Al-Zawahiri invoked his own experience in Egypt and spoke of how 'popular support is a decisive factor between victory and defeat [for] in [its] absence, the

Islamic mujahed movement would be crushed in the shadows, far from the masses who are distracted or fearful'. He told al-Zarqawi not to be seduced by the praise of the 'zealous young men' who had dubbed him 'sheikh of slaughterers', advising the younger man that 'among the things which the feelings of the Muslim populace who love and support you will never find palatable are the scenes of slaughtering the hostages'.[20] Others reminded the Jordanian of what had happened in the early 1990s in Algeria, where the militant campaign to create an Islamic state had imploded in a welter of indiscriminate violence directed largely at civilians. 'Their enemy did not defeat them . . . They destroyed themselves with their own hands by their alienation of the population with their lack of reason . . . oppression, deviance and ruthlessness,' wrote Atiyah Abd al-Rahman, a senior Libyan extremist based in Pakistan who had spent time in Algeria.[21]

Yet al-Zarqawi continued. From his perspective, what he was doing was not just rational, but obligatory, and was rooted in his conviction that his project to create a true Islamic enclave depended on ensuring the people who lived there behaved as he believed they should. Any backsliding or weakness would mean a community which would be unable to resist internal or external enemies, as countless historical examples had shown. But few communities react well to being told how to live their lives, particularly by a group of outsiders who have little understanding of local cultures and traditions. This was something the US occupying forces in Iraq were rapidly learning and the militants would also learn: that the sentiments of local people needed very sensitive handling or the consequences could be catastrophic.

By the spring of 2005 clashes were being reported between the local tribes and the foreign extremists across Anbar and beyond. This set up a spiral of violence, forcing al-Zarqawi and his associates to crack down on the growing dissent to their rule, prompting more anger, and thus more repression. The primary targets of their brutality were now the very people they were supposed to be helping. When in late 2005 many of the leaders of the tribes of western Iraq decided they needed to participate in parliamentary elections, the sputtering confrontation flared into open warfare. For the militants, participation in elections was the worst form of apostasy, with the sovereignty of popular will placed above that of God. For local Sunni communities, who had gained nothing from their insurgency, it meant the possibility of regaining a fraction of the role they had once played in the government of their nation. When the tribes accepted the US military's offer to protect voters against militant attacks, it was clear there had been a breakthrough.[22]

In January 2006, in belated recognition of the need for at least a rebranding, al-Zarqawi wrapped his al-Qaeda in the Land of the Two Rivers into a broader coalition of insurgent Islamic militant groups which was called the Majlis Shura al-Mujahideen fi al-Iraq, or Mujahideen Advisory Council of Iraq. His was the only organisation led by and composed of foreigners within the council. But this was much too little, and much too late. It was also clear that it was purely cosmetic. In February 2006, al-Zarqawi organised the bombing of the Al-Askari mosque in Samarra, one of the most holy sites to Shias in the world. This, as intended, provoked outrage and finally made it impossible for senior Shia clerics to hold back their congregations. Within months Iraq was plunged into the hellish violence of all-out civil war. By the autumn, bodies with hideous wounds from drills and blowtorches were turning up every day in their dozens on roadsides, rubbish dumps and in the Tigris. Al-Zarqawi did not live to see the full horror of the sectarian conflict he had helped unleash. In June 2006, he was killed by two 500-pound bombs dropped by a US jet.

Al-Qaeda was facing problems not only in Iraq. By early 2006, the wave of support for extremism and extremist violence in the wake of the invasions of Afghanistan and of Iraq was ebbing fast everywhere. In country after country, approval levels for bin Laden, for suicide bombing, for attacks on the US or the West were plummeting. The reasons for this were not hard to find. One of the most revealing episodes of the decade's conflicts, an event that indicated a genuine inflection point, came in Jordan in 2005 when suicide bombers attacked three luxury hotels in Amman, killing sixty people, including thirty-eight members of a wedding party. The attacks had been claimed by al-Zarqawi, on behalf of al-Qaeda. Almost all the victims were Jordanian compatriots. As polls revealed, public support for 'al-Qaeda in Iraq', for al-Zarqawi, for all strands of extremist Islam evaporated almost overnight. From 2002 to 2005 support in Jordan for violence against civilians in 'defence of Islam' had increased from 43 to 57 per cent, according to surveys by the US-based Pew Center. Another poll indicated that more than two-thirds of Jordanians considered al-Qaeda an 'armed resistance organisation', not a 'terrorist group'. Six months later, polling by Pew revealed that support for violence against civilians in Jordan had halved to 29 per cent and confidence in bin Laden had dropped from 64 to 24 per cent.[23]

The bombings in Amman showed that when violence was directed at an abstract and distant enemy, particularly the US, it was easy for people across the Islamic world to support it, but the reaction to extremist violence was very different when it was local policemen, soldiers, shopkeepers or siblings who were being killed. In every country hit by suicide bombings, backing for al-Qaeda, its ideology and methodology plunged. In Indonesia, support for radical violence had dropped six points following the bombing of a Bali nightclub in 2002 to 20 per cent, and then to 11 per cent after further attacks in 2005. In Morocco, twice as many people said suicide bombing was never justified after a spate of bloody strikes in 2004 and 2005 as before. The same could be seen in Saudi Arabia, Turkey, Egypt and many other countries too.[24] Militant groups everywhere began to weaken as the flow of recruits and money diminished. Security services, which had struggled to cope with the new wave of violence throughout the first half of the decade, now began to make real headway, bolstered by new powers, new understanding of their targets and, above all, a new flow of intelligence from communities which had now swung away from extremism. Al-Zarqawi's death was a prime example: he had been located due to intelligence given to Jordanian security services by militant sympathisers disgusted at the attack in Amman.[25]

In Iraq, this ebbing of support for the violent extremists among their fellow Sunnis continued. In August 2006, militants linked to the remnants of 'al-Qaeda in Iraq' killed a senior Anbar sheikh and dumped his body in bushes, rather than return it for immediate burial as Muslim and tribal custom demanded. The incident catalysed the formation of a coalition of Sunni tribes to battle the extremists, which became known as the 'Sahwa', or 'Awakening', Councils. These would collaborate increasingly closely with US forces, especially when the latter were reinforced with 30,000 troops during the so-called Surge of 2007 in and around Baghdad. Eventually there were 100,000 more of the Awakening auxiliaries, all paid $300 per month by the US taxpayer. By the end of 2007, the sectarian civil war was subsiding and the extremists appeared marginalised.

One reason was that there was less to fight for – the Sunnis of Baghdad, for example, were now confined to a few small enclaves. The Shia had effectively won the battle for the city. A second was a series of independent but mutually reinforcing decisions by regional powers which had all decided that their interests would not be served by the total collapse of Iraq as a state. Saudi Arabia moved to throttle the flow of its own citizens into Iraq, for instance. Tehran decided to consolidate its own massive influence in Baghdad – now effectively run by fellow Shias – through stability and continuity rather than change. Not all the death squads operating during the Iraqi civil war had been Iraqi either. US special forces, vastly aided by a streamlined process by which intelligence from raids was analysed and 'operationalised' before militants had time to react, located, killed or captured thousands of extremists, including many senior leaders.

Even though the violence declined, the social and political fabric of Iraq, already rent and tattered, had been torn apart. In 2007, in a symbolic attack on tolerance and pluralism, a suicide bomber killed thirty-eight people in Mutanabbi Street, the book market in Baghdad. Four months later came a second, equally symbolic but far more deadly assault: a series of simultaneous bombings which killed more than 800 people and injured 1,500 in a marketplace in the north-western town of Kahtaniya. The victims were largely Yazidis, from an ancient and much persecuted religious minority.

In such a vitiated environment, extremists in Iraq could survive, even if they did not thrive. The primary coalition of militant groups, known as the Islamic State in Iraq (ISI) since October 2006, retained the capacity to cause tremendous harm even in its much reduced state.[26] During August and October 2009, ISI claimed responsibility for four bombings targeting five government buildings in Baghdad which killed hundreds, as well as a series of suicide attacks targeting Shia. Even in 2010, an average of seventeen people died every day from suicide bombs or gunfire or executions in Iraq, and the country kept its position as the worst place in the world for terrorist violence.

And there were other causes for concern. Nouri al-Maliki, the Shia former Islamist activist who had been prime minister since 2006, appeared dedicated to an aggressively sectarian and authoritarian project which appeared almost deliberately designed to anger and frighten the Sunni minority.[27] Nineveh province, with its capital Mosul, remained especially troubled, the most significant base of violent extremist activism between Morocco and the Afghan–Iranian border. Contacts between ISI and al-Qaeda's senior leadership in Pakistan continued, even if bin Laden and others complained that liaison was poor and communication intermittent.[28] But Western intelligence officials nonetheless judged the threat posed by Iraqi militants to be 'relatively restricted'. ISI was 'struggling a bit', Major General Ray Odierno said. A year before the last US troops pulled out of Iraq, supposedly for good, US officials said they had killed or detained thirty-four out of forty-two of ISI's top leaders.[29] These included, in early 2010, the head of the group. A new chief was appointed: Abu Bakr al-Baghdadi.

A hagiography and former associates have described Ibrahim Awwad Ibrahim Ali al-Badri, better known as Abu Bakr al-Baghdadi, the leader of the Islamic State, as a devout, quiet youth. The truth is that we do not really know what the future leader of the Islamic State was like as a child or young man. We know he was born in the Iraqi city of Samarra in 1971. We know too that his parents were neither very rich nor very poor and that the family lived in the Al-Jibriya district of the city, a lower-middle-class neighbourhood.[30] We know, from al-Baghdadi's graduation certificate, that he did poorly in English, extremely well in mathematics and decently in most other subjects.[31] School was followed by several years at the Islamic University of Baghdad. Quite what he studied is not entirely clear, though it seems likely that, as supporters claim, he obtained a series of degrees, culminating in a PhD in Islamic studies.[32] Through the 1990s al-Baghdadi appears to have been living in Tobchi, a mixed Shia and Sunni neighbourhood on the western edges of the Iraqi capital, among the outlying districts which would become a battlefield after the US invasion of 2003.[33] He may have been preaching and teaching in a local mosque. A picture from around this time shows an impassive, bearded man with a broad forehead, smallish sharp eyes and narrow lips. Much remains unclear about al-Baghdadi's background, but what we do know is this: the environment in which he grew up during his formative years was one of religious resurgence, increasing regime brutality and corruption, ruinous Western-backed sanctions and air strikes, and extremist proselytisation. All, of course, before the invasion of 2003.

In the aftermath of the fall of Saddam Hussein, al-Baghdadi appears to have helped establish one of the first entirely indigenous militant groups motivated by extremist Islam. This drew recruits from tribal networks and neighbours in his home town and surrounding villages. Al-Baghdadi, now aged thirty-two, was picked up apparently by chance in a US sweep and interned in Camp Bucca, a vast prison built outside the southern port city of Basra. In prison he ran a sharia court, led prayers and impressed fellow inmates, guards and a US-appointed jail psychologist with his calm, quiet, serious sense of purpose. He was released from Camp Bucca after nearly a year of detention in late 2004.[34] By 2006, he appears to have gained some kind of official position on the 'sharia council' of ISI, perhaps acting as a key adviser to the group's leadership. In 2010, he was appointed the new 'emir'. This decision may not have been entirely due to his own ability or, perhaps, charisma. There is much evidence he was selected, over many older and more experienced figures, because he had religious credentials and a quiet authority which other figures, particularly a number of former senior Ba'athists involved in the group at the time, lacked.[35]

Many of these former officials were extremely competent men, with long experience in Saddam's military or intelligence services followed by almost a decade of violent insurgency. Nor was their adherence to extremist Islam superficial or pragmatic. It is very likely that some had been sympathetic to hardline ideas well before 2003, but, despite Saddam's tilt towards religion in the 1990s, had probably judged it impolitic to be too overt about their faith. It certainly should be no surprise that in post-invasion Iraq, Sunni Ba'athist officials and soldiers, forcibly demobilised and under occupation, in deteriorating economic conditions, who were engaged in an insurgency against the US and then a bitter sectarian civil war, who had seen friends and relatives killed by US troops or Shia militia, who had often been detained by the US military or Iraqi authorities for significant periods, and who had been surrounded by varying forms of anti-American, anti-Semitic and anti-Shia propaganda for their entire lives, should turn to radical Islam. The former Ba'athists brought a hard edge of military capability, organisational experience and, often, an understanding of how to run both a state and a military campaign that many Islamists lacked. There had been reports of such collaboration as early as 2004 or 2005. According to Martin Chulov, the Middle East correspondent for the *Guardian* and one of the best-informed reporters in the region, this cooperation had matured into a true partnership around 2008 or 2009. It would continue to deepen after al-Bagdadi's appointment as leader of ISI, with former Ba'athists coming to fill many of the most senior positions in the group.[36] In the June 2014 offensive against Mosul, a network of former Ba'athists led by the notorious Izzat Ibrahim al-Douri, a former vice president in Saddam's Iraq and the man who had masterminded the faith campaign in the 1990s, provided invaluable assistance to ISI fighters. As a reward, a former Ba'athist general was appointed governor of Mosul after its fall. Al-Douri praised 'the heroes and knights of al-Qaeda and the Islamic State', thus substantiating a link between Saddam Hussein and the group founded by bin Laden, al-Qaeda, nearly twelve years after the connection, non-existent at the time, was used to justified the invasion of Iraq.[37]

In time, further support for ISI came from Sunni tribes. Systematic discrimination, marginalisation and a series of broken promises had pushed Iraq's Sunnis back into open opposition to central government by the time of the elections of 2010 after which al-Maliki managed to hang on to power. Not all were aligned with ISI's goals by any means, but, in the shifting matrix of local conflict politics, many could make common cause at least temporarily. One particularly damaging failing of al-Maliki was his short-sighted treatment of those Sunnis who had earlier joined the anti-extremist Awakening Councils. These had often been organised by individual tribes and sub-tribes. Seeing them as a potential threat, al-Maliki undermined them, leaving them unemployed, unpaid and unprotected. As early as 2010, ISI had been targeting such fighters with the carrot of better pay than the government offered and the stick of an extremely unpleasant death in the case of refusal. The effort was part of a broader programme of outreach to tribes. Analysts Hassan Hassan and Michael Weiss describe an ISI tactic of offering leaders of minor tribes, or emerging younger leaders in major ones, control over an important resource, such as a particularly lucrative racket or smuggling route, if they pledged their support to the group and eliminated its opponents in their communities.[38] Al-Maliki eased the task of al-Baghdadi and his associates by continuing to stoke the Sunnis' sense that they were targets of a regional campaign of annihilation. In 2013, security forces sent by the prime minister to clear

Sunni protesters in Hawija, a town in the north of Iraq, killed scores and injured many more. The incident prompted armed clashes across much of the country. Increasingly, all ISI's leaders had to do was to organise and direct the fragmented elements of a rapidly reviving insurgency. Even in mid-2014, according to some estimates, only a third of ISI's combat strength was actually supplied by members of the group while the rest were fighters from other networks who were happy to join its armed columns as literal fellow travellers.[39]

This was of particular importance when the leaders of ISI were presented with an extraordinary opportunity to expand into Syria. The strategic decision to exploit this unforeseen chance may also have originated with the Ba'athists within the group's ranks. It led to a final break with al-Qaeda and fuelled the bitter rivalry between the two groups that exists today. It was critical to the emergence of the Islamic State as an independent, distinct entity, as well as of course to its eventual bid to re-establish a Sunni caliphate across a significant swathe of the Middle East, one of the most ambitious projects ever undertaken by an Islamic group.[40] It is a historical irony that this was only made possible by a series of uprisings led by people who explicitly rejected extremist Islam.

The 'Arab Spring' or 'Arab uprisings' began in December 2010 with the self-immolation of a Tunisian grocer, an act of spectacular violence designed to communicate a very clear message and inspire others, but one, in contrast to those orchestrated by Islamic militants over the previous decade, which harmed no one else. With their words and their deeds, the crowds that took to the streets in a succession of cities and towns across the Middle East over the following months reinforced the impression that al-Qaeda and all it stood for had been marginalised. The slogans in Egypt's Tahrir Square, in Tunis and in Manama were for democracy and human rights, not for the establishment of an Islamic state. Religion remained hugely powerful as a political, social and cultural force, but the uprisings that roiled the region through 2011 and into 2012 seemed to stand in stark opposition to Islamic militancy.

Yet, as Egypt, Libya, Syria and Yemen all descended into various degrees of anarchy and violence, it soon became clear that this sudden and powerful wave of change, though certainly a challenge to extremists, might also be the break they needed to reverse their steadily declining fortunes. Political Islamists who had long been repressed gained free rein to organise, proselytise and recruit in a way that had not been possible for decades, even taking power in some states and earning a greater government role in others.[41] Veteran extremists were released after years in prison, or returned from exile. Long-feared security services were disbanded, or remained disorientated and rudderless, suddenly unsure of the political and legal protection which had guaranteed immunity to the torturers and rapists that filled their ranks. As the first wave of euphoria turned to growing disillusion and anger, an ideal environment for recruitment, networking and activism was created.

In Syria, violent repression of peaceful demonstrators in March 2011 had prompted what rapidly became a full-scale rebellion against the long corrupt, nepotistic, brutal rule of the Assad family and their close associates. While the West dithered and moderates failed to unite, Islamists and Islamic militants stepped in. As the months went by, violence worsened and the regime worked to turn the growing conflict into a sectarian one. The Assads are Alawite, a Shia heterodox sect that comprised around an eighth of the population and was still viewed with some suspicion by many more traditional Shias around the world. Three-quarters of Syrians were Sunni, however, providing fertile ground for all those, inside and outside the rapidly disintegrating country, who saw the battle in terms of the Islamic world's most fundamental division.

The background to ISI's move into Syria was the success of Jabhat al-Nusra li-Ahl al-Sham (the Front for Protection of the Levant, JAN), the group set up by al-Qaeda's senior leadership in partnership with ISI in the early days of the uprising against the Assad regime. This was a classic move in the tradition of al-Qaeda's efforts over the decades to establish a presence wherever there was an opportunity to build capacity and spread its ideology, like a major multinational company trying to exploit a profitable new market. The venture in Syria was one of the more successful such projects. It was certainly more successful than the ill-fated joint undertaking with al-Zarqawi's Iraqi start-up a decade before. By the spring of 2013, after nearly two years of savage civil war, JAN had emerged as one of the most effective and respected of the opposition factions fighting the Assad regime. It also controlled a substantial amount of land and some highly lucrative resources such as oilfields.

The exact catalyst for ISI's attempt to assert its authority over al-Qaeda's Syrian affiliate at this time is unclear. One possibility, suggested by a suspected ISI defector in a series of tweets, is that the JAN leadership refused an order from al-Baghdadi to send a team to bomb targets in Turkey on the basis that it might jeopardise Ankara's policy of keeping their frontier with Syria open.[42] Another possibility is that the seizure of the eastern Syrian city of Raqqa by JAN and several other rebel groups in the spring of 2013 made a long-contemplated move that much more attractive and urgent. Whatever the truth, al-Baghdadi announced in an audio statement released in April 2013 that he had renamed his own organisation the Islamic State of Iraq and al-Sham (ISIS), and baldly stated that JAN was, effectively, its subsidiary. There was some justification for this claim, of course, as JAN had not only been set up by veteran fighters sent from Iraq by ISI but had been funded by their parent group since the outset.[43] However, it had then operated largely independently, and its leaders made no secret of their unwillingness to submit to their former chief. They publicly rejected al-Baghdadi's bid to assert his authority over them, saying that they recognised only al-Zawahiri, head of al-Qaeda, as their leader. When al-Zawahiri himself intervened in the dispute from his base in Pakistan, it was to tell al-Baghdadi to restrict himself to Iraq and to 'listen to and obey your emir'. The ISIS leader's response was to repudiate al-Zawahiri's authority with some of the bluntest language used by anyone in recent years of Islamic militancy. His group then launched an offensive against JAN and their allies.

By the summer of 2013, the group now known as ISIS, exploiting divisions among opposition factions and JAN's own increasing disarray, had taken control of Raqqa, the only provincial centre not held by Syrian government forces. This was a tipping point, and led to a wave of defections to al-Baghdadi's forces, particularly of foreign fighters attracted by its more aggressive approach and greater resources. These enabled further advances. Much as the Taliban had done in Afghanistan two decades before, the group now known as ISIS made rapid territorial gains as much through persuasion and coercion as through direct conquest. As its campaign gathered momentum, a range of disparate erstwhile opponents decided that their best interests lay inside the ISIS tent shooting out, rather than outside shooting in. As it had done in Iraq, the group paid particular attention to exploiting tribal conflicts to gain local allies.[44] In a region riddled with decades-old feuds and bitter competition for resources, this was not difficult to do. The powerful and fractious tribes of eastern Syria offered particularly fertile ground.[45] Fortified by the resources at its disposal, which now included the oilfields of eastern Syria and lucrative associated smuggling networks, ISIS advanced north and west, picking off successive centres of population and focusing on strategic points such as border crossings, oilfields and supply routes.

The expansion into Syria also brought them advantages on the Iraqi side of the (increasingly meaningless) border. Sunni communities there felt themselves to be part of a transnational sectarian struggle that would come to define the future of the region and their place within it. The Shia regime in Damascus was backed, diplomatically, economically and militarily, by Iran and had received assistance also from Hezbollah, the Lebanon-based Shia Islamist organisation. Tehran had also long backed al-Maliki in Baghdad, supporting his hardline sectarian policies and, as in Syria too, helping to organise a series of extremist Shia Islamist militias as auxiliaries to bolster Iraq's weak, Shia-dominated military. Sunni states backed Sunni factions, even those following hardline militant agendas, with weapons and cash. These did not include JAN or ISIS but that did not matter necessarily. In this struggle the fault lines were well known. Indeed, some had been clear for centuries, if not a millennium or more. Nor was there any sense that the battle was already won or lost. Political scientist Vali Nasr has pointed out that although the Shia account for only between 10 and 15 per cent of the world's Muslims, they constitute around half the population in the 'Islamic heartland' from Lebanon to Pakistan.[46] In this crucial zone, every effort could still count in swinging the balance one way or another, with massive long-term implications for either community.

In February 2014, al-Qaeda formally disowned ISIS. Al-Baghdadi's response was to send a suicide bomber to kill al-Zawahiri's personal envoy to Syria and allow subordinates to publicly deride the older man's leadership of al-Qaeda. Now the new resources that ISIS had acquired in Syria could be switched to the Iraqi front, which had been carefully prepared by eighteen months of intelligence work, spectacular terrorist attacks on carefully selected targets, alliance-building and propaganda. It was veterans of their offensives against JAN, other factions and, much more rarely, Assad's forces who would lead the summer offensive which saw Mosul fall and al-Baghdadi's fighters reach the outskirts of Baghdad.

Al-Baghdadi – or possibly the former Ba'athist soldiers and officials who had formulated the group's Syrian strategy – had pulled off an extraordinarily bold and aggressive manoeuvre, one that caught almost every observer, and most participants in the fight, completely unprepared. The group's next move was even more audacious, and even less expected.

4

THE ISLAMIC STATE

On 4 July 2014, the first Friday of Ramadan, the Muslim holy month, worshippers gathered at the Grand Mosque of Nur al-Din in Mosul. They talked, waited, removed their shoes, and then filed into the 750-year-old building before arranging themselves in rough lines to pray. They waited some more. The *minbar*, the high pulpit, remained empty. Then there was movement outside. A convoy of pickup trucks pulled up. Armed men opened a way through the assembled congregation. There were shouts of *Allahu Akbar*, God is Great, and Abu Bakr al-Baghdadi, dressed in flowing black robes and a black turban, walked to the front, climbed the short staircase of the *minbar* and began to address them.

He spoke for thirty-one minutes, of the importance of Ramadan, the duties of Muslims, of hellfire and salvation, and of the need to humiliate polytheism and the polytheists.[1]

'Your mujahideen brothers have been rewarded by Allah with victory and He has enabled them to assume power after long years of patience and fighting His enemies,' al-Baghdadi told the assembled men. 'He has granted them success and they have rushed to achieve their goal and to declare the caliphate . . . lost for centuries.'

He then struck a marginally more humble note.

'I have been tasked with this great burden, and this great responsibility. I was chosen to lead you, though I am not the best among you,' he said. 'If you see me as righteous, help me; if you see me straying from the straight path, correct me. Obey me as long as I obey Allah, and if I disobey Him, you should not obey me.'

The 43-year-old spoke calmly, carefully and with authority. The congregation listened attentively. This was not unsurprising. The incumbent cleric who had led prayers at the mosque until the militants had seized the city had been executed a week earlier, with a dozen other religious scholars who had refused to swear allegiance to their new rulers. At the end of his sermon, al-Baghdadi left as he had come, to shouts of *Allahu Akbar*, swept out by his bodyguards to the waiting convoy.

Since the 1960s and 70s, when this most recent wave of Islamic militancy began, strategists and thinkers within the movement have elaborated different visions of how the battle against the West, the Zionists and their local allies – and *kufr*, or 'unbelief', more generally – might play out. Some were technical, some apocalyptic, most were a mixture of both. One of the most influential of such texts, *The Management of Savagery*, was published online in 2004 and widely read by extremists. It is still referred to frequently and is reported to be part of the recommended reading for IS commanders.[2] If the exact identity of its author is still unclear, its influence is not.

The Management of Savagery described three stages of a campaign.[3] The first was '*nikayah*', when irregular forces would wage an unconventional war involving terrorist tactics to compel local authorities or occupying forces to withdraw from a given area. The second was '*tawahhush*', a mixture of unconventional and conventional tactics designed to foment civil conflict and exacerbate sectarian tension to destabilise the zone vacated by the authorities. Finally, there would be '*tamkin*', when the militants themselves moved in to take control and, through bringing a rough-and-ready form of security to desperate communities, could establish their authority and eventually consolidate a more durable base – the ultimate goal of most militants most of the time.

Over the centuries, such projects have been common in the Islamic world. All have attempted to achieve two objectives: to reform their own societies, returning those Muslims who had departed in practice and belief to the true faith, and to battle outsiders, which from the late eighteenth century on usually meant non-believers, most often Europeans. Several Islamic states were declared between 1830 and 1930 in parts of northern and eastern Africa, in the Caucasus and in the north of what is now Pakistan. Their leaders took religious titles, such as the Amir-ul Momineen, the commander of the faithful, and often set up basic institutions.[4] Minorities were oppressed and sins such as drinking or adultery were punished. None lasted very long, blown away by Western military superiority and undermined by a lack of local legitimacy.

The religious revival of the 1970s led to renewed attempts. In 1982, President Hafez al-Assad, father of Bashar, ordered the Syrian Army to put down an uprising by the Muslim Brotherhood in the city of Hama, killing tens of thousands. In 1992, extremists in a poor suburb of Cairo declared it an Islamic state – and were crushed in their turn. In Afghanistan between 1994 and 2001, the Taliban made another, marginally more successful, attempt to create an Islamic state: television and instrumental music were banned, women were forced to wear burkas, girls ordered to stay at home if strict segregation in schools could not be assured, while public executions and amputations of thieves' hands were commonplace. The campaign to 'encourage virtue and prevent vice' within the community and to defend against the threat from outside it were, the Taliban believed, intrinsically connected. As Taqi al-Din ibn Taymiyyah, the conservative thinker so often cited by today's militants, had made clear in the thirteenth century following the fall of Baghdad to the Mongols, it was Muslims' own weakness and decadence which made them so vulnerable to foreign domination.

Quite where the Islamic state that so many militants dreamed of creating should actually be located had long been a matter of dispute. Most favoured their native lands. Before he joined al-Qaeda, al-Zawahiri dismissed the 'battles going on in the far-flung regions . . . such as Chechnya, Afghanistan, Kashmir and Bosnia' as 'just the groundwork' for those 'in the heart of the Islamic world'. In 2005, he was more specific, writing that 'the victory of Islam will never take place until a Muslim state is established . . . in the Levant, Egypt and the neighbouring states of the Peninsula and Iraq'.

This had been the goal of Abu Musab al-Zarqawi too, of course.

Yet the enclave all these men were working to establish, wherever it was situated, was only a way station to another, grander destination. Abdullah Azzam had spoken of liberating areas from southern Spain to the Far East. *The Management of Savagery* tells the mujahideen that if they captured Algeria, 'they [should] begin to prepare for conquering Libya and Egypt the following morning', while 'if the mujahideen are given victory on the Arabian Peninsula, on the following day they must prepare immediately to begin conquering the smaller states which these paltry regimes in Jordan and the Gulf rule'.[5] The militant community has long been hard-wired for expansion and looks to history to justify their territorial claims.

After the Prophet's death, Islam spread rapidly. Some historians suggest it was the military superiority of the early Arab Muslim armies that was primarily responsible. The black flags under which contemporary extremists fight, use as idents on their videos and, in places like Raqqa, fly above offices deliberately recall what are imagined to be the battle banners of the earliest Muslim forces.[6] These troops' success may have been due to extremely capable battlefield leaders, the faith of the fighters, their ability to do without cumbersome supply trains, or flexible and innovative tactics. But the brutal reality of contemporary geopolitics may have been the most significant factor. Happily for the early Muslims, the faith had emerged at a time when the two superpowers of the era – Byzantine Rome and the Persians – had exhausted themselves in centuries of conflict. Riven with internal dissent, structural weakness and existential doubt, neither was in a position to defend marginal territories. This was a historic opportunity that the newly mobilised Muslim community readily seized. Armies and raiding parties surged out from the Arabian peninsula. Most headed westwards, across to the rich lands of what would be known to later conquerors as the Levant, on along the North Africa coast. Some headed north too, and into what is now Iran.

It is likely that without this expansion the new unity forged by Mohammed among Arabian tribes would have collapsed. The Prophet had stopped the tribes pursuing short-range raids on neighbours that had been a traditional part of their economic survival for centuries. If they were not to turn once more against each other, they needed new targets further afield. The expansion gathered momentum and, decade after decade, the advance of the faith never really slowed, with every military victory reinforcing their sense that Islam was indeed the project of God. Many crucial military encounters were won when opposing forces defected. Many cities just decided against resistance. Everywhere, the armies and raiding parties were preceded by preachers, mystics and traders. Huge swathes of territory were joined, nominally, to the new empire as local rulers simply sent messages pledging acceptance of their new sovereigns and often the new faith too.[7]

Whatever the reasons behind it, this extraordinary expansion meant that, from the beginning, Muslims' collective memory had a rather different tone from that of either Jews or Christians. Mohammed did not merely outline a vision of a utopian community to be realised at an unspecified future date but actually built one during his own lifetime. More importantly, that community then transformed much of the known world, through diplomacy, trade, cultural exchange and, of course, through war. While for Jews the collective memory of the earliest experience of believers is repeated exile, and for Christians it is persecution, for Sunni Muslims it is one of the most successful military and political campaigns in history.[8]

Moreover, as its early expansion slowed and its great cities expanded and its traders prospered, the new Islamic empire developed into a hugely rich and powerful civilisation. The Umayyads, who ruled from 661 to 750 from Damascus, continued to acquire new territory, extending their rule as far as the Atlantic coast of the Iberian peninsula to the west and the Indus valley in the east. They gave the new imperial entity a permanence in other ways too. Some of the most famous examples of Islamic architecture – the great mosques of Cordoba and Damascus, the Al-Aqsa mosque in Jerusalem – date from this period. The Umayyads also consolidated the Arabic language throughout their domains, and launched naval expeditions for the first time. The Abbasids, who overthrew the Umayyads in a revolt in 750, ruled from a series of cities including Baghdad, Raqqa and Samarra, and are credited with ushering in a golden age of Islamic civilisation. By the turn of the first millennium, the new empire had splintered into states run by competing dynasts, but brilliant cultural activity continued, and the various incursions of the Crusaders from the west were eventually repulsed and invasions from the east successfully resisted. Even the catastrophic sack of Baghdad by the Mongols in 1258 did not mean that the era of great Islamic rulers was over. Those who had destroyed the great city converted to Islam themselves. Within two hundred years, Constantinople would have fallen to the Ottoman Turks, who went on to conquer much of the Balkans and threaten central Europe. Even as late as the seventeenth century, no European state, with the arguable exception of Spain, came even close to rivalling the Ottoman

Empire's territorial extent, military capability, scientific knowledge and artistic achievement. From Delhi, the Mughals, an Islamic dynasty descended from Mongol converts, dominated South Asia. Their wealth and power was fabulous. Between these two superpowers, the Safavids built their Shia state in Persia. The contrast with the poor, backward, bickering, strife-torn nations of Europe is striking.

What today's commentators in London and Washington often forget – and militants repeatedly remind themselves and anyone else prepared to listen – is that the supremacy of the West is a relatively new phenomenon in historical terms. Across much of the world, for two-thirds of the last 1,300 years, the power, the glory and the wealth was, broadly speaking, Islamic. The militants seek to return the world's Muslim community to what they see as its rightful status: a global superpower. The story of the caliphate can only be understood within the context of this overarching narrative. And understanding this story – and its different versions – is essential if we are to understand the degree to which Abu Bakr al-Baghdadi and his Islamic State followers have not simply revived this 1,400-year-old institution, but also re-imagined and reinvented it.

In his book *Destiny Disrupted: A History of the World Through Islamic Eyes*, the Afghan American writer Tamim Ansary suggests that the core religious allegory of Islam – analogous to the last supper, crucifixion and resurrection of Christ, or exodus, bondage and the return to the promised land for the Jews – is not limited to the life of the Prophet but includes the rule of his four immediate successors as well.[9] These were the wise, just and affable Abu Bakr, the immensely strong warrior ascetic Omar, who oversaw much of the most rapid expansion of the Arab Islamic empire, the melancholic, austere but hugely wealthy and nepotistic Othman and finally Ali, the upright, honest son-in-law of the Prophet. These men are known as the 'rightly guided' caliphs.

When Mohammed died in 632, as mentioned in chapter 3, he not only left no clear instructions as to who should succeed him, but also gave no indication of what sort of leadership the Muslim community should expect in his absence. Many questions were unanswered. What would a successor's powers actually be? Would they have a spiritual role as well as a temporal one? Would there be a succession at all?

When the elderly Abu Bakr was chosen to lead the Muslims after long debates among the close associates of the Prophet, he was designated the caliph, which simply means deputy. No formal decision on his powers was ever taken. The caliphate was thus, from the beginning, an ad hoc arrangement, not a specific designed institution, and this is one reason why no consensus has ever been reached on exactly what role the caliph plays.

It was perhaps inevitable that the office would become the subject of fierce competition and conflict. In addition to the split over the very first succession, which became that between the Shia and the Sunnis, three of the first four caliphs died violently at the hands of fellow believers. The Umayyad Caliphate was, and remains, deeply controversial. Its replacement by the Abbasids led to the creation of a rival caliphate in Andalusia. Another arose in Egypt. This chaos and competition continued over the centuries. The title eventually ended up with the Ottoman sultans, from the sixteenth century to the twentieth. But by then these various conflicts had undermined the credibility of the entire institution. As the modern era dawned, there was little left of the original and undoubted awesome grandeur that the title had once evoked. The link to the men who had built the Islamic empire had long been broken. When Kemal Atatürk, the modernising ruler of Turkey, effectively abolished the caliphate in 1924, vesting its powers in his new state's national assembly, there was uproar in many parts of the Islamic world but no effective resistance. Atatürk dispatched the last caliph into ignominious if comfortable exile in France, and the institution lapsed into an odd sort of redundancy.[10] But within less than a decade of the caliphate's abolition, activists within the Islamic world had begun to see its restoration as the panacea to all the ills of the *umma*. One of the first to do so was Hassan al-Banna, the Egyptian schoolteacher who founded the Muslim Brotherhood in 1928.

This complicated history means no one is very sure what would allow an individual to claim to be caliph today. Many, probably the vast majority of even practising Muslims, find the whole idea of someone appointing themselves, or even being appointed, to the office risible. Others have admitted the theoretical possibility of there being a new caliph but maintain that some kind of global consensus among clerics would be essential to any actual appointment. Some have said that the simple fact of ruling justly and wisely over a sufficient mass of population and extent of territory could be enough. One condition for leadership of the *umma*, some insist, is descent from the Quraysh, the tribe of the Prophet, and contest al-Baghdadi's claim to this lineage. Some base their opposition on other points of doctrine or law. In his speech at the mosque in Mosul, Abu Bakr al-Baghdadi cited entire paragraphs taken from the acceptance speech – a reluctant one, according to most accounts – of his namesake 1,400 years earlier. That he should do so, and thus claim the legacy of a man who is revered by many Muslims, angered many. For almost everybody, al-Baghdadi's extraordinarily hubristic announcement in June 2014 does not make him caliph at all, it simply makes him the latest of a long line of religious revivalist leaders, of all faiths, who have claimed the right to lead a given religious community to redemption.

But while his claim to the title of caliph may have been dismissed by all major Islamic religious authorities, and most minor ones too, none would dispute the subtext behind it: the resurrection not simply of a title but of the power, dignity, wealth and military renown of Muslim rulers from the seventh to the eighteenth centuries.

Within days of assuming his new office, al-Baghdadi, or Caliph Ibrahim as he now called himself, issued a series of orders which gave some idea of the form his reinvented caliphate would take. First came a list of regulations determining personal behaviour of the inhabitants of Mosul, the caliphate's new capital. These were familiar from those already in force in Fallujah and Raqqa over the previous year. They also recalled those imposed on local communities in the west of Iraq during the days of al-Zarqawi's rule, in Taliban Afghanistan, and in the various Islamic states that revivalists of various kinds had tried to construct over the previous decades and centuries. Smoking and drinking were forbidden, the former punishable by amputation, the latter by death; women were only to wear 'Islamic garb' and to remain in the home unless accompanied by a close relative or their husband. Schools were ordered to rigorously segregate their pupils and teachers by gender. Men were ordered to attend prayers five times a day punctually or face lashing. The newly established religious police which patrolled Mosul was an institution familiar to Raqqa, Fallujah, Taliban Afghanistan and, of course, contemporary Saudi Arabia.

Soon after came executions. Among the first to die in Mosul were the clerics who refused to pledge allegiance to IS. These killings continued in the city through the autumn and winter. In one month alone, January 2015, four doctors were killed, possibly after refusing to treat IS fighters, two alleged homosexuals were pushed off the top of a tower block in front of a crowd in the centre of the city, and at least one woman was stoned to death for adultery. Two militants from IS itself were crucified and then shot after being found guilty of extortion at checkpoints. The majority of the killings in Mosul in the immediate aftermath of the takeover were, however, of tribesmen who had 'betrayed' the Islamic State by collaborating with government forces.[11]

Again, as in Taliban Afghanistan or in Anbar a decade earlier, the aim of this very public and brutal violence was to enforce public order. Justice needed quite literally to be seen to be done. In 1998, I had watched a Taliban cleric hold aloft the severed hands of two thieves to show them to a crowd of several hundred, possibly thousands, in a stadium in Kabul. A few minutes later a woman convicted of murder by a local court was shot dead. The Taliban hoped the severity of such punishments would compensate for their failure to administer justice in any systematic way in the parts of the country they controlled. That such punishments were visible was thus essential. The same had been true for al-Zarqawi in Anbar, who had conducted executions in the street in front of crowds rounded up by his militants. When he had the means, the leader of 'al-Qaeda in Iraq' had circulated video clips of the torture of offending local residents by hand in cities like Fallujah. But neither al-Zarqawi nor the Taliban had anything like the communications technology available to IS. The amputation of the hand of one alleged thief in Syria's Aleppo province in early 2014 was 'live-tweeted' by members of the group, in what was probably a fairly gruesome first.[12] A clip of the two alleged homosexuals being hurled from a tower block was also uploaded to the Internet. Much of the coverage in the West focused on the effect such material might have on aspirant extremists in the UK, France or elsewhere. But these were not the primary audience. The availability of the Internet and affordable Internet-enabled devices such as laptops, smartphones and tablets meant that they would be viewed locally too. The brutal justice still needed to be public, and spectacular, but would now be seen by far more people than ever before.

The violence was designed to speak to three critical audiences, with a different message for each. For those who opposed the Islamic State, the aim was to terrorise through deliberately excessive violence shocking in its cruelty. For those already committed to the cause, its aim was to mobilise: to rally them into action by demonstrating the group's power and success. And for those who remained undecided, it was designed to polarise: to force the viewer into picking a side and deciding if they would condone the violence, remain silent and thus become complicit, or oppose it.

This was why there was no effort made to hide the mass killings of captured Syrian or Iraqi government troops or Kurdish fighters. The graphic images of the massacres undermined the morale of the poorly paid, poorly armed government forces and, to a lesser extent, their Kurdish counterparts. They also indicated the ruthlessness of IS to enemies further afield, such as the Iranians, the Israelis, the Saudis and the West. They proved to those who backed the group that they had made the right choice, and also sent a clear message to local tribes still sitting on the fence: either you are with us, or against us, and made the risks of being the latter abundantly clear.

The deliberately staged killing of foreign hostages was an extension of this logic of terror, mobilisation and polarisation. It also implied a policy of continuous escalation. Though more professionally produced, these appalling films owed a clear debt to those made by al-Zarqawi in 2004 and 2005 – in their use, for example, of the orange Guantánamo Bay-style jumpsuits worn by victims. One video, broadcast in November 2014, showed the remains of a decapitated former US Army ranger turned aid worker who had apparently been executed along with eighteen Syrian Air Force pilots. The latter were lined up, while a British IS fighter delivered a diatribe against the West and the US. They were then forced to lie down to allow eighteen militants, clearly selected to represent a variety of nations, to simultaneously hack off their heads. In January 2015, a downed Jordanian pilot was locked into a cage and then burned alive.[13]

The Islamic State also exceeded any other previous group in its violence against non-Muslim communities. Even in Taliban Afghanistan, some non-Muslim communities had been tolerated, though Shias had been persecuted. This was justified by reference to early Islamic law on so-called *dhimmis*, non-Muslims who were allowed to continue practising their religion on payment of a special tax, albeit as second-class citizens with limited legal protection. A token offer along these lines was made to Christian and other communities within the territories occupied by IS but it was accompanied by threatened and real violence and almost all non-Muslims fled. One terrible example was that of the Yazidi, seen either as pagans or as apostates by the Islamic State. Large numbers – certainly hundreds, possibly thousands – of Yazidi men were killed and women abducted when the group captured the areas where they had lived for centuries. Many women were given to IS fighters as 'temporary wives' and repeatedly raped. The IS magazine, *Dabiq*, boasted that a fifth of Yazidi women captured in the wave of expansion which followed the fall of Mosul were distributed to senior commanders, and the rest split among rank-and-file fighters. This was justified on the basis of selective quotations from the Koran and holy texts detailing the treatment of captives taken in war and slaves.[14]

Along with the careful and spectacular operation of violence on people, there was violence against objects associated with other beliefs too. The primary targets of these were shrines and religious buildings which were seen as contrary to *tauheed*, the strict unicity of God. Folksy, popular practices such as worshipping at the tombs of long-dead holy men, even decorating graves, were considered a danger to the common good and therefore to the survival of the new caliphate. Al-Baghdadi, in his sermon in Mosul, had called on Allah to 'strengthen Islam and Muslims to wage war on polytheism and the polytheists', and within days of taking control of Mosul IS moved to destroy local shrines to the prophets Younis, or Jonah, and Seth, the third son of Adam and Eve. The group would have reduced many more to ruins if they had not encountered some very brave local opposition.[15] Any pre-Islamic archaeological site was a reminder of the era of *jahiliyaa*, or barbaric ignorance, and so also was a threat. In January 2015, remaining portions of the old walls of the city of Nineveh, near Mosul, were razed. Two months later, IS destroyed much of what remained of the 3,000-year-old city of Nimrud using bulldozers and explosives.

None of these measures was particularly exceptional, in anything other than the degree of rigour, brutality and violence with which they were applied. Many had been implemented before, in one form or another, by previous Islamic militant groups and, as we will see in the next chapter, in other countries such as Pakistan, Yemen, Somalia and Nigeria. But one order issued by al-Baghdadi was dramatically new. Among the very first edicts issued by the new caliph was an order that the frontier posts between Iraq and Syria be destroyed. Though previous groups such as the Taliban had carved out substantial territories, none had explicitly challenged international boundaries, even disputed ones, so directly. Nor had any such challenge been so central to their programme. Within days of Mosul's fall, a film was released showing a bulldozer breaching the sandy berm through the desert which marked the border between the two states. Entitled the 'End of the Sykes–Picot', a reference to the secret agreement between Sir Mark Sykes and François-Georges Picot of Britain and France in 1916 on what were to become the borders of Iraq and Syria, it followed a pledge from al-Baghdadi himself to 'break all the barriers of . . . all the countries'.[16]

Shortly after the seizure of Mosul, al-Baghdadi issued a message that summed up the world view not just of IS but of all Islamic militants in the early part of this century. First and foremost, the caliphate would allow Muslims to heal the damage done by centuries of Western dominance, through dismantling all the structures it had imposed. 'The Muslims were defeated after the fall of their caliphate,' al-Baghdadi wrote. 'Then their state ceased to exist, so the unbelievers were able to weaken and humiliate the Muslims, dominate them in every region, plunder their wealth and resources, and rob them of their rights. They accomplished this by attacking and occupying their lands, placing their treacherous agents in power to rule the Muslims with an iron fist, and spreading dazzling and deceptive slogans such as: civilisation, peace, coexistence, freedom, democracy, secularism, Ba'athism, nationalism and patriotism, among other falsehoods.'[17]

Surveying the Islamic world, al-Baghdadi described sectarian clashes between Burmese Buddhists and Rohingya Muslims in Myanmar, and between Christians and Muslims in the Central African Republic, mentioning pretty much every conflict in between that might be described in religious terms: the 'dismembering and disembowelling [of] Muslims in the Philippines, Indonesia, and Kashmir . . . the killing of Muslims in the Caucasus and expelling them from their lands . . . making mass graves for the Muslims in Bosnia and Herzegovina, and the slaughtering of their children'. He listed other alleged atrocities, including repression of Muslims in western China, the ban on the hijab in France, 'the destruction of Muslims' homes in Palestine, prisons everywhere full of Muslims, the seizing of Muslims' lands, the violation and desecration of Muslims' sanctuaries and families' and the 'propagation of adultery', though quite where this final crime was occurring was left unclear. All this violence was attributed to the West and aggregated into a single global conflict between belief and unbelief, between the West and their proxies in the Islamic world and true Muslims. The solution, of course, was the caliphate.

This new Islamic superpower would rival the US in political, military and cultural force and thus restore the rightful order of world affairs and the fallen honour and dignity of all Muslims. 'Raise your head high, for today – by Allah's grace – you have a state and caliphate, which will return your dignity, might, rights and leadership . . . rush O Muslims to your state. Yes, it is your state. Rush, because Syria is not for the Syrians, and Iraq is not for the Iraqis. The earth is Allah's.'

Finally, the new caliphate would mean that a Muslim who wanted to follow his faith would not have to choose between submission to the unbelievers or becoming a 'terrorist':

'Those rulers continue striving to enslave the Muslims, pulling them away from their religion with those slogans. So either the Muslim pulls away from his religion . . . living despicably and disgracefully . . . or he lives persecuted, targeted and expelled, to end up being killed, imprisoned or terribly tortured, accused of terrorism. Because terrorism is to disbelieve in those slogans and to believe in Allah. Terrorism is to refer to Allah's law for judgement. Terrorism is to worship Allah as He ordered you. Terrorism is to refuse humiliation, subjugation and subordination. Terrorism is for the Muslim to live as a Muslim, honourably with might and freedom. Terrorism is to insist upon your rights and not give them up.'

Nearly a decade before, when al-Zawahiri had written to al-Zarqawi in Iraq in his bid to moderate the younger extremist's excesses, he had repeatedly stressed one point: the importance of maintaining support among local and regional communities if the project to build an Islamic state was to succeed.

'If we look at the two short-term goals, which are removing the Americans and establishing an Islamic emirate in Iraq, or a caliphate if possible, then we will see that the strongest weapon which the mujahideen enjoy – after the help and granting of success by God – is popular support from the Muslim masses there, and the surrounding Muslim countries,' he told the Jordanian.

He had succinctly summed up the dilemma that faced all militants, including al-Baghdadi and IS as summer turned to autumn in 2014.

'We must maintain this support as best we can, and we should strive to increase it, on the condition that striving for that support does not lead to any concession in the laws of the sharia,' the al-Qaeda deputy leader said.

This tension, between application of the rigorous law the militants believe is necessary for the internal reform and thus the external strength of the community versus the desire of the people they rule to be able to decide for themselves how to live their lives has never been resolved. It is one of the fundamental weaknesses of the Islamic militant project. In the long run, it may well be what makes that project unworkable in all but the most specific conditions. Any vision dedicated to eradicating difference and diversity is always going to find the reality of human society something of a challenge.

In any given community, there might be a 'raw nerve' who finds the extremists' ideology attractive. Others might see potential for personal advantage in the rule of the militants. But actual 'popular support from the Muslim masses' depends on a community's conviction that the extremists are the only people who can protect its economic, social and cultural well-being.

This was made much easier if communities believed they were facing an existential threat which the militants were uniquely qualified to counter. In the Sunni-dominated areas of Syria and Iraq, this threat, of course, was Shia hegemony. But to maintain support was harder, as al-Zarqawi had found out when the tribes began to turn against him in Anbar province in 2005. One option would be to replicate the vast network of informers, surveillance and terror of the brutal authoritarian regimes that had ruled Iraq and Syria for the last four decades. In April 2015, *Spiegel* magazine published a cache of documents revealing the extensive system of repression IS set up across Syria, even in zones it did not actually control. It was bureaucratic, systematic and apparently effective. Unsurprisingly, the man who had designed it was a former senior intelligence officer in Saddam Hussein's air defence force.[18]

Reporting of IS has focused, justifiably, on the horrific and systematic human rights abuses the group commits, as well as on its military capabilities. What has received less attention is the model of governance IS seems to be developing. If one aim of the project is, as al-Baghdadi has clearly indicated, to show Muslims and the world in general that the revolution it is implementing is a universal panacea to all man's ills, it has to be effective as well as righteous, respected as well as feared. The new Islamic state needs to do what states in the region have so often failed to do: it must provide, in some measure, for its citizens.

Where IS differs dramatically from any previous project to create a new, extremist Islamic state is in the scale of its operations, the size of the territory it administers and the resources it has at its disposal. This means a much greater ability to order and structure the lives of the several million people living under its authority than any previous group has ever had. It also means more money to spend on what could be called its 'soft power' and 'outreach' efforts, or propaganda. (Of course, it also means it has much higher expenses than most of the other militant organisations existing over the last two to three decades.[19])

IS gets its money from a number of sources. Historically, private donors elsewhere in the Islamic world have provided significant financial assistance. Typically, these will be tapped for funds for a particular operation. This is not unlike a major charity in the West launching an appeal during a particular disaster or for a special cause. In 2013, IS, JAN and other opposition factions launched an offensive near Latakia on the Mediterranean coast. One cleric in Kuwait provided hundreds of thousands of dollars of funding while others in Saudi Arabia, the United Arab Emirates and Qatar also appear to have contributed to the multimillion-dollar cost of the push. The short campaign saw, among other atrocities, the killing of 190 civilians, including fifty-seven women and at least eighteen children and fourteen elderly men, in a single day.[20]

The flow of funds to IS from the Gulf has prompted repeated speculation that it has been directly funded by one or more states, particularly Qatar or Kuwait. Such suspicions are understandable given that both states are known to have generously backed other factions in Syria and elsewhere, but remain unfounded.[21] Nor has any firm proof emerged that the authorities in such states have given their tacit approval to private donations by residents to al-Baghdadi's organisation. In recent years, Western intelligence officials believe, such donations have dropped away and private giving now provides a negligible proportion of the group's income.[22]

For as IS has expanded territorially, it has carefully prioritised the acquisition of lucrative resources. The most obvious has been oil, and the majority of the oilfields of eastern Syria are currently under its nominal control as well as some in Iraq. Most is used for internal consumption, but some is sold through long-established smuggling routes, mainly through Kurdish areas of northern Iraq and into Turkey, though also into regime-controlled zones. Despite fetching a price which is only around a fifth of market values, these sales may have brought in more than $40 million every month in the summer of 2014, according to the United Nations. In comparison, the personal wealth of Osama bin Laden was estimated at between $5 million and $30 million, with the reality almost certainly at the bottom end of this scale. The revenue of the Taliban, derived from the vast Afghan drug trade as well as donations, protection rackets and levies on activities ranging from marble mining to human trafficking, may have reached around $400 million in 2011. It seems probable that the revenue IS earned from oil declined substantially by the middle of 2015 as the US bombing campaign and other measures took effect, though it still may earn the group several million dollars every month.[23]

This may not matter. Hydrocarbons are far from the only resource to be exploited. Large sums are also made from trafficking wheat, seized cotton and antiquities smuggled by criminal gangs who buy a 'licence' to excavate and traffic from IS authorities.[24] Ransoms for hostages have brought in, it is thought, tens of millions of dollars, though as these are sold, killed or otherwise freed, this flow of cash will dry up. As IS has advanced it has seized very large quantities of arms and ammunition, vehicles, generators, industrial plant and construction equipment. Some of this too is sold, raising further large sums, as has much of the private property that has been 'requisitioned', particularly from members of religious minorities. This resource is rapidly exhausted, however, and only renewed through expansion.

But most important in terms of income generation are the 'taxes' levied on businesses and individuals. Some are traditional, such as the customary levy for charitable works, which at 2.5 per cent or thereabouts of revenue is often less onerous than many of those raised by the Syrian or Iraqi regimes when they were in power.[25] Government employees – some still paid by national exchequers in Damascus and Baghdad – are taxed on their salaries. Together these may bring in a million or so dollars every day, though reliable figures are difficult to come by.[26] Other taxes are less systematic, but still involve very significant sums. These are a form of protection racket, accompanied by explicit threats of extreme violence if they are not paid but also on the understanding that IS will ensure the security of businesses or individuals from bandits, thieves or other extortionists if the money is handed over. Well before the fall of Mosul, the city's inhabitants were paying between $8 million and $12 million each month to IS, US officials and others estimated. Reuters news agency reported that a standard payment – described as 'support to the Mujahideen' by IS on the receipts they scrupulously issued – was around $100 per month for a shopkeeper. Bigger businessmen paid much, much more of course.[27]

Such fees are also levied on trucks and private cars travelling through Syria and Iraq. The transport business across the zone that is now under the nominal control of IS has long been run by Sunni tribes for whom illegally moving fridges, microwaves, air-conditioning units, livestock, petrol, foodstuffs, shampoo, people, drugs and lots more besides across the desert to Baghdad is a primary source of revenue. A decade ago, al-Zarqawi and his extremists alienated local tribal sheikhs in western Iraq by brusquely appropriating many of their smuggling networks. Charles Lister, of the Brookings Institution in Qatar, points out that IS has been more careful, forgoing revenue by demanding relatively light payments for passage and thus not only guaranteeing the tribes' security for their business but allowing them to make more money than when they had to deal with corrupt regime officials in either Syria or Iraq. IS may earn less this way, but gain a priceless collaborative relationship with local communities and, particularly, with local Sunni powerbrokers.[28]

What then does IS do with this immense flow of cash? The answer, predictably, is that it does what many rudimentary states with a revolutionary agenda do: funds an administration, social services and a military as well as a variety of cultural or educational initiatives designed to shape the values, norms and world view of the people it governs.

The administration relies on co-opted or coerced local officials who have been unable or unwilling to leave, reinforced by volunteers, both local and foreign, and all overseen by IS 'cadres'. Courts are of course Islamic, with religious judges. These provide a rapid adjudication of often long-standing disputes and do not demand bribes. In the population centres they command, IS officials have moved rapidly to gain almost total dominance over the supply of daily necessities, particularly bread, cooking oil and fuel. This monopoly of distribution and production of the basics for everyday existence is a powerful tool of social as well as economic control, as many other regimes in the region have long recognised.[29] IS appears to prefer subsidies to outright handouts, however, though it nonetheless apparently tries to make sure that no one goes hungry. Bread produced in the bakeries run by the group is usually sold relatively cheaply. In some towns, IS has offered low-cost food for families, including cut-price meat for the 'poor and needy'.[30] When functioning smoothly, such programmes are an effective way of building community support, and allow any opposition to be punished by the denial of basic means of sustenance. But if such schemes break down, the credibility of IS as administrators, such as it is, risks significant damage.

Yet even before the invasion of 2003 and the chaos that has followed, basic services in urban and rural areas of Syria and Iraq were already grossly inadequate, in part due to a drastic shortage of trained and competent administrators. IS also lacks the personnel needed. In July 2014, al-Baghdadi appealed to 'judges, as well as people with military, administrative and service expertise, and medical doctors and engineers of all different specialisations and fields' to migrate to the caliphate from overseas.[31] Few came. The maintenance of the infrastructure alone in the areas ruled by IS in Iraq was estimated to cost around $200 million per month.[32] The implacable laws of the market still functioned too, even in a revolutionary religious proto-state. So, for example, air strikes on oil production infrastructure had pushed up the price of fuel in IS-controlled zones by spring 2015. In Mosul, locals reported, IS was forced to introduce price caps on gas and petrol.[33] Electricity supply everywhere was intermittent, hospitals were short of basic medical equipment and rubbish collection systems, always a weak point for municipal authorities in even stable middle-income countries in the developing world, had broken down. Clean water was rare due to a lack of chlorine and available from the tap for only a few hours per week. 'We use the river water for washing, but it's very dirty. Children . . . are getting sick of [from] it,' one resident said.[34]

Such problems make IS's other areas of expenditure all the more important. One is religious proselytisation and education: after all, the righteous-minded can reasonably be expected to accept a certain amount of privation if they believe it necessary for the creation of the perfect religious community. These are often the first initiatives introduced in any given area identified by the group for a subsequent takeover. At their most basic they comprise very simple events of faith-based outreach, involving public Koranic recitation and sermons explaining the project and beliefs of IS, with participants offered refreshments and a break in the tedium of the day. Such proselytisation is often mixed with more innocuous activities, such as a tug of war or some kind of sporting competition, and usually aimed at young men and boys. More elaborate efforts involve the establishing of camps where a select group might be educated over a period of days.

More broadly, education is seen as part of a campaign not just to win 'hearts and minds' but to 'reform' them. Some government schools continue to function, with their original staff, but with strict segregation of teachers and students and a curriculum purged of more or less anything but study of the Koran, the deeds and sayings of the Prophet and Islamic law. Foreign languages, mathematics, social sciences and references to nation states have all been banned from lessons. The long-term aim is the quintessence of totalitarianism: to eliminate all possibility of alternative viewpoints, particularly among the young, and to raise a new generation of utterly loyal, unquestioning 'citizens' of the caliphate. Naturally, force, or the threat of force, is used to achieve this aim. In one incident in May 2014, ISIS abducted more than 150 schoolchildren aged between thirteen and sixteen in Manbij, in the north-west of Syria, and held them for weeks.

The boys were beaten, forced to pray five times a day and to spend hours learning the Koran, and made to watch videos of ISIS behead-ings and attacks.[35] Even young children are involved in horrific violence, including executions. There are very few examples of 'brainwashing', a much-misused word, in Islamic militancy but this kind of effort must come close to qualifying as one.

One aim of this propaganda is simply to encourage recruits. IS casualties are difficult to estimate but even top-end estimates of up to 10,000 being killed in fighting between September 2014 and June 2015, for example, are still unlikely to mean a shortage of manpower given the number of unemployed, angry young Sunni men in Syria and Iraq.[36]

Another aim is the sustaining and spreading of a culture of martyrdom and suicide attacks. Suicide bombing is neither a cheap weapon, as often said, nor the spontaneous, organic expression of the inchoate rage of a people. It is a tactic, adopted for specific strategic reasons by terrorists, and which involves the commitment of significant resources if it is going to be successful. The extremist organisations that pioneered the use of the tactic – such as Hamas, Hezbollah and the Sri Lankan Tamil Tigers – rapidly learned that few communities naturally accept the voluntary death of their teenagers. The individual who becomes a human bomb may cost an organisation less than a missile but any militant hoping to deploy suicide attackers needs to invest heavily and systematically in propaganda designed to build and then maintain a 'cult of the martyr' if they are to avoid a backlash from relatives, friends and their wider circle. It is not natural for a mother or a father to celebrate the death of a child, and the idea that young men, or increasingly women, should kill themselves in order to kill others, often civilians, has to be normalised. In interviews with dozens of bereaved parents of suicide bombers over the last fifteen years, I have heard the identical response: 'I am sad that my son has gone but I am happy because of his sacrifice.' This has to be learned, and the victims need to be turned from other human beings into a faceless, dehumanised enemy. In practical terms, meanwhile, the fam-ilies of 'martyrs' need to be looked after; funerals organised and paid for; valedictory films produced and broadcast; a dedicated infra-structure to find, isolate and condition 'martyrs' set up and run. This effort must be constant and places a considerable strain on a group's resources. Many Islamic extremist organisations, including IS, make disproportionate use of foreign volunteers as suicide attackers. One reason may well be to make a powerful statement about the extent of their support around the globe. But another may simply be that the foreigners are cheaper.

For the biggest expenditure of IS is, inevitably, war. Estimates of the number of fighters IS could deploy at any one time vary from a few thousand to tens of thousands. In September 2014, the CIA reportedly suggested a figure of between 20,000 and 31,500. Most are paid somewhere between $200 and $600 every month, meaning a maximum total wage bill of somewhere between $4 million and $21 million, with allowances for food and lodging adding a further financial burden. But many fighters do not receive a salary in the conventional sense. There is a hard core of ideologically motivated full-timers but many of those deployed either to the front lines or used to perform more mundane duties in the rear are auxiliaries mobilised through tribal networks, by other groups who happen to be currently aligned with IS or simply by individual villages for use in a local operation. Such fighters are rewarded materially, usually by their own patrons and leaders, but do not necessarily receive cash from the central treasury.

What is clear is that the majority are Syrians and Iraqis, despite the international media's focus on volunteers from overseas. This is not to minimise the importance of the phenomenon of 'foreign fighters' within IS but simply to emphasise that for most participants the conflict remains a local one. It might have been framed as part of a broader sectarian struggle, or one against unbelievers or tyrants, but the actual factors which lead individuals and communities to be mobilised are often more immediate.

One study of Syrian fighters joining militant groups including IS found that they did so 'primarily for instrumental purposes' – meaning with a specific aim in mind rather than out of a general ideological motivation. One reason for this is that Islamic militant groups were perceived as better equipped, led and organised. They were therefore seen as more capable of defeating the Assad regime, which remained the priority of most Syrian rebels. Richard Barrett, a former head of counter-terrorism at MI6 and author of the study, described how 'fighters' individual motivation for joining has more to do with the dynamics of a social network that provides direction, identity, purpose, belonging, empowerment and excitement, than it does with religious understanding'.[37] This is also the case for every other militant volunteer, group, network and cell described in this book.

As well as soldiers, war requires weapons. These IS appears to have in astonishing abundance. No previous Islamic militant group has had such reserves of armoured vehicles and possessed such sophisticated weapons systems, even if IS appears unable to use many of them. Reports from interrogated militants who have returned to Europe do not mention any problems obtaining ammunition, something that has crippled many such organisations' military efforts previously. Some reveal a surplus that would be the envy of many conventional forces. Nor does there appear to be any shortage of light arms, needed in vast numbers for the kind of tactics IS favours and the type of force it habitually deploys. One Indian former IS militant told police he had been sent to attack Kurdish peshmerga positions armed with an AK-47 assault rifle with three hundred rounds, four hand grenades, a Glock handgun with fifty cartridges and a knife. Others in his small assault group were equipped similarly but also carried a sniper rifle, a light machine gun with a thousand rounds, and rocket-propelled grenade launchers and ammunitions. This small armoury was not intended to be reused – the volunteers were told to fight to the last bullet and then their deaths – and was worth many thousands of dollars.[38]

Then, of course, there is the Islamic State's media department, responsible for the videos that have been so instrumental in establishing the image of IS overseas, and particularly among the young Muslim men, and some women, who travel to Syria to be part of the new caliphate. Though these films have attracted much international attention, most of the media department's output is directed at local viewers and varies according to the degree of control IS has over a given area. The degree of violence shown is carefully calibrated. Productions promoted in, for example, Raqqa, where IS is firmly in control, have highlighted governance, aiming to mobilise support. In Kirkuk and Diyala provinces in Iraq, on the other hand, both of which are frontier zones where control is fiercely contested, the emphasis has been very different, with graphic images of the execution of alleged criminals and spies being used to terrify the local population into submission.[39]

This propaganda is produced in multiple languages and disseminated by thousands of sympathisers across social media.[40] The Islamic
State has even developed its own Arabic-language app – Dawn
of Glad Tidings – allowing a user to automatically retweet its
communications using specified hashtags.[41] Despite its centralising,
totalitarian culture, IS appears to allow, if not actively encourage, a
constant stream of material about it to be uploaded onto social
media by foreign volunteers who have joined it – for example onto
the social media pages of specific units within the group – which
turn them into powerful recruiting tools in distant lands. The tolerance extended by the otherwise obsessively authoritarian IS to this
kind of effort may simply be pragmatic. Beyond confiscating the
phones and tablets of all recruits, there would seem to be little the
group could otherwise do.

Another and important use of social media is to allow followers
and potential sympathisers around the world to engage with, and
thus become complicit in, the Islamic State's atrocities. One
example was the 'crowd-sourcing' of the means of executing the
Jordanian pilot captured in January 2015. The degree to which IS
itself was responsible for the hashtag 'Suggest ways to kill Jordanian
pig' is unclear, but responses ranged from impaling to execution
with an axe.[42]

This then is the proto-state which has emerged, chaotic and opaque
but nonetheless clearly recognisable, in the area formerly known as
eastern Syria and western Iraq. It is of a type and ambition and
capability that has simply never existed before. The nearest equivalents
– such as the Taliban in Afghanistan, or the Islamic Courts Union
which seized power in much of Somalia in 2006 – were less organised,
ambitious and aggressive. They were also much poorer and much
more isolated. They certainly never had either the conventional or
non-conventional military strength of IS. Both, crucially, were confined
to relatively marginal areas of the globe and had limited capability to
project influence or power beyond the frontiers of the remote locations which they controlled.

But, despite its many innovations, the Islamic State may be considerably less revolutionary than it likes to pretend and observers often
claim. In many respects its emerging form does not recall the community in the earliest decades of the faith, or that ruled by the four

'rightly guided' successors of Mohammed, or the state constructed by the magnificent potentates of the Umayyads or the Abbasids, as its leaders clearly imagine.[43] Nor, as the author and academic Charles Tripp has pointed out, does it present as radical an alternative to modern nation states in terms of governance or administration as may seem the case at first sight. IS rules a frightened, fragmented populace through a mix of blackmail, bribes, paternalism and terror. It seeks to bind inhabitants together with an ideology based on a selective reading of specific texts, a hate-filled sectarian agenda, paranoia about the designs of external actors and deep-rooted anti-Western sentiment fused with anti-Semitism and anti-Zionism. Capital punishment, sometimes in public, is common. Violence is systematically employed to intimidate and terrorise entire communities. It develops and sustains a cult of martyrdom and suicide attacking, jealously controls the basic means of subsistence for millions of people, runs a semi-command economy with widespread use of price-capping, subsidies and other measures which interfere with the functioning of the free market. Its tax system is extractive, predatory and often arbitrary. Divisions between traditional communities such as tribes are exacerbated and exploited. Prominent families are co-opted or coerced. Dissent of any form is savagely punished, religious minorities are systematically persecuted, while education and information are seen only as means to reinforce its leaders' own position through the eradication of any ways of thinking that might allow a cowed population to imagine alternatives to their continued rule. It is economically fragile, lacks skilled workers, has problems providing basic services to its population, and suffers both from massive underinvestment in infrastructure and a prodigiously unequal distribution of wealth. Despite huge expenditure on security forces, law and order is in reality patchy and it is detested and feared by all its neighbours. None of these problems are exactly unfamiliar in the region. Indeed, they could even be said to characterise many nations within it.

In this sense, IS is, despite its own rhetoric, an entirely contemporary phenomenon, its emergence and its form determined by a specific environment at a very specific time.[44]

This undoubtedly helps explain its spectacular local success. Yet it begs an obvious question: can that success be exported? Can a group establish networks and affiliations overseas? Can a group 'go global'? In the next chapters, al-Qaeda's and the Islamic State's efforts to build bases, capacity and influence around the Muslim world are examined. Here, we will learn that what bring militants success 'at home' does not always guarantee it abroad.

5

THE AFFILIATES

Osama bin Laden died very early on the morning of 2 May 2011 when he was shot in the head by a US Navy SEAL. The assault on the compound in northern Pakistan had lasted less than twenty minutes. His remains were later dropped from an aircraft carrier into the Arabian Sea.

The house where the al-Qaeda leader died, in the garrison town of Abbottabad, was surrounded by a high wall and cut off from all connections with the outside world except for the messages delivered by a single man. It was by following this courier, identified through the painstaking collation of leads from multiple sources, including tips from foreign services, interrogations and surveillance intercepts, that the CIA eventually located the most wanted man on the planet.[1]

Bin Laden's sudden death set off a power struggle within al-Qaeda. His eventual successor was Ayman al-Zawahiri, the veteran Egyptian who had been more than a deputy and less than a co-leader for many years. Al-Zawahiri, an abrasive and stubborn man without the charisma of his predecessor, was not a unanimous choice.[2] At least one meeting of al-Qaeda's leadership council was convened – a high-risk enterprise given the consequences if detected and targeted – but failed to reach a clear decision. In the end, it was the decisions of al-Qaeda's affiliates thousands of miles away which swung the debates in favour of al-Zawahiri.

The affiliates had been established over the best part of a decade – in Iraq in 2004, in the Maghreb in 2006, in the Arabian peninsula in 2009. Each was the result of months of negotiations, as the terms of the relationship were worked out in a series of back-and-forth clandestine communications. In each instance, the potential partners in these joint ventures were already well known to each other, and the eventual agreements were less a new departure than the formal recognition by the al-Qaeda senior leadership of a long-standing relationship with groups or individuals who had usually been very active, and often very violent, for several years. The only affiliate which appears to have demurred from endorsement of al-Zawahiri as leader was that in Iraq. Abu Bakr al-Baghdadi merely deputed a spokesman to send congratulations when, six weeks after bin Laden's death, al-Zawahiri's succession was announced.

The transition at the highest levels in al-Qaeda was not simply about personalities. It was about strategy too. It meant a significant shift away from al-Qaeda's historic focus on attacking the US – the 'Far Enemy' – and towards attacking local regimes around the Islamic world – the 'Near Enemy'. It also meant a new emphasis on seizing and holding territory.

This was in part due to al-Zawahiri's own background. Born in Cairo in 1951 to a prestigious family fallen on hard times, the al-Qaeda leader had been a devout and studious youth who had grown up amid the religious revival of the 1960s and 70s and was first drawn into its more moderate activist strand, political Islamism, before swiftly becoming involved in the fragmented networks that constituted the violent extremist fringe in Egypt at the time.

Al-Zawahiri had been aware of the 1981 plot to kill President Sadat though not actually involved in it. Following the assassination, he attempted to flee Egypt but was arrested. Tortured in prison, he may have been forced to betray close associates. When released, he travelled to Peshawar, where he worked in a Kuwaiti government-funded clinic looking after Afghan refugees but spent more time lecturing, writing and running his own relatively small group, Egyptian Islamic Jihad (EIJ). He was not involved in the foundation of al-Qaeda and was not particularly close to bin Laden during this period, though the two men ended up together in Khartoum, Sudan, when forced out of Pakistan and Saudi Arabia respectively in the early 1990s. Like all militants of his generation, al-Zawahiri was heavily influenced by Abdullah Azzam, and repeatedly quoted the older man's insistence that the 'mujahideen' needed a 'solid base' which would act as a launch pad for their operations.[3]

While bin Laden had been making efforts to overcome the disunity that had long characterised the movement of violent Islamic extremism, al-Zawahiri, by contrast, focused his efforts on his homeland. He recognised the practical difficulties of operating in Egypt, where the inhospitable desert denied militants sanctuary outside a narrow, heavily populated strip along the Nile, leaving them exposed to the ruthless security services, but nonetheless insisted that 'the way to Jerusalem ran through Cairo'. Successive bids to overthrow the un-Islamic tyrants of his homeland had failed, he argued, because the 'solid base' had never been established.

By the middle of the nineties, after launching a series of abortive attempts to kill Hosni Mubarak, who had succeeded Sadat as president, he had run out of funds, backers, operatives and places to live. Forced out of Sudan, unwelcome in Bosnia, wanted throughout the Middle East, al-Zawahiri fetched up in Afghanistan where, out of necessity, he joined bin Laden's Global Front against Crusaders and Zionists, an alliance of independent groups, in 1998. Eventually, only four months before the 9/11 attacks, he folded what was left of his Egyptian Islamic Jihad group into al-Qaeda.

Even then, at this high point in bin Laden's campaign against the US, al-Zawahiri's focus remained the gritty business of winning and holding territory, arguing bluntly that 'the jihadist Islamic movement will not achieve victory against the global infidel alliance without possessing a base . . . in which to establish a defensible Islamic state'.

After the 9/11 attacks and the war which followed them, as bin Laden continued to prioritise his international terrorist campaign, al-Zawahiri quietly managed relationships with the new affiliates. It was he who was charged with trying to moderate the excesses of 'al-Qaeda in Iraq'. Al-Zawahiri's clear concerns about al-Qaeda's focus on the Far Enemy seem to have grown as the decade passed. It is apparent from documents seized when bin Laden was killed that by 2010 al-Zawahiri was suggesting a moratorium on attempts to strike the US in the US because 'the homeland' was simply too well defended. Bin Laden, on the other hand, was plotting to assassinate the US vice president.[4] Their diverging views meant that the two men saw the chaos sown across much of the Middle East by the uprisings of the Arab Spring in 2011 and 2012 rather differently. For bin Laden, they challenged his strategy of instigation. The demonstrators across the Islamic world were demanding democracy, after all, not Islamic law.

But for al-Zawahiri the new upheavals were full of opportunities. Shortly after the Tunisian President Zein al-Abidine Ben Ali had been forced out, President Hosni Mubarak had resigned in Egypt. Half a dozen other rulers were looking vulnerable. Less than three months later, bin Laden was dead and al-Zawahiri took charge of al-Qaeda.

Within fifteen months, he had sent envoys to Libya and Egypt to build contacts with local networks there and offer them assistance, he had accepted a pledge of allegiance from the leader of the al-Shabaab organisation in Somalia (which bin Laden had repeatedly rejected) and thus created a fourth affiliate, and he had collaborated with Abu Bakr al-Baghdadi in Iraq to send experienced and capable operators into Syria to set up a fifth, Jabhat al-Nusra. In 2013, al-Zawahiri issued new guidelines for the entire Islamic militant movement, laying out the principles of his strategy. The overall goals of al-Qaeda – the destruction of the Far Enemy, the fall of the local 'apostate, hypocrite tyrants' in the Islamic world and the eventual establishment of a new caliphate – remained the same but the emphasis on how to reach them had changed dramatically. If targeting the US remained at the top of the list – this was al-Qaeda's niche specialism after all and where it had had its greatest historic success – most of his recommendations focused on the operations of the group's affiliates in the Islamic world. In 2014, he stated his belief that 'the party that does not withdraw from its land is winning the battle'.[5]

Of all the various affiliates or allies established by al-Qaeda in the last decade there is only one that Western officials consider a clear and present danger: al-Qaeda in the Arabian Peninsula.

The Arabian peninsula is an area of around a million square miles, bordered to the north by the Persian Gulf, to the south-west by the Red Sea and to the east by the Arabian Sea. It is divided into seven individual states which range in size from Saudi Arabia, with more than a third of the peninsula's total population of 80 million and a land mass spanning almost the entire interior, to Bahrain, which has 1.2 million inhabitants living in 262 square miles. Somewhere between 15 and 20 per cent of the inhabitants of the peninsula are Shia, though the exact number is unclear. The strategic significance of the peninsula comes from three sources. The first is its position within the Middle East and at the pivot of Asia, Europe and Africa, and more specifically across the trade routes, now shipping lanes, linking the Atlantic and the Mediterranean to the Indian and Pacific oceans. The second is of course its vast carbon fuel resources – a third of the world's known oil reserves and, in recent years, around a fifth of global oil production. The third is religious. The peninsula is the birthplace of Islam, the site of two of the three holiest sites for Muslims and the destination of the haj pilgrimage which is obligatory for all believers who are sufficiently healthy to bear the (now fairly painless) journey.

The peninsula has known successive waves of religious revivalism, many accompanied by violence of one sort or another. The most significant was that of Mohammed ibn Abd al-Wahhab in the eighteenth century, and then of his followers at the end of the nineteenth. They were Salafi, following the example of the *salaf*, the 'ancestors', the first generations of Muslims, and sought to purge Islamic practice of all *bida*, innovation, and *shirk*, polytheism, in order to reform their community and usher in a utopian age of social justice, power and glory.[6]

The first wave of 'Wahhabis', as detractors dubbed these devout and puritanical revivalists, had little impact outside the Najd, the arid central plateau of the Arabian peninsula. The second wave, in the late nineteenth century, had consequences which reverberate today. As described in chapter 2, a minor tribal chief called Abdulaziz ibn Saud, who lived near modern-day Riyadh, used these authentically fanatical fighters as the military cutting edge of his own bid to unite and rule the fractious and disparate local communities of the region. Ibn Saud, reinforced battlefield successes with marriage alliances and, by the late 1920s, was close to declaring the foundation of a united Arabian kingdom. The Wahhabis had now served their purpose and their desire for new campaigns further afield needed to be curbed. Ibn Saud offered them a deal. In return for support for his temporal power, they would be granted effective control of education and religious matters within the new state, plus given generous financial support. Those that did not agree to the terms were gunned down at a one-sided battle.

Over the following decade the extent of the new kingdom's oil reserves became clear and in 1945 US President Franklin Roosevelt concluded a momentous strategic alliance with the ageing ibn Saud at a meeting on a US warship in the middle of the Suez Canal. In return for US military protection, Saudi Arabia would guarantee cheap and stable oil for the world market. As described in chapter one, the huge amounts of money flowing in brought extraordinarily rapid change. This generated massive internal tensions, and the 1960s saw a growing resurgence of religious activism of every type. Successive rulers also struggled to reconcile the kingdom's strategic alliance with the US both with generally hostile domestic sentiment and with the role the kingdom sought to play as leader of the Arab and Islamic worlds. The crisis came with the 1973 Arab–Israeli war, when US aid may have saved the Jewish state. The Saudis led the Arab world in imposing an oil embargo, which sent the price of the precious commodity rocketing, destabilising Western economies and sending so-called 'petrodollars' gushing through the Middle East. Some of the effects were immediately visible to the West. This was the moment when the legend of the fabulously rich Saudi potentate with the gold-plated Rolls Royce, four entire floors at the Ritz, and an entourage that filled not one but two 747s, was created. It was not without foundation. King Fahd, the kingdom's effective ruler from 1975, bought dozens of palaces across Europe which he never visited and was an inveterate gambler who regularly lost vast sums at tables in Monte Carlo, Paris and London.[7]

But the kingdom's extraordinary wealth did not bring stability. In 1979 came the seizure of the Grand Mosque in Mecca, the invasion of Afghanistan and the Iranian revolution. As we have seen, each of these events revealed a different threat, and one reaction of the house of Saud at the time was to funnel their new-found riches into an extensive programme of proselytisation of their own conservative strand of Islam throughout the Muslim world.

Another response was to bankroll part of the Afghan mujahideen. Once more this aligned them with the US. The rapprochement paid off in 1990 when President George Bush deployed US troops to the kingdom to defend it from Saddam Hussein's 'million-man army' following the latter's invasion of Kuwait. There was a domestic cost to the call for US protection, however. The decision provoked much anger within the kingdom and badly damaged the monarchy's credibility. After the war, to compound the problems, oil prices dropped, cutting revenues and thus necessitating a reduction in the generous welfare payments on which most Saudis depended. An emerging wave of extremist clerics found receptive audiences, particularly among the kingdom's young and (relatively) poor.

But though there was growing violence through the 1990s, it was only after 2001 that al-Qaeda made its real entrance in Saudi Arabia. Bin Laden sent a small group of veterans to organise and energise existing local militants. Under pressure from their overall leader to strike swiftly, this new network, a first version of al-Qaeda in the Arabian Peninsula, launched a premature campaign of attacks in 2002 and 2003, hitting both Western and local targets. Any public sympathy for the extremists – always limited among a generally law-abiding population – rapidly evaporated when Saudi civilians started to die. The militants also made a series of amateurish mistakes which allowed the increasingly effective Saudi counter-terrorist services to rapidly round them up. A second wave of violence, prompted in part by returning veterans from the war in Iraq, was also swiftly crushed. Survivors among the militants fled to Yemen.

Yemen too had been traversed by revivalist movements over recent centuries, but had never been exposed to rigorous puritanism with the same intensity as most other parts of the Arabian peninsula. Most communities in the country followed the Shafi school, which is marginally more moderate than the ultra-conservative Hanbali school from which Wahhabism emerged. Exposure to traders along the coast also tempered the rigorous outlook of the tribes of the interior. But by the early 1990s, like so many countries in the region, Yemen had also suffered decades of traumatic social change and internal conflict. For young men in seething cities like Sana'a, the capital, or even far-flung villages, the message of the hard-line preachers who were appearing in the local mosques or going from home to home was fresh and convincing.

The early 1990s saw the return of veterans from the war in Afghanistan. In Yemen, these former combatants were co-opted by President Ali Abdullah Saleh to act, rather like the Wahhabis had done for Abdulaziz seventy or eighty years before, as shock troops in his campaign to reunify the country under his rule. Welcomed as heroes, they were thus allowed to establish bases, train and fight against the forces of the nominally socialist south. This was all in stark contrast to what had happened in other Middle Eastern countries, where such men had launched campaigns of violence against local authorities in a bid to establish Islamic rule. By the end of the decade, the Afghan veterans were well entrenched in parts of the restive and anarchic west and south, with broad networks of support among local tribes.

But Saleh had been playing with fire – or dancing on the heads of snakes, as he colourfully put it. When a new wave of militants arrived from Afghanistan in early 2002, they did what their forebears had not done and launched an offensive which directly targeted the president and his allies. Though the violence had subsided by around 2005, a combination of the war in Iraq, clumsy US policy, a mass prison break, grave economic problems and the influx of hardened militants fleeing the crackdown in Saudi Arabia gave the militants new momentum. One particular commander – Nasir al-Wuhayshi, a diminutive former religious student who had been bin Laden's personal secretary for four years in Afghanistan – proved extremely effective.[8] He swiftly set about establishing new bases, building relationships with tribal leaders and consolidating networks of support among other local power-brokers.[9] Al-Wuhayshi then looked to expand. In 2009, having absorbed a further influx of extremists fleeing Saudi Arabia, he declared the foundation of a new 'al-Qaeda in the Arabian Peninsula', formally announced his allegiance to bin Laden, and sent a young Nigerian recruit to the US to blow up a plane with a sophisticated bomb sewn into his underwear. The would-be suicide attacker attempted to deton-ate the device aboard a flight to Detroit containing 290 people shortly after take-off, but it failed to ignite. The bid nonetheless brought America close to a major mass-casualty attack approaching the scale of 9/11. 'We dodged a bullet,' the newly elected President Barack Obama was reported to have told his top security officials.

The attempt was just the first of a series of increasingly sophisti-cated attempts by AQAP to execute spectacular mass-casualty attacks in the West. One man played a critical role in turning the group into such a grave international threat. This was the man who the failed plane bomber, now in detention, said had 'greatly inspired' him. He was called Anwar al-Awlaki.[10]

Al-Awlaki was born in New Mexico, US, in 1971, while his father, from a prominent Yemeni family, was studying agriculture there.[11] He moved to Yemen with his parents at the age of seven and spent his teens in

Sana'a before travelling back to the US on a scholarship to follow a course in civil engineering at Colorado State University. By the mid-1990s al-Awlaki was teaching and preaching at a mosque in San Diego despite having had no formal religious education. During this period he developed a relationship with two of the future 9/11 hijackers which has never been fully understood, and appears to have been a compulsive user of prostitutes. In the aftermath of the attacks of September 2001, al-Awlaki was interviewed repeatedly by US media and described the operation as un-Islamic but a response to US foreign policy. He also warned that bin Laden, 'who was considered an extremist . . . could end up becoming mainstream'.[12]

When it looked like he was to be arrested for visa fraud, Awlaki returned to Yemen. However, he continued to make frequent trips to the West, particularly the UK where he focused his efforts on Islamic centres and student societies, which were under less surveillance than mosques from either security forces or mainstream religious figures. His sermons were typical of many such preachers – a mix of half-understood radical theology, politics and self-help – and show the influence of the usual extremist thinkers such as Qutb and Azzam. Undoubtedly charismatic, bilingual in English and Arabic, al-Awlaki's lectures were straightforward, clear and sometimes witty. The contrast with the traditional oratory of established clerics and prayer leaders was dramatic and al-Awlaki rapidly built a substantial following. His trips to Europe had become less frequent by the middle of the decade and in 2006 he was imprisoned in Yemen on terrorism charges. Released in December 2007 following lobbying by senior members of his tribe, al-Awlaki moved to his family's ancestral home in the rugged and remote Shabwa Mountains south-west of the capital. This did not end his outreach efforts. He had been using the Internet extensively for years, and though the intermittent electricity supply and poor download speeds were a hindrance, he could still receive and send emails and upload lectures and texts. His output was prolific.

Al-Awlaki was of course simply the latest in a long line of men who had formulated a new interpretation of the holy texts of Islam that he felt more pertinent to the contemporary world and used the latest technology to disseminate it. But few propagandists before him have had quite such influence from such a remote location.[13] A text he published on his blog called '44 Ways to Support Jihad' became one of the most successful Internet hits of the online extremist movement, and in February 2009 he launched a slick Internet magazine named *Inspire*, which not only explicitly called on Muslims around the world to launch attacks but was full of practical tips to help them do so. Al-Awlaki was an avid user of social media and also became an online mentor to hundreds of people around the world. One was Nidal Malik Hasan, the psychologically troubled US Army officer who killed thirteen people and wounded thirty at Fort Hood, Texas, in November 2009. Hasan had exchanged dozens of emails with al-Awlaki, though did not receive direct instructions from him. Another possible protégé may have been Faisal Shahzad, a Pakistani-American who pleaded guilty to an attempt in May 2010 to detonate a car bomb in Times Square, New York, and was sentenced to life in prison. Al-Awlaki was also cited as a key influence by Roshonara Choudhry, a British student who, in May 2010, stabbed an MP after spending weeks watching scores of al-Awlaki's speeches online. He also met volunteers who made it to Yemen. One was the young Nigerian who had tried to kill 290 people flying to Detroit.

By 2010, al-Awlaki had thus become one of the best-known figures in the world of Islamic extremism, despite a thin CV compared to others in the field. This provoked some resentment in what had always been a jealous and competitive community. Bin Laden himself vetoed a suggestion that the younger man be appointed head of the al-Qaeda affiliate in Yemen, icily asking for 'the résumé, in detail and length, of brother Anwar al-Awlaki, as well as the facts . . . relied on when recommending him'.[14] It was inevitable, then, that US security efforts in Yemen should focus on eliminating al-Awlaki. The forty-year-old became the first US citizen to be placed on the CIA's 'kill or capture' list and died in a drone strike in September 2011.

For all the troubling legal questions it raised, and the obvious risk of creating a martyr, this long-range assassination ended a growing threat posed by a major figure of Islamic militancy. But, as had so often been the case over the previous decade or so, their focus on the direct threat to the West had distracted Western officials from other militants who were of far greater significance from al-Qaeda's point of view in terms of their local aim – to make and consolidate territorial gains – in the Islamic world. Al-Awlaki was dead, but Nasir al-Wuhayshi, the very capable leader of al-Qaeda in the Arabian Peninsula, was alive and thriving.

In late 2010, al-Wuhayshi had outlined a plan to bin Laden in Pakistan for a major operation that would allow AQAP to break out of the high mountains and deserts to which it had been confined for several years. Bin Laden had told him to wait, arguing that there was insufficient popular support for such a venture.[15] Al-Wuhayshi obeyed the order, though he sent a series of small groups of fighters to make probing attacks around government positions in coastal settlements about sixty miles north-east of the port city of Aden over the winter months. By February, despite the instructions from bin Laden, the black flags of the mujahideen had been raised over government buildings at the centre of Ja'ar, a small district centre with a long history of on–off control by extremists. No one appeared to notice. But then came the Arab Spring. By April 2011 revolts were roiling the region. Following demonstrations in Yemen's capital prompted by the ouster of Mubarak in Egypt two months earlier, the 33-year rule of President Saleh was crumbling. Yemen's military, meanwhile, was split between rival factions and unlikely to fight for anything much beyond its own power or influence. It was a clear opportunity for something more ambitious than the seizure of a single scruffy settlement. Al-Wuhayshi could evidently wait no longer and, apparently without telling bin Laden what he was doing, began sending fighters into the outlying districts of the town of Zinjibar, capital of the governorate of Abyan with a population of between 50,000 and 80,000 people and a port. By mid-May bin Laden was dead, and by the end of the month the black flags flew over Zinjibar's pitted roads, dilapidated government buildings and poorly constructed breeze-block homes. No serious attempt to retake the town would be mounted for almost a year.

The regime AQAP established in their new territories was familiar to anyone who had watched militants take territory in Pakistan, Afghanistan or Iraq over the previous decade. The fighters declared an Islamic emirate, an Islamic state ruled by an emir, which does not claim to be the seat of the unique caliphate.[16] The usual rules and regulations would be enforced by a new religious police. They set about collecting taxes and told women not to leave their homes without a male guardian and then only for essential errands. Sharia courts were set up and dealt rapidly with many petty disputes and a handful of more serious ones. A thief had a hand amputated in public. Men were flogged for possession of alcohol. Spies were executed. An alleged 'witch' was decapitated. There was little mention of the global struggle of the *umma*, beyond accusations, broadcast through loudspeakers, that President Saleh was an apostate in the pay of the Americans who were themselves in the pay of the Jews.

Abyan and its surrounding villages had long been alienated from Yemen's central authority dominated by northerners. This ill-will had been compounded by corrupt and inefficient local officials sent or appointed by the government in Sana'a and a predatory police force. The semi-anarchy that had prevailed in Abyan for several years meant that there was at least some immediate local support for the militants and the austere order they were able to impose. To some extent, the rigorous new codes governing attire and behaviour weren't too far removed from those already in place. This was a deeply conservative society governed by tribal codes of honour and retribution in which women were seen as the possessions of the menfolk and female literacy levels were around 50 per cent.[17] It also helped that al-Wuhayshi's men made an effort to maintain good relations with local powerbrokers. The aid of local tribes had been crucial to the seizure of the town in the first place. Indeed, one crucial advantage al-Wuhayshi had was that most of his men were themselves locals. He himself had actually been born in Abyan and was literally on home ground.

One important measure was to avoid any mention of al-Qaeda entirely. Those in charge of Zinjibar called themselves Ansar al-Sharia (Partisans of Islamic Law) instead. This deliberate hiding of the reality of the group's affiliation was proof of quite how tarnished al-Qaeda's global brand had become. And besides, when building local support, or at least establishing local consent or acquiescence, there was no great advantage to be had from portraying their struggle as part of a vast global or even cosmic one. Instead, the militants worked to restore public services and even spoke of attracting investors. Morten Storm, a Danish convert who infiltrated AQAP for Western intelligence services, visited the area while it was under AQAP control and described the group 'handing out food, digging wells and storage tanks, driving water trucks around, bringing in free electricity to areas that had never known it, and providing other services that the central government in Sana'a had neglected for decades'.[18]

But this was the very stumbling block that would turn AQAP's apparent victory in southern Yemen into a setback, if not a major strategic defeat. When a new president, Abd Rabu Mansur Hadi, finally succeeded Saleh in February 2012, months of uncertainty and political wrangling were brought to an end and the military was unified under one commander.[19] Hadi openly solicited, and received, US military assistance. A month after Hadi took control, government forces massed for an offensive in Abyan. There would be no more dancing on the heads of snakes, at least for the moment.

At the same time, despite AQAP's strategic efforts, local resentment was growing at the failures and excesses of the extremist administration. There was, unsurprisingly, little sign of the investments that AQAP had promised would come, and there was a limit to what Wuhayshi's deputies could do to restore services. Few had any genuine administrative capabilities. Their presence also exposed local people to the government's indiscriminate bombing. The national military forces might be deeply unpopular, but it was AQAP who took the blame for prompting the fighting and, in part, for the many civilian casualties. There was also a limit to the extent that the group could moderate its policies, even if it wanted to. Popular shrines to local saints were destroyed. The body of a local man accused of espionage was left crucified by a roadside for days. Bans on women teaching boys older than six led to protests, but most schools remained shut.[20] In the end, to defend their emirate, the militants needed the active support of local people, not just their passive acquiescence. But when the government troops finally did move in under the cover of US air strikes in the spring of 2012, the auxiliaries who had swept into Zinjibar alongside the extremists stayed out of the fight.[21] Just as the Taliban had done over a decade before when faced with the US-backed Northern Alliance outside Kabul, the militants did not risk a confrontation with the superior conventional forces but, after a show of resistance, slipped away back to their mountain strongholds to the north and east. By May 2012, the Yemeni national flag had replaced the black banners.

In a letter to the leader of a faction of al-Qaeda in the Maghreb, al-Wuhayshi spoke of the costs of the campaign and the lessons that could be drawn from it.

'Control of these areas during one year cost us 500 martyrs, 700 wounded, 10 cases of hand or leg amputation and nearly $20 million,' he said. The spoils of war, from taxation and booty to hostage ransoms, had made the campaign more or less self-financing, he explained, and offered his counterpart advice on ways to 'make [the population] sympathise . . . and feel that their fate is tied to ours'. These included efficient rubbish collection, something which seems to be a perennial problem for Islamic militant groups, and 'only enforcing Islamic law, when you are forced to do so'. All this had brought 'good results', al-Wuhayshi said. But he also stressed the need always to ensure a secure fallback position before undertaking such a campaign. 'Despite their undeniable benefit, [these battles] are exhausting in terms of money, men and weapons . . . [so] Hold on to your previous bases in the mountains, forests and deserts and prepare other refuges for the worst-case scenario.'[22] For the next three years, AQAP would keep to their mountain strongholds, reverting to a strategy based on bombings, including several ambitious and complex operations against high-profile targets, and intense use of social media.

If AQAP's bid to establish a secure hold on territory and communities in Yemen was short-lived, their counterparts in Syria had more success, until they confronted an enemy unlike any that had ever threatened an al-Qaeda affiliate before.

In the summer of 2011, shortly after AQAP had seized Zinjibar in Yemen, a small group of men belonging to what was then still the Islamic State in Iraq crossed into Syria with a very sensitive mission. Their task was to set up a new organisation to fight against the Assad regime. The Syrian civil war was then gathering momentum and someone – though whether it was Ayman al-Zawahiri or Abu Bakr al-Baghdadi is still a mystery – had decided that the fractious and disorganised rebels needed an efficacy, discipline and agenda that only Islamic extremists could bring. Quite whether the new group would owe its ultimate allegiance to ISI or to the al-Qaeda central leadership was unclear. As seen in chapter 3, this would have very significant repercussions.[23]

All the men were hand-picked from within the ranks of ISI and were highly capable. They were led by a man in his mid-thirties who called himself Abu Muhammad al-Golani, suggesting that he was from the Golan hills in the west of Syria.[24] Al-Golani is thought to have come to Iraq to fight US occupiers there in 2003 or 2004 and then remained, eventually joining ISI when it was formed. He may have been detained in a US prison camp for several years, but there is no confirmation of this. The men with him were also Syrian, from different parts of the country, and all veterans too.

The story of this small band crossing the border to create an organisation from scratch, repeated in interviews by al-Golani himself, may be slightly romanticised. There were plenty of experienced local Islamist activists, violent or otherwise, in Syria in the summer of 2011. Hundreds had been released from jails by the Syrian authorities as part of a strategy seeking to 'Islamicise' the opposition, thus allowing the regime to portray itself as battling violent extremism as opposed to doctors, shopkeepers, mechanics and farmers seeking to exercise basic human rights. Others had been working underground. Whether al-Golani was sent simply to lead an existing network or whether he and his half-dozen or so veterans created that network is unclear. Whatever the case, Jabhat al-Nusra li-Ahl al-Sham was up and running by the early autumn of 2011 and had begun to build up contacts and capacity. They would be joined by further senior operatives from Iraq – and several sent by al-Qaeda central from Afghanistan and Pakistan – over winter.[25]

From the beginning Jabhat al-Nusra sought to avoid the mistakes made by earlier militants in the region. One measure was to deny any link to al-Qaeda, just as AQAP had done, to avoid prompting an adverse reaction from local communities. Other measures included strict internal discipline, a rigorous vetting process of recruits, and above all careful coordination with other factions fighting the regime, including even secular outfits. When it was clear that the 'collateral damage' of JAN's bombing attacks on the regime in urban areas was provoking the anger and concern of local people, the tactic was dropped. JAN fighters also showed themselves to be very effective and, partly as a result, they attracted significant numbers of foreign volunteers and of overseas donations.[26] The group admitted its al-Qaeda affiliation in the summer of 2012. When the US designated JAN a terrorist organisation, in December of that year, it prompted protest marches by opposition groups and civilians across Syria, who shouted, 'We are all Jabhat al-Nusra.'

JAN began to take over substantial amounts of territory, but remained pragmatic. Public executions occurred in JAN-controlled areas, as did killings of opposing tribes, regime troops and others, but excesses were, supposedly, kept to a minimum. Capital punishment, stoning, lashing, amputation and other sanctions were not enforced, on the basis that Islamic law permitted their suspension during 'wartime'.[27] JAN's sectarian rhetoric remained relatively muted, even as the conflict became one increasingly between Sunni and Shia. Pledges were made publicly to respect the rights of minorities in any post-war Syria. As the Islamic State would later discover, literally providing a population's daily bread could be a useful tool to build support and control, so JAN started organising bakeries too. By early 2013, the organisation had become the most significant single force in the fractured opposition, exerting nominal authority over areas in the north-west, south-west and, most importantly, along the ribbon of inhabited land running east through the centre of the country into Iraq. This included Raqqa, a city of more than 200,000, and lucrative oilfields further east at Deir Ezzor. 'We started with eight fighters and now can talk about entire liberated regions,' al-Golani boasted to an interviewer from Al Jazeera.[28]

It may have been JAN's success that prompted Abu Bakr al-Baghdadi to attempt to assert his authority over his former associates in January 2013. As described in chapter 3, this was resisted by JAN's leaders, rejected by al-Zawahiri and led ultimately to al-Baghdadi's declaration of the independence of his own group – ISI – from al-Qaeda. Serious fighting between ISI and JAN erupted the moment al-Zawahiri made his decision known. For a moment it looked as if JAN might hold off the onslaught, but it soon became clear that al-Golani's organisation, even with the assistance of allies among other rebel factions, was no match for al-Baghdadi's forces. By early summer 2014, JAN had been forced out of eastern and central Syria, and from most of its positions around the city of Aleppo. The donations, volunteers, tribal allegiances and respect from minor local commanders all started to flow away from the official al-Qaeda affiliate and towards ISI. The subsequent expansion of al-Baghdadi's breakaway group only reinforced the growing disparity between the financial resources, territory and military capacity of the two organisations.

Like AQAP's in Yemen, JAN's success in Syria was short-lived. But al-Qaeda had two other affiliates that might still prove useful. One was al-Qaeda in the Maghreb, an Arabic term for all of North Africa between Egypt's western border and the Atlantic. The other was the Harakut al-Shabaab al-Mujahideen, the Mujahideen Youth Movement, but better known simply as al-Shabaab.

Al-Shabaab had emerged from the remnants of what was known as the Islamic Courts Union (ICU), a rough coalition of Islamic groups of varying extremism which in the summer of 2006 had swept feuding warlords and an internationally backed provisional government aside to capture large parts of the centre and south of Somalia. After almost two decades of civil conflict, the relative stability that ICU brought was welcomed by many communities, particularly businessmen. However, the movement was suspected by US policy-makers of far deeper links to al-Qaeda than was actually the case at the time, was bitterly opposed by several neighbouring powers, and had significantly less support within Somalia than is sometimes claimed. When it was eventually forced out of Mogadishu by the Ethiopian Army in a US-backed offensive in December 2006, the ICU broke up.

Among its more aggressive and extreme elements were several commanders associated with its youth wing, al-Shabaab. These kept fighting and eventually managed to claw back some of the territory they had lost. Once again, a familiar mix of 'civil affairs' programmes such as food handouts, the co-opting of local powerbrokers, the rapid delivery of justice and, of course, straight coercion allowed al-Shabaab to consolidate their hold on desperate communities shattered by years of war. Their task was made easier by the heavy-handed military tactics of the Ethiopian Army, which included artillery bombardments of civilian areas, and by the rapacity and incompetence of the officials it protected.

By 2009, al-Shabaab had regrouped and moved out of their rural strongholds, eventually seizing the important southern town of Kismayo, with its lucrative port facilities, and most of Mogadishu.

Once again, however, they were unable to hold on to their gains. Though they could enforce mosque attendance and a rudimentary rule of law, the militants proved incapable of supplying more than the very basic needs of local populations, despite a very significant income from protection money, tax, trafficking and piracy. An innate brutality, poor discipline, the extensive use of suicide bombs and a disregard for civilian casualties undermined any popular support. When a graduation ceremony for medical students in Mogadishu was attacked in December 2009, even al-Shabaab knew it had gone too far and denied responsibility. Repression increased, violence intensified and support declined still further. Internal divisions multiplied. Some hardliners wanted teenage 'adulterers' stoned to death; others sought moderation. One commander favoured terrorist strikes in those foreign African states that were involved in the military campaign against them, or even against the US; a second wanted to focus on Somalia alone; a third wanted to do both.

Over the years, bin Laden had deflected the various appeals of different al-Shabaab commanders for a formal recognition of the organisation. Becoming an affiliate of al-Qaeda is not a straight-forward business. 'Al-Qaeda in Iraq', a particularly complex case admittedly, only came into existence after eight months of negoti-ations. One problem is that the oath of allegiance, the *bayat*, can only be made by one individual to another individual; it cannot be made binding for an entire organisation. Nor can it be transferred, if a leader dies, for example. In private, bin Laden admitted grave concerns about the unpredictability of al-Shabaab and its tendency to use violence against other Muslims. In public, he used progres-sively thinner excuses, arguing shortly before his death that an affiliate bearing the al-Qaeda name would attract greater attention from global and regional powers and find it harder to distribute aid to the needy as a result.

Al-Zawahiri was more enthusiastic about a formal association, though, and negotiations appear to have started between al-Qaeda and various al-Shabaab commanders in the summer of 2011. When in early 2012 Ahmed Abdi Godane, the most extreme of al-Shabaab's rival commanders, made a public pledge to follow his 'sheikh' al-Zawa-hiri, he was rewarded by an almost instantaneous response confirming that the group, or at least his faction, had been accepted as an official affiliate. This news, al-Zawahiri said, showed the 'jihadi movement is growing with God's help' and would 'delight the believers and anger the crusaders'.[29]

It did not, however, help al-Shabaab in the battles raging across southern Somalia. A new offensive, this time led by a regional force composed of troops from Kenya, Uganda, Burundi as well as Ethiopia, forced al-Shabaab out of both Kismayo and Mogadishu by the autumn of 2012. The loss of the port city in particular denied the group many of its most important funding streams. A year later, it launched a spectacular attack on the luxury Westgate Mall in Nairobi in which sixty-seven people died. This may have been a bid to shift operations to neighbouring Kenya by radicalising local Somalian immigrants and other potential sympathisers there. It may have been a bid to turn the movement's flagging military fortunes around by convincing the Kenyan state to cease its operations in Somalia. Or it may simply have been a bid to impress al-Qaeda's senior leadership and live up to the new status of official affiliate. The fact that the Westgate operation came shortly after a purge of the movement's more moderate elements may also have been an important factor. At any rate, Godane, the hard-line commander who ordered the attack, was killed by a US drone shortly afterwards.[30]

Though some of its other commanders have since made their own pledges of allegiance to al-Zawahiri, they do not have Godane's overall authority. Further strikes have also killed several of these men too, leaving the exact status of the relationship between al-Shabaab and al-Qaeda very unclear. Their capacity for violence remains, however. In April 2015, gunmen from the group massacred more than 140 students at a Kenyan university.

If the exact links between al-Qaeda and al-Shabaab are difficult to pin down, then those between al-Zawahiri's organisation and the rough coalition of militant groups labelled 'al-Qaeda in the Maghreb' are even more opaque. This affiliate came into being in late 2006 when the remnants of the Algerian militants who had been fighting to overthrow local authorities for almost twenty-five years announced their allegiance to bin Laden. Like al-Shabaab's pledge of allegiance to al-Qaeda, the decision to enter into a formal alliance with the international group was taken at a time of relative weakness, not strength. It was greeted with similar rhetoric from al-Qaeda leaders. 'We pray to Allah that this [alliance] will be a thorn in the neck of the American and French crusaders and their allies, and an arrow in the heart of the French traitors and apostates,' al-Zawahiri said.

The leaders of the new al-Qaeda in the Maghreb appeared to have been motivated primarily by a desire for a much-needed rebranding after a series of setbacks. 'We saw the merger . . . as giving us the breathing space we badly needed . . . a new authority in people's eyes [and] an image of us as a new group,' one senior Algerian militant later recalled.

Initially, the merger looked like something of a disaster for all concerned. Al-Qaeda appears to have hoped that the Algerians would act as a platform for attacks in Europe and would provide organisation across the region. It proved incapable of either. The series of massive suicide bombs on targets such as the United Nations that the Algerian militants undertook instead killed large numbers of civilians and simply made any comeback for the group even harder. Al-Zawahiri's attempts to encourage regional cooperation foundered on the deep parochialism of the new affiliate's leaders, who showed little interest in liaising with counterparts in Libya, Tunisia, Egypt or pretty much anywhere else, while al-Qaeda's efforts to make its agenda look more local by invoking the name of mythic figures from Algeria's history – such as a Berber general who led Muslim forces into Spain in 711 – in public statements just looked opportunist. The Algerian militants continued to be split between a southern faction, which tended to ignore ideology in favour of trafficking and robbery, and northern groups who were marginally less criminally minded. By 2010, few outside observers expected AQIM to do much more than fade further into a well-deserved obscurity.[31]

But, once again, the wave of change and anarchy that broke across the region through 2011 and 2012 offered a huge new opportunity. Authorities in Algeria itself were never threatened by any uprising – which given their corruption, inefficiency and ruthlessness suggests people vividly remembered the atrocious violence of the 1990s – but events in neighbouring countries provided all that was necessary for a resurgence. The breakdown of law and order in Libya, the flow of weapons from Gaddafi's armouries and vehicles from his garages, the arrival of envoys sent by al-Zawahiri from Afghanistan and a political crisis in Mali allowed Algerian militants to establish new networks along the North African coast, to regroup in scattered enclaves inland, and, most spectacularly, to take advantage of an upsurge of ethnic unrest in northern Mali to join with two other independent Islamic militant outfits in 2012 and seize the cities of Gao and Timbuktu. As others had done previously in Iraq, Somalia, Yemen and Pakistan, to name but a few examples, militants carefully leveraged existing local rivalries and conflicts to their advantage. And like the others before them, the militants imposed strictures on the behaviour of those who fell to their control and set about purging their new domains of anything deemed to be 'un-Islamic'. In Mali there was a particular emphasis, derived directly from Gulf 'Wahhabism', on destroying the rich architectural and cultural heritage of the more pluralist and tolerant forms of Islam which had long been dominant in the region. The great libraries and globally known shrines of Timbuktu were a particular target.

Its new swathes of territory allowed AQIM to broaden its involvement in a range of lucrative illicit activities too. Everywhere al-Qaeda was developing a more extensive range of criminal contacts than it had ever had before. In part, this was the inevitable consequence of collusion with local powerbrokers. It may also have been motivated by a lack of local or international donors and the difficulty of transferring money after a decade of measures designed to restrict such financial flows. AQIM became involved in a huge variety of immensely profitable criminal activities including extortion rackets, kidnap for ransom and the trafficking of pretty much everything from narcotics to people.[32]

But for all their funds, AQIM commanders were unable to avoid the same trap that had been the undoing of affiliates everywhere. Having never established a firm foundation of popular support, they were soon forced to rely entirely on coercion and intimidation to maintain their authority. They also proved incapable of fighting any conventional military force that showed a bare minimum of motivation. By early 2013, just as AQAP had been forced out of Zinjibar and Ja'ar, and al-Shabaab had lost Kismayo and Mogadishu, AQIM had lost almost all its gains in Mali to a French-led counter-offensive. The most spectacular act of terrorism against Western interests in the Sahel – the seizure of a gas facility in south-east Algeria in January 2013 – was the work not of AQIM itself but a breakaway faction led by a disgruntled former AQIM commander who had struck out on his own after a dispute with the coalition's overall commander.[33]

Through 2014 and 2015, AQIM's offensive activities were limited to a series of roadside bombings, assaults and ambushes on peacekeepers and government troops in Mali.[34]

What, then, can we conclude from this survey of al-Qaeda's affiliates?

At first glance, al-Zawahiri's decision to 'go local' brought some significant successes. In the summer of 2011, the senior leadership of al-Qaeda had been in serious trouble. Restricted to a narrow belt of inaccessible hills running along Pakistan's border with Afghanistan, they had little capacity for training, the stream of volunteers had largely dried up and many of their best people were dead or detained. Cash flow was unpredictable and money was often tight.[35] In the words of Western security officials, the 'bench' below the leadership had been 'hollowed out' by four years of drone strikes, and the men who now filled relatively senior positions had limited experience or credibility among other extremists.[36] Even its affiliates at the time – AQIM, AQAP and al-Qaeda in Iraq – appeared weakened. Around the Islamic world, major thinkers and groups that had pioneered the new wave of militancy in the 1980s and 90s were publicly rejecting violence and giving up the armed struggle.[37] In 2015, although the al-Qaeda senior leadership has yet to regenerate many of the capabilities it has lost, its global network has certainly expanded dramatically. Its former affiliate in Iraq may have broken away and become spectacularly successful, but it has AQAP, JAN, AQIM and a relationship with al-Shabaab. Overall, the affiliates, whatever the complexities of their relationships with the senior leadership, give the organisation a presence and a profile in four of the most important ongoing conflicts in the Islamic world today.

But while al-Qaeda's subsidiaries have proved that they are capable of taking territory, their overall record is patchy, to say the least. Their conquests are limited to zones where no organised or at least efficient and honest governance exists, such as those created by the chaos of the Arab uprisings of 2010 and 2011, and they have been unable to bring any long-term governance of their own. None has developed the military, political, social or administrative capabilities that would allow it to maintain territory or to resist conventional military forces (or, in the case of JAN, the 'quasi-conventional' forces of the Islamic

State). AQAP have recently been given another chance to expand in Yemen by political chaos and the threat of civil war there. Whether they have somehow found the means to hold on to gains over the long term has yet to be seen.

AQAP is also the only one of the affiliates to have shown a proven capability and will to strike the West in the West – still fundamental to al-Qaeda's overall strategy. Significantly most of these attempts occurred *before* it started trying to seize territory, and AQAP not only made no mention of the West during its Abyan operation but even appears to have suspended attempts to launch international strikes between spring 2011, when it seized Zinjibar, and May 2012, a month or so after it was forced to withdraw from the town.[38]

Al-Shabaab killed Westerners in their attack on the Westgate Mall in Nairobi, but the primary target was Kenya and Kenyans. AQIM elements have fought French soldiers, attacked local Western commercial interests and have taken Western hostages, but, despite much angry posturing, have not actually launched violent strikes in Europe or elsewhere. The group's attacks on international targets in Algeria proved profoundly counter-productive, due to the collateral damage among civilians, and have been avoided since. In Syria, JAN has not been linked to any direct attempt to strike the West and has repeatedly said it has no intention to do so. In fact, all of al-Qaeda's affiliates over recent years appear to have been most successful when playing down global rhetoric. Admittedly, AQAP's decision not to strike in Europe or the US was tactical, and tactics change. Even groups which currently lack an international capacity could develop one with relative ease. JAN could deploy foreign volunteers, after training in any one of the numerous camps they run already, or collaborate with the so-called 'Khorasan group', a small network of senior al-Qaeda veterans who made their way to Syria between 2012 and 2014 looking to use the country as a platform from which to launch strikes on neighbouring countries, Europe and further afield. But for now, leaders of the affiliates appear to believe that attacking the West in the West is incompatible with, or at least distracting from, their local project. Even leaders who are deeply committed to killing Westerners appear prepared to put the global jihad on hold.

One important development which has gone largely unnoticed

outside specialist circles is that the various affiliates have established
a practice of communicating among themselves without passing
through the central leadership. AQAP have long had strong
independent links with al-Shabaab, for example. Storm, the convert-
cum-agent, described liaising between the two groups on issues
ranging from weapons deals to explosives training.[39] Al-Wuhayshi,
the AQAP chief, sent his letters of advice to Mali-based members
of AQIM. Leaders of al-Shabaab have established independent
contact with counterparts in Algeria too. In September 2014, the
two affiliates in Yemen and the Maghreb issued an unprecedented
joint statement calling for extremists in Iraq and Syria to unite
against the common threat from the newly formed US-led coalition.[40] This suggests power is shifting away from al-Qaeda central.
If al-Zawahiri suffers the fate of his predecessor, bin Laden, it is
entirely possible that the senior leadership simply disintegrates. This
would see al-Qaeda becoming nothing more than a collection of
different regional groups, an ironic end for an organisation founded
to overcome the parochialism and particularism which has always
been so characteristic of Islamic militancy.

Al-Zawahiri apparently continues to believe the role of the senior
leadership is as important as ever. In September 2014, he announced
the formation of a new affiliate: al-Qaeda in South Asia, supposedly
spanning the territory once ruled by the Mughal emperors at their
height, from Afghanistan to Bangladesh, and home to more than a
third of the world's Muslims. If the move was meant to reassert the
power and influence of the old guard of the organisation it was a
failure, serving more to draw attention to continuing weaknesses than
durable strengths. There was no significant existing group on the
ground ready to be incorporated into the al-Qaeda network, as there
had been with the creation of all previous affiliates, and it remained
unclear exactly who or what actually constituted 'AQSA'. Its leader
was a little-known propagandist who appeared to have few, if any,
extant followers.[41] An ambitious attempt to publicise the new group
by hijacking a warship in Karachi, the Pakistani port city, was foiled by
local security forces at the last minute. The sense that al-Qaeda had
yet to adapt to a new era was reinforced by the hour-long video that
had announced the foundation of the new affiliate. This differed in
no appreciable way from those produced by al-Qaeda a decade or so

before, down to the lengthy diatribe from the bespectacled 63-year-old al-Zawahiri himself, and contrasted dramatically with the clever, exciting videos being produced by the Islamic State to highlight its own global outreach campaign.[42]

Indeed, for the first time in the recent history of Islamic militancy, al-Qaeda was not the only group keen on developing a 'solid base' around the world.

6

THE CALIPHATE'S CAVALCADE

They left in small groups, walking through the narrow streets of their neighbourhood, past the hotels, banks and restaurants near the jetty, then, after paying their ten rufiyaa each for the fare, onto the ferry across the glassy blue water to the airport. There, they waited with the tourists, a handful of young local men amid the hundreds of wealthy, sunburnt foreigners returning from their thousand-dollar-a-day holidays. An hour or so later they were gone, heading first to Malaysia or Dubai, and then, they hoped, on to their final destination: Syria and the new caliphate of the Islamic State. Few had ever ventured overseas before. None ever expected to see their homeland again.

The dozen or so men – and handful of women – who left the Maldives in January 2015 were not the first extremists to travel the 3,000 miles to Syria from the island nation, better known for its luxury resorts than its burgeoning problem with Islamic militancy. Several Maldivians had already died fighting in Syria and Iraq. 'Save Syria' slogans had adorned walls in Malé, the capital of the Indian Ocean archipelago, since 2012. Some had also gone to Syria to deliver money, carefully collected in the Sunni nation's mosques, to hard-line groups. But those travelling in the first weeks of 2015 were part of a new wave of departures, much more numerous than any before, and all inspired by the apparent success of the Islamic State and its declaration of a caliphate.

The near one million foreign tourists who visit the Maldives annually meet few of the 400,000 inhabitants other than staff at their resorts, where consumption of alcohol is tolerated though it is banned elsewhere. They fly into the main airport and then leave directly for the atolls where they will spend their holidays.

Hardly any even visit Malé, a city of 150,000 packed onto a tiny two-mile-square island. Almost all the foreigners are unaware of the 900-year-old Muslim culture. Animists converted by Arab traders, the people of the archipelago remained a sultanate for many centuries, though a British protectorate from 1887 until full independence in 1965. After a period of instability, Maumoon Abdul Gayoom took power in 1978 and ruled for thirty years. Gayoom clamped down on all unsanctioned opinion, whether religious or otherwise, but encouraged 'moderate' Islamist views, which matched his own and bolstered his authority.

Following the pattern of so many Muslim countries, conservative and more politicised strands of Muslim practice and thought have made inroads over recent decades into what had previously been a tolerant, syncretic and quietist tradition. The outward signs of this are familiar – increased attendance at mosques, more men growing beards as a sign of devotion, and more women forgoing colourful traditional dress and donning headscarves. Equally familiar are the reasons for the change: a new exposure to events elsewhere in the Islamic world through satellite TV and the Internet over the last decade, the often violent nature of those events and the strong emotions they provoked, and, inevitably, the influence of wealthy Gulf States. Conservative clerics from the Gulf are frequent visitors to the Maldives and have a close relationship with the Ministry for Religious Affairs. In a single donation in 2013, Saudi Arabia gave $1.5 million for building half a dozen mosques in the Maldives and the Crown Prince Salman, who became king in January 2015, promised to build ten more of 'world class'. He also reportedly booked out all the resorts on two islands for dozens of minor royals for a holiday costing an estimated $10 million.[1]

The ouster of Gayoom in 2008 led to the end of strict controls on mosques and clerics and free elections for the first time in decades. But the new democratic era has been troubled. Rapid economic development, political instability and wide-reaching social change, accompanied by unemployment, overcrowding, drug abuse, a new gang culture and rising crime, have disorientated many Maldivians, particularly the young. Some have sought refuge in the rigid certainties of conservative religion, others have turned to faith-inspired political activism and a small minority have chosen instead to commit themselves to a violent 'jihad'.

Throughout the last decade, instances of extreme militancy at home remained rare.[2] The only terrorist attack in the Maldives was a small bomb in 2007 and, though frequently rumoured, there was little evidence that regional groups such as those based in Pakistan had gained any purchase on the islands.[3] Though Maldivians did occasionally become actively involved in conflicts around the Islamic world, their numbers remained negligible with perhaps only a few score travelling to Pakistan, Afghanistan or elsewhere between 2001 and 2012.

Extremism was undoubtedly growing, however. Between 2011 and 2014 there had been a series of attacks on liberal bloggers and other public figures. These came amid successive political confrontations, some violent, in the young democracy. In 2012, the progressive, pro-Western president, human rights campaigner and climate change activist Mohamed Nasheed, was ousted by former regime elements allied with Islamists and conservative religious parties who claimed that he was a threat to the 'traditional Islamic values of the Maldives'. Gangs, hired by political parties to break up opposition rallies and intimidate opponents, played a significant role in the crisis. In one incident, twelfth-century Buddhist statues from the nation's pre-Islamic past were destroyed by attackers linked to a local group of known militants.[4] The most serious incident was the fatal stabbing of a parliamentarian and moderate cleric. The culprits were gang members who had become interested in extremism while in prison.

A network of hard-line Islamic preachers and organisers in the Maldives was increasingly active too. Some had existed for years but now grew fast, energised by the early phases of the conflict in Syria. Some were involved in humanitarian assistance, raising funds for projects in the conflict-hit country itself or in the refugee camps in neighbouring states, which by the beginning of 2014 held four million Syrians. 'The Muslim *umma* is like one body. If there is pain in one part, the rest should feel it,' said a thirty-year-old businessman in Malé.

Others helped young men who wanted to reach the conflict zone to fight. Not many actually made it to Syria but some that did created a web page which became extremely popular back home. Among much sectarian invective, in both English and the local language of

Dhivehi, and calls for reform of the *jahiliyya*, or pagan, ignorant Maldives, the page lionised Abu Turab, a 44-year-old Maldivian who was killed in a suicide operation near Idlib with Jabhat al-Nusra in May 2014.[5] Tracts were also being distributed by extremists, calling for violent resistance to the West, the Zionists and the defence of the *umma*. Self-appointed activists harassed alleged homosexuals and so-called 'secularists', particularly bloggers, and intimidated journalists.

The seizure of Mosul and the declaration of the caliphate catalysed all this varied but inchoate activity. Previously, much of the activism had lacked a specific focus, and Jabhat al-Nusra had been the most popular single group among any Maldivians drawn to Syria as a cause. By late summer, clandestine Islamic State support groups had formed. Some met in private homes. Others daubed walls with pro-IS graffiti. A well-known journalist who wrote about 'jihadis' and was involved in a campaign for a 'secular' Maldives was abducted and probably killed. In September 2014, around a hundred men and women marched through the centre of Malé carrying ISIS flags and banners saying 'Islam will dominate the world' and 'To Hell with Democracy'.

In the autumn, there was a surge in the number of Maldivians travelling to Syria, and dying there. Two were killed in suicide operations in September 2014, then another in November.[6] From a negligible dozen or so trying to reach Syria in 2012, the total had climbed to around a hundred by the end of 2014, even before a further wave of departures in the new year. Some of those who left were men like one 27-year-old from one remote island who had long derided the 'corruption' of his homeland and had practised a rigorous, puritanical faith by himself. He took his mother, younger sister and wife with him, sending word to a stunned father that he was 'making a new life' where 'pure Islam' had been realised. His father blamed hours spent on religious and jihadi websites.[7]

But the lives of many others had been more dissolute, and their interest in radical Islam more recent. Those who left in January 2015 included a dozen or so members of a well-known gang from the Kuda Henveiru neighbourhood. Most had a range of charges outstanding against them or previous convictions for trafficking, assault and murder.[8] Several had been radicalised in prison.[9]

Family members of one gang member who travelled in January 2015 said he had been told by local preachers that it 'was better to die in the way of God than to go to prison in the Maldives'. The 26-year-old had previously been detained for offences relating to drugs and violence. 'After becoming religious, he was a really good boy, working hard and not misbehaving,' said his father. 'But he kept saying how the Maldives was not a land for Muslims and was talking about going to paradise.'[10] Old media played a role in convincing his son of this new view of the world too. The young man had spent hours on the Internet, consulting a site run by Maldivian fighters in Syria, but an equal if not greater amount of time with an 84-page booklet called 'The Blessings of Jihad'. Distributed outside a mosque in recent weeks, it repeated the arguments of Qutb, Farraj and al-Awlaki that young people do not need the authority of a cleric, sovereign or their parents to go and fight.

The inspirational effect of the emergence of the Islamic State was felt elsewhere in South Asia too, even if the region was seen as marginal to the ongoing resurgence of militancy in the Islamic world. Only a handful of young men had either travelled or attempted to travel to Syria between 2011 and mid-2014 from India, for example. The declaration of the caliphate prompted a surge there too, with around two hundred volunteers leaving their homes by the end of the year. Militancy in India had been a largely domestic affair, with significant involvement from Pakistan-based groups, but IS had brought a new global element to both rhetoric and activism, local officials said.[11] In the disputed region of Kashmir, where a bloody conflict had pitted Islamic militants and separatists, many based in and backed by Pakistan, against Indian security forces for almost thirty years, pro-IS graffiti was seen and IS flags waved at demonstrations. A software engineer in the central Indian city of Bangalore was unmasked as a prolific social media activist for the group, though he had no direct connection with them, simply retweeting thousands of pro-IS messages. The numbers of those involved were negligible compared to India's overall Muslim population of 180 million, or even compared to those thought linked to long-established militant networks in the vast country. However, the effect of IS was considered significant enough for Western officials charged with protecting their citizens in India to increase security at schools, embassies and businesses.

In Bangladesh, the world's third biggest Muslim-majority nation, a small network of pro-IS sympathisers was broken up, though, as in India, most militancy remained a very local matter. In Pakistan, slogans painted on walls from Karachi in the south to Gilgit in the north were reported, and a video released in late 2014 showed female students and teachers of a religious school attached to Islamabad's infamous Red Mosque, a long-standing centre of extremism, sitting under an Islamic State flag, and pledging support to al-Baghdadi.[12] Elsewhere, pamphlets were distributed and an imam in the eastern city of Lahore who charged each volunteer $600 to send him to join the Islamic State was arrested.[13] Around five hundred Pakistanis were estimated to have travelled to Syria to fight by January 2015. If, like in other parts of the region, IS-related activity was marginal, it was still a new element which had clear potential, particularly in an environment as volatile as Pakistan's, to evolve into something much more threatening.

But South Asians made up only a tiny fraction of the foreign fighters to reach Syria. Far more came from countries in the Middle East. These constituted around half of the 20,000 believed to have fought with Sunni militant organisations over the course of the conflict up to the beginning of 2015. Another 3,000 were from states of the former Soviet Union and around 4,000 from Western Europe. The largest individual country contingents were from Tunisia, Jordan, Morocco and Saudi Arabia. A significant number came from Libya too. Much fewer came from Egypt or Turkey. The total, as several observers pointed out, was greater than the estimated number of foreign fighters who had travelled to take part in the war against the Soviets in Afghanistan in the 1980s.[14] Some, particularly in the early phases of the conflict, were experienced fighters, often veterans of the battles against US troops in Iraq or Afghanistan or, as the perceptive analyst Aaron Zelin noted in a review of online 'martyrdom' announcements in 2013, the chaotic campaign to oust Gaddafi in Libya.[15] But the vast proportion, especially as time went on, had never seen any kind of combat before. The influx to Syria increased significantly in the autumn and winter of 2014 and early 2015 following the declaration of the caliphate, US officials said. The variety among the fighters that had been graphically highlighted by the notorious Islamic State video of November 2014, which featured men from an assortment of different countries decapitating Syrian Army prisoners, did not diminish.[16] The executioners, clearly identifiable, appeared to have been carefully chosen to demonstrate the range of the group's supposed support across the Islamic world and beyond. IS also made an effort to publicise the deaths of foreigners in 'martyrdom operations', giving special prominence to announcements of their deaths online.

Why did the war in Syria exert such a pull on so many? There were multiple factors of course but several, shared in varying degrees across the Islamic world, will by now be familiar: the long-term resurgence of Islamic identities and practice; the growing dominance of the more rigorous, conservative strands within that more general revival of faith; an increasingly global vision of the responsibilities of the members of the *umma* to one another; the powerful example of the Prophet Mohammed's flight from Mecca – the 'Hegira' – repeatedly referred to by al-Baghdadi in his calls to Muslims to join IS; the sense of the Muslims' collective loss of power and glory and its current 'humiliation'; the higher levels of radicalisation and mobilisation seen across the Islamic world since 2001. Although, a decade or more after the 9/11 attacks, overall support for violent extremism of the type represented by al-Qaeda still remained low, this did not mean any less anti-US sentiment.[17] In the Middle East, a median of just 21 per cent saw America positively in 2013, and only 14 per cent of Jordanians and 16 per cent of Egyptians.[18] A significant minority everywhere believed most Christians are hostile to Muslims.[19] One consequence of the invasions of Afghanistan and, particularly, Iraq was that the idea that the West was set on the division and humiliation of Muslims had become so well established as to be almost a commonplace amid hundreds of millions of people.[20] Concepts such as the 'defensive jihad' and the responsibility of the individual to take up arms, once confined to fringe thinkers such as Abdel Salam Farraj or Abdullah Azzam, had also become much more widely accepted, even if they were still far from 'mainstream'. Support for sharia law was also high, around 74 per cent in Middle Eastern states in 2013, and similar levels in South and Far East Asia.[21] None of this translated directly into support for the Islamic State, but made the basic principles on which its project and world view appeared to be based significantly easier to accept.

A further element was the growing popularity of apocalyptic prophecy in the Middle East, as many veteran commentators on extremist Islam noted.[22] This can be overplayed but it is clear that both IS statements and propaganda stress the apocalyptic in a way that few previous Sunni militants had done. Islamic State videos had shown executions against a carefully selected backdrop identified as a dusty field on the outskirts of the small but symbolic Syrian town of Dabiq, the supposed site of the forthcoming final battle between the *umma* and 'Rome'. Dabiq had been a key objective of the Islamic State fighters as they made their way across Syria in 2013 and was now firmly under their control. References to Judgement Day, to the coming of the 'black flags' from the east as a herald of the end-times, and especially to the imminence of the final battle of belief and unbelief, had a broad resonance. As scholar Jean-Pierre Filiu has noted, millenarian thinking once limited to poor and ill-educated Shia communities and eschatological literature once consigned to a 'lunatic fringe' of Sunnis had become much more widespread over recent decades. Video clips predicting the coming of the 'Great Slaughter' received almost as many viewings as those describing the major historical victories of Muslim armies over the Crusaders, the Byzantines or the Mongols. Both often use images from Western-made films, dubbed with Arabic subtitles and religious songs, an especially important way of drawing those with minimal knowledge of the Islamic faith, or indeed political awareness, into the extremist project. The Islamic State also benefited from a new network of younger clerics and propagandists around the world who had emerged over previous years but whose support for al-Qaeda had been tepid at best, and whose narrative was distinctly more apoca-lyptic than al-Qaeda's had ever been. They too were powerful adver-tisers of the brand that the Islamic State was able to construct as its successes piled up.

But perhaps the most important element was the newly virulent sectarianism. Throughout the 1990s, violence towards the Shia had risen in parallel with the growing animosity towards the West, and growing intolerance towards other Sunnis who did not follow the more conservative, rigorous schools. In Afghanistan, in Pakistan and elsewhere, Shia minorities had been targeted by extremists in a new wave of sectarian violence fuelled in part by the rivalry between Saudi Arabia and Iran for leadership of the Islamic world but also by much more local factors, such as historic land-ownership patterns. Iraq had seen a savage outbreak of what was in effect sectarian violence when in 1991 a revolt amongst Shias against Saddam's rule was bloodily crushed by Sunni military units loyal to the dictator.[23] As described in earlier chapters, events in Iraq since 2003 had progressively exacerbated local and regional Sunni fears. The sectarian battle lines drawn in Syria since 2011, particularly as Shia foreign fighters from Hezbollah in Lebanon and beyond joined Assad's forces, had simply reinforced this anxiety. This alignment extended beyond Syria and Iraq, of course, and beyond the two states' immediate neighbours. The conflict in the Levant and Mesopotamia was the fulcrum around which a vast battle for influence and power was being played out, by Iran and Saudi Arabia, the pre-eminent Shia and Sunni powers of the region, and by actors across most of the Islamic world. Again, the Islamic State, with its avowed and aggressive sectarian prejudice, was perfectly positioned to capitalise on fears prompted among Sunnis by an apparently resurgent Shia Islam. That Sunni states such as Turkey, Saudi Arabia, Qatar and Kuwait did both actively and passively support some hard-line groups in Syria – though not the Islamic State or Jabhat al-Nusra – did not help either.[24]

Then there were the demographics of the region. One factor working in the favour of the Islamic State, as it had done once for al-Qaeda, was the huge number of very young people. In 2011, North Africa and the Middle East had the second highest percentage of young people in the world, trailing only sub-Saharan Africa. Sixty per cent of the region's people are under thirty. Significantly, all the countries which have gone through a revolution, coup attempt or civil war from 2011 to 2012 had a median age of twenty-four or younger. Though it is difficult to be exact, the average age of the volunteers travelling to Syria was probably around twenty-two or twenty-three. These were young men for whom the 9/11 attacks were ancient history, a childhood memory at best. Their formative experiences had been the conflicts of more recent years, in which al-Qaeda had played a diminishing role, and the Arab Spring uprisings. Across the region, young people faced the same challenges: grotesque levels of unemployment, crumbling educational facilities, limited opportunities for constructive use of leisure time, sexual frustration but social constraints on cohabitation or pre-marital relationships too. In many Moroccan cities, for example, more than half of young men were neither employed nor studying in 2012.[25] Elsewhere, unemployment among male graduates – a key recurring cohort among the volunteers, and extremists more generally – had reached 35 per cent by 2013 and was significantly higher in some places than it had been a decade before. There may be no direct link between poverty and extremism, but such circumstances must surely have contributed to the appeal of the brutal solutions proposed by Islamic State, given the propaganda surging through the region. 'The Islamic State is a true caliphate, a system that is fair and just, where you don't have to follow somebody's orders because he is rich or powerful,' one young Tunisian told a reporter from the *New York Times* in October 2014.[26]

In addition, millions of young people had experienced a vast surge of hope and aspiration during the heady days of the Arab uprisings, only to be rapidly disillusioned. If the previous fifty years had seen the discrediting of socialism, Arab nationalism and communism, the fifty months from early 2011 to mid-2015 saw the discrediting of almost every possible ideology or system one could imagine as regimes collapsed, governments failed, the international community stood by as tens of thousands died and conditions for most people in the region steadily deteriorated. Several cases came to light of relatively Westernised pro-democracy activists who had played prominent roles in the uprisings of 2011 and 2012 turning to violent Islamic militancy.[27]

An important distinction with foreign volunteers who had joined local militant groups around the Islamic world over the previous decade was that those who joined IS did not sign up for a lengthy period of enforced celibacy. In fact, fighting with IS appeared to offer significant sexual opportunities. The organisation encouraged marriages between volunteers from overseas – a small but notable proportion of the foreigners were women – and of course provided captive 'wives' to be systematically raped. This policy not only avoided the problems of outsiders causing enormous resentment among local communities by taking local women as 'temporary' wives but also meant that the possibility of sexual 'conquest', or welcome nuptials, was thus added to a powerful package which already included the excitement of battle, camaraderie and status among peers which could be enjoyed online even while still in the conflict zone as friends and family read your Facebook posts or mails. Fighting in Syria, though not quite the 'five-star jihad' sometimes reported, was considerably more comfortable than in Afghanistan, Yemen, Somalia or the Pakistani tribal areas. It was also, even as successive governments began to clamp down from 2013 onwards, much, much easier to reach.

Some married volunteers brought their families with them, convinced by clever propaganda that the IS-run 'caliphate' was a better place to bring up children 'in the way of God'. Much of the 'softer' propaganda produced by the Islamic State was ignored as media attention, especially in the West, focused on the appalling images of violence that some films contained. But a significant amount of the videos being uploaded by IS and its supporters avoided all martial imagery, aiming instead to portray life in the territories the group controlled as an Islamic idyll, devoid of any of the stresses and concerns of daily existence elsewhere in the Middle East. A survey of IS propaganda videos in early 2015 found nearly half concentrated on highlighting governance efforts, infrastructure projects, the work of traffic police, the provision of health care, courts and agriculture. One featured images of children at a mall and amusement park north of Mosul. Another, subtitled in Arabic, showed an Australian paediatrician volunteer in a neo-natal clinic in Raqqa with facilities rare anywhere in the developing world. Not only was care free and available to all but there were Western-trained doctors too, the clip implied. Much of this output was directed at local populations, but it could, obviously, be viewed across the planet. It was supported by huge quantities of what could be called 'unorganised propaganda', that disseminated by individual volunteers, which emphasised the 'quality of life' in Raqqa particularly but also elsewhere. Tweets of food, for example, were common, or, inevitably, happy children. If the slick and graphic videos of violence appealed to one group, those promoting the 'family atmosphere' of IS appealed to another. Both appear to have been effective.[28]

Many of the volunteers came from middle-ranking, provincial

towns and poor neighbourhoods in capital cities. These were places like the impoverished southern town of Ma'an and the slums of industrial Zarqa in Jordan; the conservative small towns of the central Najd Desert in Saudi Arabia; Tizi Ouzou, in the Kabylie region in north-east Algeria; a series of towns in the north of Morocco. In Tunisia, two key sites of recruitment were Sidi Bouzid, a scruffy central town, and Ben Gardane, on the Libyan border. Other examples are the tough quarter of Haci Bayram in Ankara, the Turkish capital, and Douar Hicher, a poor district at the edge of Tunis.[29]

All these places share certain characteristics. The first is that they are outside the political, economic and cultural mainstream. Ma'an is a world away from the luxury hotels, the palaces and the tourist sites of Amman, for example. Towns like Buraydah, in central Saudi Arabia, are markedly different in atmosphere and culture even from Riyadh, let alone more cosmopolitan cities such as Jeddah. Frequently they are physically distant too. Sidi Bouzid is 160 miles from Tunis and Ben Gardane 220 miles. Tetouan is 170 miles from Rabat, the Moroccan capital, and 220 miles from Casablanca, the country's commercial centre. These are places where people speak with regional accents, drive on poorer roads, send their children to less well-funded schools, get less electricity, drink worse water, and are often watched over by suspicious police officers sent to what are considered hardship postings by worried administrations. Sometimes the inhabitants are largely from a minority tribe or ethnicity. The north-east of Algeria and the north of Morocco are strongholds of the Berbers, who inhabited the North African coastline before the Arab invasions. Ma'an is a Bedouin town. Neighbourhoods like Douar Hicher are not physically distant, but they are peripheral in cultural and economic terms. The frequency with which such towns appear as sources for the foreign volunteers attracted by IS, as well as other militant groups in Syria, underlines the role of social and economic factors, even if, as stated above, there is no essential and direct connection between extremism and poverty. The rate of graduate unemployment in Sidi Bouzid had reached 57 per cent by 2013, well above the national average. It was reported to be at a similar level in Ma'an.

These are also places which have been associated with violent and non-violent activism for decades, indeed sometimes centuries. The north of Morocco and north-east of Algeria have both posed law and order problems for successive regimes, going back to the days of European rule. Buraydah, the conservative town in central Saudi Arabia which has been a key source of volunteers for Syrian Islamist groups, saw violent demonstrations against reforms in the 1960s and 70s, and was home to a series of radical clerics in subsequent decades. Ma'an was placed under curfew in 1998 after violent protests against the threat of a US attack on Iraq and was the scene of intense armed clashes with security forces in 2002.[30] In the last decade, many of these places were the source for large numbers of fighters in Iraq, or even recruits for al-Qaeda central. Tetouan, set in the hills of northern Morocco just back from the Mediterranean coast, became known as the city of 'suicide bombers'. Not all the violence associated with these places has been 'Islamic', however. It was in Sidi Bouzid that a young grocer self-immolated in December 2010, thus setting off the revolt in Tunisia and the chain of uprisings across the Middle East. The Douar Hicher neighbourhood in Tunis was heavily involved in the Jasmine revolution, contributing four 'martyrs' in the unrest. Since 2012, many have developed strong networks of support for Syria too. The role of such towns and cities also underlines how a broader history of local activism, whether Islamic or other, clearly encourages new generations to become involved, violently or otherwise, in new causes.

And finally it underlines the importance of connections in modern Islamic militancy. Commentators and analysts in the late 1990s systematically referred to Afghanistan as isolated. Yet, as seen at the end of chapter 2, it was in fact well connected to a variety of informal global networks which had contributed significantly to the 9/11 attacks. A similar series of intersecting criminal, ideological, religious and extremist networks connect towns like Ma'an, Tetouan, Ben Gardane, even Malé, the capital of the Maldives. For one more characteristic of these places is a deserved reputation for clandestine activity of all kinds. Many are sited next to international frontiers, ports or other useful transport nodes. The cities of northern Morocco, such as Tetouan or Fnideq, have long been plugged into a range of regional networks which have been smuggling people, drugs and much else around the Mediterranean for decades. Militant clerics and organisers from around the region and beyond have been travelling to these towns along well organised routes for many years, and disseminating propaganda through equally well-established systems of communication. Ben Gardane, which is a major source of volunteers, has been a base of trafficking networks for years. Ma'an is known for illicit cross-border trade.[31] Such networks enable young men who would otherwise be defeated by the sheer logistics of international travel to make their way to conflict zones. Marginalisation locally no longer means marginalisation globally. If the young men from these places pose a threat, it is not because they are unconnected from the myriad networks which constitute our contemporary world, but because, they are very much connected to them.

Of the young men from the Kuda Henveiru neighbourhood of Malé who reached their destination, only one of them subsequently contacted his family, and then simply to tell his father that he had 'no regrets'.

Forty men stumble along a beach, treading a narrow strip of grey sand between the dark rocks and the subdued waves. The sun is low and casts almost no shadow. The camera swings up smoothly then tracks across. Half the men are wearing orange jumpsuits and are led by an identical number of armed men in black, faces obscured by balaclavas. Their leader wears pale desert camouflage combat fatigues and brandishes a large black combat knife. The men in the jumpsuits are forced to lie chest down in the sand and their necks pulled back for the knives. Their eyes are blank. Their heads are severed – the camera pausing on a blade carving through cartilage and flesh – and placed on their bodies. The leader of the killers addresses the camera, spitting threats against the 'Crusaders', invoking the memory of 'the martyr' Osama bin Laden and the prospect of blood-red seas. The final images are of the water stained with the blood of the twenty-one Coptic Christian fishermen murdered by the Islamic State, not in Syria or Iraq but on what appears to be the southern coastline of the Mediterranean.

The video, released in late January 2015, was not merely a message delivered, like so many others by militants over the years, through spectacular and appalling violence with the aim of terrorising the enemy, mobilising followers and polarising anyone in between. It was a statement of territorial possession. In the video, entitled 'A Message Signed in Blood to the Nation of the Cross', the leader made explicitly clear, in perfect English, that the message it contained was being sent 'from south of Rome'. This was almost certainly Libya, and most probably the coastline somewhere near Derna, less than three hundred miles from the nearest European Union territory. Analysis by Western officials later identified a cove with distinctive rock types north-east of the city of 100,000.[32] It was a reminder that the IS motto was still 'remain and expand' and that its caliphate was not, and would never be, limited to Iraq and Syria.

The priority for IS during the fighting of 2013 and early 2014 had been to attain local objectives, and most of the group's propaganda directed at audiences beyond the group's core territories had sought to convince them to come to the caliphate, not that the caliphate was coming to them. But that the territory ruled by the new caliph would one day cover that once ruled by great Islamic empires over the previous thousand or so years had always been intrinsic to al-Baghdadi's vision, as it had been to that of generations of militant leaders before him. In Mosul, al-Baghdadi had spoken of the coming conquest of 'Rome'. How was this to be achieved? The Umayyads, the Abbasids, the Mughals and the Ottomans had led long campaigns of military conquest, successively subjugating princes, sultans, kings and lords across the Middle East, the Maghreb and, in the other direction, as far as modern-day Myanmar. There was little chance IS, even given the momentum it had generated and the conventional firepower it had amassed, was going to be able to fight its way across Turkey, Jordan, Iran or the rest of Iraq. If a conventional campaign was out of the question, something unconventional was called for.

By the early autumn of 2014, three months after the declaration of the caliphate, a strategy was taking shape. The model that al-Qaeda had followed in recent years was adapted. There would be no patient acquisition of territory through lengthy negotiation with existing established groups in far-flung lands. Instead the Islamic State would rely primarily on the inspirational power of its apparent success in Iraq and Syria to convince existing independent actors to pledge their allegiance, to break others away from different established groups or simply to bring new actors into existence who could represent the Islamic State around the Muslim world. This was a new version of the 'propaganda by deed' strategy pioneered by bin Laden almost twenty years before, except the 'deeds' were not an act of spectacular violence against international targets but the declaration of a new caliphate and the seizure of Mosul, continuing military victories and repeated videos of atrocities of escalating horror.

But as with al-Qaeda's project of expansion and outreach, IS saw no immediate need for contiguous territory. The provinces of the new caliphate did not need to be physically connected, at least not yet. Instead series of individual nodes of support scattered across several thousand miles would coalesce over time. This was an Islamic militant version of a strategy elaborated by Mao, Che Guevara and Western counter-insurgency specialists, among others, based on the creation of 'ink spots' of revolutionary activity or good governance that would steadily grow until eventually merging to create more sizeable blocs of unified 'liberated' or 'governed' territory. The fragmentation of the territory that the Islamic State sought to bring under its control thus was not an impediment. Indeed it was an advantage. The countries adjacent to Iraq and Syria could be ignored in favour of more distant objectives where conditions were propitious to an intervention and which were of sufficient strategic importance to be worth the effort. These outposts of this 'pop-up' caliphate could be created wherever sufficient people loyal to the caliph existed. The new Islamic empire would be created by the people who decided to live in it. It would, at least in part, be crowd-sourced.

Throughout early 2014, a score or so of groups around the Islamic world had come out with public statements of support for the Islamic State, of which around a dozen had pledged allegiance to al-Baghdadi.[33] In the late summer and early autumn the Islamic State sent envoys to work with these local sympathisers in key areas. Individuals or small groups travelled to Libya, Egypt, to a meeting with representatives of hard-line Sunni groups from Pakistan somewhere along the Iranian frontier, and possibly to Algeria, Tunisia, Yemen and into Afghanistan too. These were all places where militants had endorsed the idea of the caliphate even before it had actually been declared. This support was recognised in November when al-Baghdadi announced that IS was accepting declarations of allegiance from local mujahideen and creating a series of 'wilayat', a word which had been used by the Ottoman Empire to describe semi-autonomous provinces under loyal but independent rulers and could also be translated as 'governorates' or simply 'territories'. These, he explained, had been formally established where support for the caliphate was considered sufficiently robust and where 'direct lines' of communication with local organisations existed. The frontiers of the seven new governorates – in Saudi Arabia, Egypt, Yemen, Algeria and three in Libya – were for the most part not defined by boundaries drawn by Western colonial administrators but by their ninth- or tenth-century Muslim counterparts. So the governorate in Egypt was the 'Wilayat al-Sinai', while that in Saudi Arabia was the 'Wilayat al-Haramayn', or of the 'Two Sanctuaries' of Mecca and Medina. Two months later IS issued a new audio statement, announcing to the mujahideen the 'good news of the Islamic State's expansion to Khorasan'. The term was, like so much else, borrowed from the era of the early-Islamic empires and referred to a swathe of land comprising eastern Iran, Afghanistan, western Pakistan and southern parts of what are now Turkmenistan, Uzbekistan and Tajikistan. It also had a variety of millenarian resonances. Further wilayat in the Caucasus, Indonesia and the Philippines were promised at a later date.[34]

Of the new structures the most important were in Egypt and Libya.

Egypt was, of course, where it had all started, forty years before, with Qutb, Farraj and the assassination of Sadat. With hindsight, it was inevitable that Islamic militancy would emerge resurgent from the disorder that followed the 2011 ouster of Hosni Mubarak. All the requisite factors were present: very high numbers of very bored young men, spectacular levels of graduate unemployment, disillusionment after the false hopes of the early days of the democratic era, economic chaos, a crumbling infrastructure and the release or return of long-imprisoned or long-exiled veteran militants.[35] But though there appeared to be some growth in extremism in urban areas, the main focus of the new militancy was not the seething cities where it had taken hold in the 1970s and 80s. It was in remote, poor and resentful Sinai, from where groups had launched a wave of bombings around a decade before but which had been relatively calm since.[36]

At first, violence in Sinai seemed to be largely confined to the restive Bedouin tribes, and the bombing of pipelines in the summer of 2011 and spring of 2012 appeared simply a return to a traditional means of putting pressure on central government to take note of local demands for better services. This rapidly evolved, however, as militants moved in, either recruiting among the tribes or similarly taking advantage of the security vacuum themselves. Among the varied mix of groups operating in the deserts and scrubs of Sinai were some claiming allegiance to al-Qaeda. One faction, or set of factions, which seemed to be marginally more organised than any other, called itself Ansar Beit al-Maqdis (which very roughly translates as 'Partisans of Jerusalem').[37]

This group claimed responsibility for a series of attacks through 2012, including rockets fired at the southern Israeli resort of Eilat, an operation targeting an Israeli border patrol, and another attack which killed sixteen Egyptian soldiers. Though based in Sinai, the group drew fighters from across Egypt. Two of those involved in the attack on the patrol were educated, middle-class men from a village in the Nile delta.[38]

The violence escalated significantly after the Muslim Brotherhood's Mohamed Morsi, the first democratically elected president in Egyptian history, was forced from power after a year in office by the Egyptian Army in July 2013. This event reverberated throughout the Middle East and wider Islamic world, framed as definitive proof that the bullet not the ballot box was the only way to achieve an Islamic state. In one of the most high-profile attacks, the Ansar Beit al-Maqdis (ABM) tried to assassinate the minister of the interior with a huge car bomb and struck a police station in Cairo. Abdel Fattah al-Sisi, the former general who was the new president, sent troops into Sinai, where their heavy-handed tactics simply made a bad situation worse.

As elsewhere, the Islamic State's seizure of Mosul and declaration of the caliphate galvanised and polarised militants in Sinai.[39] ABM had suffered the loss of a number of leaders, which had, as elsewhere, strengthened the hand of remaining hardliners. These turned increasingly to IS. The influence of the group on ABM was evident when, in August 2014, it broadcast a carefully choreographed and edited video showing the beheading of four alleged spies. In October, it attacked an Egyptian Army base and killed twenty-eight soldiers, inflicting the military's worst single loss for decades.[40] Following the formal announcement of allegiance, and the renaming as the Islamic State's Sinai *wilayat*, the group's propaganda output became even closer to that of the new caliphate. So too did the style, and efficacy, of its military operations. After a short period of calm, there came a new series of strikes against military targets in Sinai, which left another thirty dead.[41]

Yet, if much of the attention focused on Egypt, it was hundreds of miles to the west that the Islamic State appeared to be having its greatest success, in its newly declared governorates of Cyrenaica, Fezzan and Tripolitania, known collectively since the end of the Second World War as Libya and, by early 2015, in as much of a mess as anywhere in the Middle East outside Syria or western Iraq.

Here was a toxic brew of many of the conditions fuelling Islamic militancy's resurgence elsewhere. There was a long and rich history of Islamic militancy in Libya, reaching back to the tenacious resistance to Italian colonisers by tribesmen in the first half of the twentieth century. This had often been framed within a religious narrative and primarily organised by religious networks.[42] Muammar Gaddafi, the mid-ranking army officer who took power in 1969, inherited a country which faced many of the challenges of other states in the region in the period and was as subject as any to consequences of the religious revival under way at the time. The deep faith and Islamic identity of many Libyans was obscured by Gaddafi's bizarre mixture of nationalism, socialism and personality cult, but extremist cells and networks formed in the 1970s, as they had done in Egypt and elsewhere, and a Libyan contingent fought in Afghanistan against the Soviets the following decade. Veterans of that conflict then launched an unsuccessful campaign to overthrow the regime in the early 1990s. The Libyan Islamic Fighting Group just about survived into the next decade, despite a prison massacre in which hundreds of them were killed, before concluding that the armed struggle would never succeed and eventually agreeing to give up their fight in return for an amnesty in 2009.[43] This would have been a major blow against Islamic militancy in the country had it not been for the new mobilisation prompted by the Iraq war. Hundreds, probably thousands, of young Libyans travelled to fight US troops and Iraqi government forces. Survivors returned to build new extremist networks which were particularly strong in the east and in the city of Derna.

Close to the frontier, far from the capital, poor and isolated, long known for trafficking, conservatism, extremism and violence, and well connected to international networks, Derna is yet another example of those provincial centres which play such an outsize role in Islamic militancy today. It too, like Tizi Ouzou in neighbouring Algeria and so many similar places where militancy thrived, had a history of resistance to colonial occupiers in earlier eras. According to records seized from an al-Qaeda base in Iraq and to US officials, Derna, despite a population of only 100,000, was one of the most significant regional contributors of fighters to Iraq between 2003 and 2011. In the chaos that followed Gaddafi's fall, with the area awash with guns and devoid of any government authority, the city and the surrounding area saw intense extremist activity. A series of well-armed, well-trained and combat-experienced militias following radical Islamic agendas rapidly emerged, in Derna and elsewhere. Al-Qaeda's senior command in Pakistan spotted an opportunity and sent a series of veterans as emissaries and leaders to start building a network.[44] Atiyah Abd al-Rahman, the Libyan al-Qaeda veteran who had once tried to moderate al-Zarqawi's murderous savagery in Iraq, had made the group's aim in his homeland very clear in a written document in early 2011 entitled 'The Arab Revolutions and the Season of Harvest'. This was to effect 'a real, radical, and revolutionary change that would affirm the supremacy of Allah's words and the dominance of sharia'.[45] The most dramatic demonstration of the rising power of the extremists, few of whom were affiliated to any major group, came in September 2012 when a US diplomatic compound in Benghazi was attacked by local militants and the country's ambassador to Libya was killed.[46]

By then, Libyan fighters were making their way to Syria in significant numbers and the country had become a key transit and training point for volunteers. The familiar post-Arab Spring cocktail, of political chaos, collapsing governance, networks of radical clerics and organisers, easily available weaponry and propaganda, continued to fuel militancy across much of the country. Many extremist groups provided basic security and services where no one else would, or could, as well as brutally suppressing any dissent. Benghazi and Derna were effectively run by a series of battling, ill-disciplined militant factions.

There was already a network of semi-organised support for the Islamic State, and considerable popular enthusiasm for the group, in eastern Libya well before al-Baghdadi's announcement of the *wilayat* there in November 2014. Three months earlier, extremists had held a public execution in Derna.[47] By October, a faction on the Shura Council, the committee composed of representatives of different militant groups which ran Derna, had publicly sworn allegiance to the Islamic State. Islamic courts were set up and an Islamic police organised. Opposing officials were shot; others were threatened and resigned, clearing further space for the extremists. In November, three activists who had criticised the militants on social media were beheaded. In the new year, a series of more audacious attacks were launched by militants thought to be affiliated with the Islamic State, including one on a luxury hotel in Tripoli and another on the Mabruk oilfield. Then came the video of the killing of the Coptic Christians. Five days later two suicide bombers killed forty people. Violent clashes were also reported in the cities of Sirte and Benghazi, where fighters loyal to the Islamic State were increasingly active and aggressive. According to an internal State Department document, reported by Reuters, the number of Islamic State fighters operating in Libya ranged from 1,000 to 3,000 with around 800 based in the Derna area alone, including up to 300 who had previously fought in Syria or Iraq.

The successive declarations of the Islamic State's various *wilayat* allowed observers and allied propagandists alike to create terrifying representations of the new extent of the caliphate with entire countries coloured in red or black. But there was less to the Islamic State's capabilities in Algeria, Libya, Egypt and certainly in Pakistan or Afghanistan than met the eye. In Khorasan, many extremist fighters and leaders were undoubtedly impressed by the achievements of al-Baghdadi. 'Look, we have been fighting for years but we don't have an inch of land in our possession in Afghanistan. On the other hand, [the Islamic State], within limited time, captured vast areas in Iraq and Syria and established Sharia,' said one senior commander, in the Afghan province of Kunar.[48] But this did not translate into any broad-based support for IS or its project, either among local militants or among the population more generally. Recruits were relatively low-grade. The overall leader of the Khorasan *wilayat*, Hafiz Khan Saeed, had approached the Islamic State only after coming off worse in a battle with a rival to take the leadership of the battered and fractured Pakistani Taliban, while another high-profile recruit had been expelled from the Afghan Taliban for running an unauthorised kidnap and ransom racket.[49] The creation of the *wilayat* had little immediate impact, not least because the group's most senior commander in Afghanistan was killed by a US drone strike within weeks of his loyalty becoming public knowledge. Afghan security officials did not deny the suggestion that his location had been betrayed to them, and then passed on to the Americans, by the Taliban who remained very much the dominant militant power in the country.[50]

The extent of the IS presence in Saudi Arabia was difficult to judge. Local authorities made hundreds of arrests of people for recruiting or sending money to unnamed 'extremist groups overseas', detained others for making explosives and broke up at least one local network which officials said was explicitly linked to al-Baghdadi's group. IS did also claim the bombing of Shia mosques in the kingdom in May 2015, indicating growing capacity to kill and maim. Saudi officials, probably accurately, described the local IS activity as 'limited but worrying' with the potential to grow into a wave of violence like that seen a decade or more earlier unless it was rapidly countered.[51] In Yemen, the situation was similar and, in March 2015, local militants claiming to be part of IS bombed mosques in Sana'a killing 140 Shia worshippers. A cleric linked to the al-Qaeda affiliate in the country angrily criticised IS for spreading fitna among militants there. But there was still no evidence of any substantial IS presence even if the potential for growth was obvious. In Algeria, the supposed 'governorate' appeared to consist of little more than a small faction of militants estranged from al-Qaeda in the Maghreb which was effectively annihilated within weeks by the army and police.[52]

By the spring of 2015, the Islamic State's outreach efforts thus seemed to have had inconclusive results. In each new zone of expansion, the group loyal to IS was only one of many militant outfits vying for space, attention and power, with a tenuous hold on territory and fragile access to key resources such as weapons or cash. Nowhere had they yet been seriously tested, either by local security forces or by local communities, and wherever their declaration of allegiance had prompted an effective response from local authorities or rivals, such as in Algeria and Afghanistan, they had suffered significant setbacks. Nowhere had any of the IS militants in the various governorates been forced to actually govern, and the targets they had attacked were, if sometimes high profile, broadly soft ones. There was certainly no sign that the various enclaves they were working to establish might somehow soon be transformed into miniature Islamic States, let alone attract large numbers of migrants eager to live in righteous communities that, once joined together, would constitute a new Muslim superpower stretching across much of the Islamic world. One document posted by an extremist in Derna in January 2015 underlined the gap between aspiration and what was actually happening on the ground. It was entitled 'The Land of Caliphate in Libya Between the Calls for Hijra [migration] and the Challenge of Reality'.[53]

The leaders of IS gave no sign that they doubted their expansion strategy. In mid-March, they took their biggest gamble yet and accepted the *bayat* of Abubakar Shekau, the volatile and brutal leader of the Nigerian-based Al Jamaatu Ahl us-Sunnah Lid Dawa Wal Jihad (the Union of the People of the Law for Jihad and Proselysation), better known to the world as Boko Haram.

The militants arrived at the Government Secondary School in the north-eastern Nigerian town of Chibok shortly before midnight on 14 April 2014. One group attacked the local government offices, rapidly putting the detachment of fifteen fearful, poorly armed, poorly trained soldiers, who were supposed to defend the town's many thousands of inhabitants, to flight. A second group torched a church and several other buildings. A third headed to what appeared to be their main target.[54] The school was almost undefended and the attackers made straight for the main dormitory, where several hundred girls aged between sixteen and eighteen were sleeping. They rounded up 276, forced them to march through the surrounding brush to where a column of pickup trucks was waiting. Then the girls were driven to a camp seven hours away through the scrubby plains and forest. Most were Christian.

It took some time for the news of the abduction to circulate and two weeks before Nigeria's president, Goodluck Jonathan, made an official statement. The day before the kidnappings, a massive bomb had killed more than seventy-five commuters on the outskirts of the capital, Abuja, five hundred miles to the south, and little attention was focused on a remote provincial town where what appeared to be simply the latest in a string of kidnappings had occurred. As the scale of the abduction became clear – fifty-seven girls managed to escape while being led to the vehicles, leaving more than two hundred in captivity – local and global outrage began to grow. A social media campaign, spearheaded by the Twitter theme #bringbackourgirls, gathered momentum. Almost three weeks after the attack, there was a claim of responsibility, though few unbiased observers had ever doubted who had been behind the abduction. In a typically incoherent hour-long speech, Abubakar Shekau, the leader of Boko Haram, told the world that he was the one who had 'captured your girls'. 'I will sell them in the market. I am selling the girls like Allah said until we soak the ground of Nigeria with [the blood of] infidels and so-called Muslims contradicting Islam.'[55]

Under pressure, Jonathan assured the international community that the abduction of the girls would mean the 'beginning of the end of terror' in Nigeria, the most populous African state and the continent's biggest economy. Almost as he spoke, reports came in of a new atrocity: a militant attack on another remote small town in the north-east in which between one hundred and three hundred had died. Local politicians said the town had been left unguarded because soldiers based there had been redeployed in an effort to rescue the Chibok schoolgirls. 'Some bodies are burnt beyond recognition,' Babagana Goni, a resident, told the Agence France-Presse. 'Some of the bodies were shot while others had their throats slit, which made me sick. I couldn't continue the count.'[56]

Of all the violent extremist movements described in these pages, Boko Haram remains one of the least understood, and the most complex. It operates in the far north-east of Nigeria, has no defined command structure or obvious programme beyond the release of Boko

Haram prisoners and the creation of an Islamic state in place of 'Western democracy', is internally fractured, and has a well-deserved reputation for apparently random savagery. But though it might be an outlier among militant groups active today, many of the historical factors which have contributed to its growth are depressingly familiar.

Boko Haram – the name means 'No to Western Education' in the local Hausa language – launched its violent campaign in 2010.[57] However, it is only the latest of a series of revivalist movements, both violent and non-violent, that have swept northern Nigeria, over decades. Once again, the same pattern emerges: a resurgence of Islamic faith and identity in the 1960s and 70s, given a strongly conservative inflection by the efforts of missionaries and groups funded by Gulf-based organisations. Some of these – financed by Saudi Arabian institutions – were explicitly dedicated to purging the north of Nigeria of its more tolerant, pluralist traditions and imposing the rigorous literalism of Wahhabi Islam.[58] Helped by the construction of mosques and religious schools with Gulf funds, these organisations grew in strength through the 1980s and 90s. Meanwhile, ethnic and sectarian competition over land and water exacerbated communal tensions. When military rule in Nigeria ended in 1999, a powerful movement, backed by many northern politicians, demanded the imposition of sharia law in Muslim-majority areas. Others shunned political process altogether, withdrawing to create isolated communities where 'pure Islam' could be practised.

In 2002, a young charismatic preacher called Muhammad Yusuf broke away from a more moderate group of clerics and set up a mosque in a tough neighbourhood of Maiduguri, the capital of the miserable north-eastern Borno state and his birthplace. He rapidly gained followers, both from the town and surrounding villages, arguing that democracy was an alien construction imposed by British colonial rulers and maintained by a corrupt and exploitative elite. Given the relative poverty of the region, the brutality of the police, the venality and incompetence of the bureaucracy and the broader context of radicalisation created both by the sharia movement locally and the aftermath of the 9/11 attacks globally, it is not difficult to see why this was, once again, convincing to many poor, if not desperate, young men. If the movement was ostensibly non-violent, the fact that Yusuf named his mosque after Ibn Taymiyyah, the thirteenth-century scholar venerated by extremists from Syed Qutb to bin Laden, gave an indication of his world view. By 2007 or 2008, Boko Haram was very definitely violent, however, and in 2009, after an escalating series of clashes, security forces moved in on the Maiduguri mosque. More than eight hundred people were killed in the operation, which involved indiscriminate firing in civilian areas and significant numbers of executions. Yusuf was among those shot dead after being captured.[59]

Nigerian authorities believed this was the end of the problem. It was not. After a year regrouping, one of the various factions loosely joined together in Boko Haram launched new operations, including a series of assassinations and a prison raid which freed hundreds of detained militants. The attackers were led by Shekau, probably aged around thirty at the time. In 2011 came Nigeria's first suicide bombing. In 2012 came the most spectacular strike yet: a coordinated assault by scores of extremists hurling bombs and shooting on Nigeria's second largest city, Kano, in which 185 people were killed.[60] 'I enjoy killing anyone God commands me to kill, the way I enjoy killing chickens or rams,' Shekau said in a videoed speech. Previously, targets had largely been representative of an unjust and corrupt state. From 2013, attacks on Christians, on schools, and particularly on Muslims deemed insufficiently obser-vant or collaborators, including supposedly pro-establishment clerics, multiplied. So did kidnappings for ransom, abductions of women and bank robberies.

A new element of internationalism crept into some of Shekau's statements too, with increasing references to the US, the UK or, after the French intervention in Mali, to France.[61] One faction of Boko Haram, which had distanced itself from Shekau, appeared to be in contact with al-Qaeda in the Maghreb. A new sophistication in bombing and coordinated military assaults became evident as well, leading many observers to suggest that some Boko Haram fighters had received training from the more experienced AQIM or even al-Shabaab in Somalia.[62] The savagery was undiminished. In attacks on schools, teenage pupils were burnt alive when their dormitories were locked and torched; others were simply stabbed to death; girls were raped. Increasingly indiscriminate suicide bombings continued, killing hundreds. In one attack alone, on a busy marketplace in the central city of Jos, more than 120 people were killed and many more injured. Most were women and children. Forty-four died when a mosque was bombed. Successive offensives by the underprepared, undertrained, demoralised and brutal military did strip the militants of some of their territorial gains but, as the Chibok abduction showed, neither they nor the emergence of quasi-organised 'civilian defence groups' made any lasting impact on Boko Haram's continuing campaign of violence. At least 2,053 civilians were killed by Boko Haram in the first half of 2014 alone.

Quite when, or why, Shekau or his associates entered into contact with the Islamic State is unclear. One strong possibility is that the reabsorption of the splinter group that had previously developed links with al-Qaeda in the Maghreb and other militant organisations further afield may have allowed Boko Haram to establish contact with al-Baghdadi's organisation sometime in late 2014. Certainly some degree of convergence was indicated by the increasing quality of its media output around this time.[63] Two months after al-Baghdadi's announcement of the new caliphate, Shekau issued a statement saying the newly captured town of Gwoza, one of the largest in Borno state, was now 'part of our Islamic Caliphate'. As Shekau was careful to call himself simply the 'emir', it seems that this was a unilateral declaration of another province of al-Baghdadi's caliphate rather than an entirely new entity. Further declarations of support followed, though the most explicit came in early March 2015. This was formally accepted by the Islamic State ten days later.

Explaining the apparent union is not straightforward. Shekau may well have been looking for advantage over rivals within Boko Haram and hoped to bolster his position with the new credibility, and the new resources, such an alliance with the internationally (in)famous IS might bring. Militants had certainly frequently been motivated by such considerations when joining al-Qaeda in earlier periods. Though Boko Haram was active over a significant swathe of land, they had hitherto been more focused on hit-and-run tactics designed primarily to destabilise their opponents, advance their inchoate agenda and gain recruits, women, money and weapons. The occupation of Gwoza may have been an indication of a new interest in holding territory which might also have orientated Shekau towards IS. Equally, the recapture of the town along with several others in the spring of 2015, in an offensive led by the Nigerian Army in conjunction with neighbouring states, undoubtedly put Boko Haram on the defensive, making outside assistance more attractive.

However, Shekau's public statements and his decision-making give little indication of any strategic thinking, or real understanding of what any link with the Islamic State might actually mean in practice. The internal workings of Boko Haram, particularly the relationships between the various factions which it comprises, remain unclear. Its leader's personal ambition, a megalomania similar to that of al-Zarqawi a decade before, a world view barely rooted in reality, may all have been more significant factors than any reasoned appraisal of his move-ment's current strengths or weaknesses.

For the Islamic State, one attraction of the new relationship with Boko Haram may have been the desire to steal a march on al-Qaeda. Al-Baghdadi may also simply have been impressed by Shekau's record of appalling violence, so similar to the increas-ingly horrific atrocities which had become a hallmark of his own organisation. Either way, the alliance with Boko Haram gave IS a more global dimension, adding a large new ink spot in a region where the caliphate had been for the most part unrepresented. This alone was reason enough. That those swearing allegiance to IS around the Muslim world were often minor actors or factions with little capability on the ground, that their international reach was minimal, that their hold on terrain was tenuous, did not matter. IS was true to its motto: remain and expand. The new relationship with Boko Haram also maintained the momentum, and the concomitant aura of invulnerability, which was such an essential part of its appeal to volunteers and to other groups. When Mohammad al-Adnani, the chief spokesman, announced that Boko Haram had joined 'the caliphate's cavalcade', he called for migrants to join the new outpost of the empire, and imagined how 'all [enemies of Islam] are now watching, asking in amaze-ment: how it is possible for the caliphate to survive . . . despite our troops, arsenals, airplanes, tanks, rockets, vessels and demoli-tion weapons [and] our satellite channels, sorcerers, scientists, sheikhs and fatwas?'

The answer was quite simple, he suggested. 'If our ancestors have fought the Persians, Romans and apostates, whether on the same fronts or on separate ones, we take pride in fighting them today in a single battlefield, under one united leadership.'[64] The caliphate, he said, would endure 'until Judgment Day'.

As we have repeatedly seen, the broad phenomenon of Islamic militancy contains a multitude of different strands. Most have goals that, in the short term at least, are primarily local. A few have focused their violence primarily on the West in order to bring about change in the Islamic world more generally. But in the last decade a potent new strand of activism has emerged. Its adherents view distinctions between the Near Enemy and the Far Enemy, or between local targets and global ones, rather differently than any of their predecessors. This is for the simple reason that they are Westerners living in the West, and it is to them that we now turn.

7

LEADERLESS JIHAD

On the morning of 22 May 2013, at around 9 a.m., Michael Adebolajo, an unemployed 28-year-old living in the nondescript south-east London suburb of Lewisham, parked his car close to a local authority housing block where his friend, 22-year-old Michael Adebowale, shared a fourth-floor flat with his mother.

Both men were converts to Islam, having been raised as Christians by devout Nigerian-born parents. They had met a year or so previously.

The two men drove back to Adebolajo's nearby flat, where they remained for the rest of the morning, going out once to buy some food from a local grocer's. At 1 p.m., they left in the blue Vauxhall Tigra and headed north-east towards the River Thames and the historic if slightly run-down neighbourhood of Woolwich, where they parked the car opposite the Royal Artillery Barracks, a military base. Then they waited. At around 2.20 p.m., the two men saw Lee Rigby, a 25-year-old soldier who had served in Afghanistan some years earlier, walking out of the exit of the Woolwich Arsenal railway station, around 150 metres from his home in the barracks and 50 metres from the car. Rigby, in civilian dress, was on his way home from the recruiting office at the Tower of London where he worked. Adebolajo, in the Vauxhall's driving seat, accelerated hard to around 40 mph and ran the soldier down from behind, breaking five vertebrae in his back and five of his ribs. The speeding car skidded across the road, mounted the kerb, smashed into a road sign and then stopped, dropping Rigby, unconscious, to the ground.

Adebolajo and Adebowale got out of the car carrying three of the five knives they had bought for £44.98 from a local Argos discount store the previous day and an old unloaded handgun obtained from criminals, and attacked Rigby's inert body. One hacked at the soldier's neck, first with a meat cleaver and then with another smaller blade, in an apparent attempt to decapitate him. The other repeatedly plunged his knife into the man's chest in what was described later in court as a 'frenzied attack'.[1]

After three minutes, the two men stopped stabbing and cutting to drag Rigby's body into the road and left it there. As a small crowd gathered, Adebolajo handed out a pre-prepared written statement, then stood with the knife in one hand and the cleaver in the other, hands red with blood, and delivered a speech into a mobile phone held by a stunned passer-by. 'The only reason we have killed this man today is because Muslims are dying daily by British soldiers . . . We swear by the almighty Allah we will never stop fighting you until you leave us alone. So what if we want to live by the sharia in Muslim lands? Why does that mean you must follow us and chase us and call us extremists and kill us?' he said, speaking with a strong south London accent.

'Many passages in the . . . Koran [say] we must fight them as they fight us. An eye for an eye, a tooth for a tooth . . . You people will never be safe. Remove your governments, they don't care about you. You think David Cameron is going to get caught in the street when we start busting our guns? You think politicians are going to die? No, it's going to be the average guy, like you and your children. So get rid of them. Tell them to bring our troops back so can all live in peace. So leave our lands and we can all live in peace. That's all I have to say. Allah's peace and blessings be upon you.'[2]

Armed police arrived on the scene thirteen minutes after Adebolajo and Adebowale had run Rigby down. They shot and wounded the two attackers, then gave them first aid, while colleagues worked to save the young soldier's life. But he was very badly injured and had already lost a lot of blood. Rigby was the first Briton to be killed by Islamic militant violence in the UK for eight years.

The killing prompted another round of heated debate. This centred on issues which had become familiar over the previous decade or so: the integration of migrant communities in the UK, the apparent social and economic problems of some, the success of others, the need for 'British values' to be reasserted, and the reasons why some individuals become drawn to violent extremism. Many of the contributions cast little light, not least because of continuing confusion about the origins of terrorist attacks in the West by Islamic extremists. As we have seen, al-Qaeda, IS and their respective affiliates have no significant presence outside the Islamic world, and with the exception of AQAP, the focus of their activity is essentially local. How is it, then, that young men, born and raised in countries such as Britain, France and Spain, perpetrate such atrocious acts apparently in sympathy with those distant militants' cause? Are they merely damaged individuals looking for a way to vent their alienation and frustration, or are they the product of carefully orchestrated efforts from afar? What is the link between these young men and the rest of the *umma*? What is their connection with organisations such as al-Qaeda? How do they become 'radicalised' and what motivates them then to such appalling violence?

If there were small Muslim communities in the UK from the early nineteenth century, it was only in the 1950s and 60s that these grew to be a significant presence. In the years after the Second World War, all European powers were in desperate need of cheap labour and looked to their overseas possessions to help them reconstruct shattered cities, infrastructure, factories and economies. For Britain this meant the Caribbean, newly independent India, Pakistan (particularly lowland areas near Kashmir) and what was to become, in 1971, Bangladesh. These workers were thought unlikely to remain permanently and almost no consideration was given to their impact on the broader existing community.[3] By the 1960s, restrictions began to be introduced to limit the number of relatives joining migrants who now looked to be staying for longer than originally envisaged. Further limits were imposed as the post-war economic boom gave way to the crises of the 1970s. By the early 1990s, the number of Britons declaring themselves Muslim had reached a million (out of a total of around 60 million). Half of these were either themselves from South Asia, or the children of South Asian-born parents. Most of the rest were British-born and of British-born parents. Ten years later, by 2001, the total of Muslims in the UK was around 1.5 million, but this bald figure masks a community of enormous diversity.[4]

Like all immigrants, those in the UK's growing Muslim community continued to be influenced by events in their (or their parents', or their grandparents') countries of origin. Consequently, what happened 'over there' was important 'over here'. So, the religious revival of the 1960s and 70s that had been so powerful in the Muslim world had, in part, been imported to the UK. In the early 1980s, there was excitement among some at the Iranian revolution and a wave of support for the mujahideen fighting in Afghanistan. The end of that decade saw an outburst of assertive faith identity when the Ayatollah Khomeini gave his infamous fatwa calling on Muslims across the world to kill Salman Rushdie, the Indian-born British author of the controversial and allegedly blasphemous *The Satanic Verses*. With the discrediting of socialism and communism that culminated in the collapse of the Soviet Union, young 'British-Pakistanis', for example, were increasingly likely to use their Muslim identity to explain the problems they often faced rather than frame their grievances in terms of class or race.[5] Major Islamist groups such as the Jamaat Islami of Pakistan and various Muslim Brotherhood offshoots became a political force for the first time.

Nor was the British Muslim community unaffected by the power struggle between the contesting strands of religious practice in the Islamic World. Saudi Arabia's funds poured into bursaries and mosque construction in Europe and the US, promoting their rigorously conservative brand of Islam. In the UK, mosques went from fifty-one in 1979 to 329 six years later.[6] Perhaps half of the new mosques being built, especially in areas dominated by communities with roots in Pakistan, were of the Deobandi school of Islam, the extremely conservative strand of observance that had originated in India in the late nineteenth century and had steadily spread across much of Pakistan and Afghanistan; the Afghan Taliban, for example, are all Deobandi. Bankrolled in part by donors in the Gulf, the numbers of Deobandi madrassas had increased hugely in the countries of origin of many British immigrants and their hard-line views were imported into the UK by preachers through the 1990s. Just as significant was the Ahl-e-Hadith movement, which was also similar to Gulf-style Wahhabism and had grown powerful in Pakistan through the later decades of the twentieth century at the expense of more tolerant schools of observance, particularly that known as Barelvi. In the UK too, Barelvi clerics found themselves pushed aside by their better-funded, less tolerant counterparts, whose message often appealed to a younger, more assertive generation.

The sense among some British Muslims of a global Islamic identity infused with a strong anti-American or anti-Western sentiment was reinforced through the mid- and late 1990s by the war in the former Yugoslavia, which was seen by many in the Islamic world as one pitting Christian Serbs against local Muslims left unprotected until it was too late, the conflict in Chechnya and the second Palestinian Intifada. The membership of groups like Hizb ut-Tahrir, an international organisation founded in the 1950s and dedicated to the restoration of the caliphate through peaceful activism, rose steeply, even if the numbers involved, a few thousand, were a tiny proportion of the UK Muslim population. Some British Muslims even became directly involved in these conflicts. One of the most notorious was Omar Saeed Sheikh, a graduate of LSE who had become interested in violent militancy when an aid worker in Bosnia in the early 1990s, but then, like many others, became involved in Pakistani extremist groups fighting in Kashmir and elsewhere.[7] By the end of the decade, radical organisers claimed that 1,800 British Muslims took part in 'military service' each year, recruited at mosques and university campuses across the country.[8] The number was perhaps inflated, but that increasing numbers of young Britons were actively engaged in violence overseas through Islamic groups was indubitable.[9] Inevitably, South Asia was a particular focus. A Briton died in a suicide bombing in Srinagar, the summer capital of Kashmir, in 2000. In October 2001, two young Britons from families of Pakistani origin who had joined the Taliban in Afghanistan were killed in Kabul in a missile strike.[10] Two months later a young British convert who had travelled to Afghanistan in 2000 and been trained in Afghan camps tried to blow himself up on a transatlantic jet, but failed to detonate the explosives concealed in his shoes.

The 1990s also saw the arrival in the UK of a wave of extremist ideologues and organisers. Many were fleeing the repression of the violent campaigns veterans from the Afghan war had catalysed in their native lands throughout the Middle East in the early years of the decade.[11] Britain, which had a long tradition of accepting political dissidents and relatively generous social welfare systems, and which had long been a favoured destination of English-speaking dissidents in the Arab world, was a popular choice. Though many were virulently anti-Western in their views, most were entirely focused on striking the 'local enemy' back home in Algeria, Jordan, Syria, Libya, Saudi

Arabia or elsewhere in the region and were not seen as a threat by
the UK's security services. Many were simply content to have a base
where they could organise and communicate without fearing a knock
on the door at midnight. But some had a wider vision and more
ambitious plans and believed that targeting the West was an essential
part of any long-term strategy.

The foremost such thinker was Mustafa Setmariam Nasar, better
known as Abu Musab al-Suri. If al-Awlaki was the propagandist who
did most to shape today's threat against the West, and al-Zawahiri
and al-Baghdadi are currently the most influential commanders, then
al-Suri is the strategist of greatest relevance. Born in Aleppo, Syria's
most populous city, in 1958, al-Suri was a qualified engineer and the
son of educated, prosperous, conservative parents. He was drawn into
the underground 'Islamic resistance groups' agitating against the
nationalist, secular, Ba'athist regime of Hafez al-Assad and was forced
to flee Syria when the Islamists were bloodily crushed in 1982. By
1988, he was supporting the local fighters and Arab volunteers in
Afghanistan from Peshawar, where he knew bin Laden and al-Zawahiri
but maintained his distance from both. By 1992, he was on the move
again, and eventually fetched up in London, via Spain, in 1995.

In the UK, al-Suri became involved with the network of support
for Algerian militants, then in the middle of their savage insurgency.
After three years – and an acrimonious dispute with some of the other
activists in the British capital – al-Suri moved on once more. By 1999,
he was in Afghanistan, where he ran a kind of rudimentary think tank
in Kabul and wrote prolifically.[12] His relations with bin Laden remained
chilly – he had no prior warning of the 9/11 attacks – but he did spend
a lot of time considering how al-Qaeda, or other groups, might bring
about the 'global Islamic revolution' he wanted to see in his homeland
of Syria and elsewhere. This, he decided, would only be brought about
by a dramatic shift in understanding the way Islamic militant groups
should work.

'Al-Qaeda is not an organisation, it is not a group, nor do we want
it to be,' al-Suri wrote in his 1,600-page work *The Call for Global Islamic
Resistance*. 'It is a call, a reference, a methodology.' This had always
been the case to a certain extent of course. From the start, the al-Qaeda
phenomenon has been multivalent – partly a revolutionary vanguard,
partly a network of bases or trainings camps, partly a broader move-

ment of sympathisers, fellow travellers and motivated individual actors – bound together by ideology.[13]

Al-Suri's strategy took this to a further extreme. His vision was of a popular uprising that was entirely self-organising, without leaders or structure, one that would be led by scattered and only loosely connected cells of active militants. These would unite together for specific attacks and then disperse once more. Shared principles could be provided on a collective basis through texts, such as his own, uploaded to the Internet for general consultation. The texts would give guidance as to what targets were considered legitimate, for example, or what form attacks should take. But there would be no overall authority and no orders from self-appointed leaders.

Bin Laden's thinking was closer to al-Suri's than either man appeared prepared to admit. The 9/11 attacks were not, of course, self-organising. They were extremely complex, involving scores, if not hundreds of people, on three continents, but they were ultimately conceptualised and run by key personnel from within the core of al-Qaeda itself. However, what the two men did share was a vision of the principal aims of such operations: to inspire further attacks elsewhere. 'Every Muslim has [now] to rush to make his religion victorious,' bin Laden said in his first message after 9/11, a videotaped speech broadcast by Al Jazeera on 3 November 2001. And if an immediate mass uprising was unrealistic, then the mobilisation of hundreds, or even thousands, of young men in the West, all of whom could strike a single blow, was at the very least a significant step towards achieving the ultimate aim of convincing the Western powers to end their support for Middle Eastern despots, weakening the latter sufficiently for their regimes to collapse, and thus expediting the establishment of true Islamic states and an eventual caliphate.

This was al-Suri's belief too. The cumulative impact of all the dispersed activity would inevitably lead to further radicalisation and mobilisation and thus advance the cause. Its sum would be greater than its 'leaderless' parts. Al-Suri summed up his thinking with a pithy motto: Nizam la Tanzim, System not Organisation. Western commentators dubbed it 'leaderless jihad'.

The first major Islamic extremist strike in Western Europe was the bombing of commuter trains in Madrid's Atocha station in March

2004. Nearly 200 people were killed, more than 2,000 hurt and the death toll would have been much higher if the bombs had exploded, as intended, inside the station instead of on its approaches. They still did horrific damage, and the scores of mobile phones ringing hopelessly in the pockets of the dead as news of the attack spread to worried relatives must count among the most haunting images of the last decade or so of violence. The network responsible was largely composed of Tunisian and Moroccan immigrants, some present in Spain for a while, but some newly arrived. One possible trigger for the attack, though it came when preparations were already well advanced, was a document posted on the Internet by al-Qaeda calling for a strike against Spain to force the nation to withdraw its troops from Iraq.

A year later, on 7 July 2005, four suicide bombers killed fifty-two on Tube trains and a bus in London. More than seven hundred were injured and rescue workers described horrifying scenes in carriages wrecked by the home-made explosives deep underground.[14] This time the attackers were all very much 'home-grown', in the newly emerging parlance, and all British citizens. Astonished reporters related how the ringleader, a thirty-year-old care worker from Leeds called Mohammad Sidique Khan, liked football and fish and chips.

Extremist strategists saw the two attacks as evidence of a ground-swell of anger and alienation among European Muslims. Al-Suri immediately posted a long statement on the Internet describing how happy he had been 'when the attacks on the historic stronghold of oppression and darkness [London] took place' and calling on 'mujahideen in Europe . . . to act quickly and strike'. He appeared certain that his strategy of 'leaderless jihad' was working, that the uprising had started and that victory was close. 'We are at the height of the war, and the enemy is on the verge of defeat, as many signs clearly indicate. Whoever stays asleep now may not be able to participate on waking up,' he wrote.

The reality, however, was much more complex. True, the Madrid attacks had only the most tangential connection to al-Qaeda central, but neither did they involve Spanish citizens, and so they hardly indicated radicalisation among European Muslim communities. And while the 7/7 attacks involved second-generation immigrants, suggesting something genuinely 'home-grown', they also involved al-Qaeda, which suggests the opposite. Certainly Mohammad Sidique Khan had become interested in extremist ideas over a period of years and entirely independently of any 'global terrorist organisation'. But he had also, as became clear in the months after the bombing, made repeated journeys to Pakistan to meet senior al-Qaeda leaders. There he had been turned from an angry young man hoping to fight with the Taliban against international forces in Afghanistan into a skilled, dedicated and highly motivated terrorist. The gulf between participating in combat against foreign troops in a distant country and killing scores of civilians in one's own is immense, and without the intervention of the al-Qaeda high command, it is likely that Khan would never have bridged it. He returned from Pakistan and recruited friends who themselves were dispatched to training camps there. Not all the bombers travelled overseas, but the conspiracy is likely to have taken a different, much less dangerous, form without the direct input of the experienced and dedicated militants working closely with bin Laden at the time.

This led analysts and commentators, as well as security officials and policymakers, to emphasise the continuing threat from bin Laden's group, an impression that was reinforced over the following two or three years. Two weeks after the bombings of 7 July, another atrocity was narrowly averted when explosive devices carried onto Tube trains by a second wave of bombers failed to detonate. This network too was composed of young men resident in the UK led by someone who had travelled to Pakistan to meet leaders of al-Qaeda. Most were recent immigrants themselves, and thus differed from the 7/7 attackers, but again, the input of al-Qaeda was important in converting an inchoate desire to act into the capability to cause massive harm.

Then came the discovery of a hugely ambitious bid to bring down a dozen US-bound planes with liquid explosives mixed by passengers inside the aircraft – the reason we are still not allowed to bring fluids through airport security. This conspiracy too had been run by al-Qaeda from Pakistan. There were several more plots during this period, of which at least half involved young Britons who had successfully sought out and spent time with al-Qaeda in the unstable South Asian state.

In retrospect, these attacks and attempted attacks in the middle years of the last decade were the climax of al-Qaeda's campaign to strike Europe. By 2007, as the group's efforts began to weaken elsewhere, there were signs that the threat in the UK was diversi-fying. In the summer of that year, a small group of extremists attempted a double bombing of a nightclub in London. This failed and two of its members, an Indian-born doctor and an Iraqi engineer, later drove a car full of gas and petrol into Glasgow airport. They had no connection with any established militant organisation, big or small, affiliated or independent. Other plans for major mass-casualty attacks, some linked to Pakistan and al-Qaeda, some autonomous, were uncovered over the following years, though all were broken up before reaching the stage of actu-ally making bombs. What is truly notable about the threat to the UK and the West at this time is how few attacks ever came close to fruition, despite the fact that MI5 officials said there were at least two such plots annually.[15]

That none of these various efforts successfully achieved their aim of killing large numbers of Britons was, not unfairly, judged a victory for security services. Those charged with keeping the UK safe had been caught largely unprepared by the 9/11 attacks and had taken several years to develop the resources necessary to better face what was a significant challenge. Prior to 2001, watching Islamic militancy was the job of junior MI6 station staff overseas, while in the UK a third of MI5's 1,500 staff were focused on Irish republican terrorism.[16] The domestic service had few offices outside London, and none in areas where Muslim communities were concentrated, while 'the number of Urdu or Arabic speakers could be counted on half a hand'.[17] The result of these failings was clear. Eliza Manningham-Buller, then head of MI5, had spoken in 2003 of the threat coming from terrorist sleeper cells hiding 'in plain sight' composed of 'individuals . . . that blend into society . . . who live normal, routine lives until called upon for specific tasks'. A key focus of MI5, Manningham-Buller revealed, was to track down people in the UK who might offer logistic help to overseas militants planning strikes abroad.[18] Her analysis was an indi-cation of quite how deficient the security services' understanding of the threat they faced was. Most of those involved in Islamic militancy in Britain led normal lives because they were normal people, and the threat came from local extremists receiving help from overseas to strike locally, not vice versa. The police were even less well informed, with officers admitting, even as late as 2005, that they really didn't 'have a handle' on the problem. The result of these failings was made all too clear.

However, particularly after the London bombings of 2005, the injection of considerable resources, intellectual as well as financial, led to improvement. By the end of the decade, MI5 had officers based in police stations around the UK, exploiting the growing flow of intelligence from concerned local communities, and were using their own behavioural science unit to develop a more accurate understanding of what led individuals into extremism. They, and the police, were also able to benefit from newly legal powers – to monitor and question suspects, for example. Cooperation between intelligence services within Britain and internationally had advanced rapidly in the years after 9/11 while the declining use of torture by the US removed a significant impediment to close collaboration between agencies on either side of the Atlantic. Though there were serious problems with the British government's 'counter-radicalisation' strategy, named Prevent, the need for some kind of effort to tackle the problem of extremism at a community level had at least been recognised. The departures from power, in 2007 and 2009 respectively, of both Tony Blair and President George Bush, allowed work to begin on countering the 'single narrative' of an aggressive West set on the humiliation, oppression and division of the Islamic world. Though the change brought by the election of President Barack Obama in the US may have been less substantive in policy terms than some had hoped, the change in tone was definitely dramatic. In the UK, officials had been told in 2006 not to use the term 'war on terror'.[19] However, only when Blair was gone could the vocabulary of the previous five years or so be set aside, and a genuine attempt be made to convince all citizens of the UK that the effort to keep the West safe, and combat violent Islamic extremism everywhere, was a collective fight that was in the interests of everyone.

But it wasn't just the success of British security efforts that accounts for the failure of the various attempts to execute mass-casualty attacks in the UK. One of the main reasons was the genuine decline in al-Qaeda's ability to do harm anywhere from the middle of the decade onwards. This weakness was particularly evident when it came to attacking Britain. The militants' strategy here had involved forging a direct connection, preferably in person, between the extremists in Pakistan and British volunteers. But this link was getting harder and harder to establish. From 2008, the pressure brought to bear on al-Qaeda in their bases in western Pakistan by drone strikes increased steadily as every month passed, restricting movement, prompting internal secur-ity scares and inexorably eliminating many of the organisation's most capable people. Successive offensives by Pakistani military forces along the rugged frontier with Afghanistan were also causing significant problems. Though local security forces left the toughest zone around the town of Miranshah in north Waziristan well alone, other key areas were being denied to militants. The process was haphazard – an offensive that I watched in the high valleys of Mohmand simply pushed veteran extremists across the border into Afghanistan while angering local communities – but did deny al-Qaeda the leisure to plan, organ-ise and operate that they had earlier enjoyed. Tighter travel restrictions helped too, as did ongoing cooperation between the Pakistani intel-ligence services and their British counterparts. These were often diffi-cult and tense, but the various local agencies proved relatively effective when dealing with individual British militants who neither nation wanted at liberty.[20]

In these conditions, just reaching al-Qaeda was much more difficult for Britons, let alone actually being accepted, trained and given a mission by the organisation. Several tried but failed to establish the critical connections. Even those that succeeded appeared much less competent than earlier groups on their return. In September 2011, police broke up a network of young Britons, all the children of migrants from Pakistan, in Birmingham who had been plotting to plant up to eight bombs to turn the UK into a 'war zone'. Several among them had made their way to Pakistan at least once. Two, the leaders, had managed to contact people close to an al-Qaeda leader and had, they claimed, been intensively trained, taking forty pages of notes during a month of instruction.[21] If so, they had retained little, as they made a series of basic mistakes in what spies called 'tradecraft', particularly the steps taken to avoid detection. One reason for this weakness was probably the rudimentary nature of the facilities al-Qaeda was reduced to using. These were very different from the training camps that were being run just a few years earlier, let alone a decade before in Taliban-run Afghanistan. The ringleader of one network was recorded by MI5, describing how al-Qaeda 'hasn't got no more camps now . . . the brothers used to be in the mountains [but] the drones just get them straight away, they just bomb the camps, so . . . they taught us inside houses . . . They were restricted to one place most of the time: One place to eat, sleep, go to toilet and do everything.'[22]

Nor were the volunteers arriving in Pakistan always particularly well received, or indeed motivated. The same ringleader was recorded boasting to a friend of how he faked stomach aches to avoid 'lessons' and spent his days watching 'jihadi videos'. 'After dawn prayers they would come to our room . . . we used to say we were ill . . . after two months they threw us out,' he said to a friend, laughing.[23] It is little wonder, perhaps, that the advice given to the departing volunteers was 'don't send anyone [more to us]'.[24] Significantly too, the Birmingham plotters do not appear to have had any contact with anyone in Pakistan once they had returned to Britain, indicating that communications were difficult to maintain or that no one in al-Qaeda had any desire to talk to them again. The former appears more likely, though we cannot be sure. None of the dozen or so individuals involved in two major plots uncovered in 2012 had any serious link to any extremists in South Asia at all.

If Pakistan was an increasingly problematic destination for aspirant terrorists, a growing number of young British men did travel to Somalia, or Yemen, with several killed in both locations. One militant, when his hopes to travel to South Asia appeared unlikely to be fulfilled, even suggested Mali as a destination. But of the various al-Qaeda affiliates in 2011 or early 2012 which might have offered any serious training to aspirant British bombers, only AQAP appeared to pose a serious threat with its track record of sophisticated attempts to hit Western targets. Senior officials genuinely felt they had turned a very significant corner in the fight against Islamic militancy and quietly celebrated. 'If you'd told me five years ago that we'd be where we are now, I'd have been very happy,' said one MI6 official in 2011.[25] The London Olympics of 2012, despite being described by counter-terrorist officials as 'the biggest peacetime security challenge since the Second World War', was untroubled by any extremist violence.

The killing of Rigby challenged this new optimism and confidence. Security service officials had been aware for some time of a new form of terrorist attack that was emerging alongside the older 'hybrid' type, although they were unsure exactly what sort of threat it might pose.

This new type of operations involved individuals attacking seemingly random targets with weaponry limited to whatever they could make, steal, find or buy themselves. Entirely without any connection to major groups like al-Qaeda, or even minor ones, they were said to herald a new wave of violence. Borrowing a term from the US security services' analysis of domestic right-wing extremist violence in the 1990s and its perpetrators' own texts, they were given the name 'lone wolves'.[26] It was a profoundly misleading one.

Michael Adebolajo was Romford-born and -bred, growing up on the ragged eastern edge of London's urban sprawl, in a family of devout and hard-working Nigerian immigrants who took him, his brother and his sister to church every Sunday and read the Bible most evenings. He was 'a typical teenager', playing football, listening to rap and hip hop, and had friends from all the various local communities in a very mixed neighbourhood. Tall, good-looking, popular, he initially did well at school and teachers remembered nothing out of the ordinary about him until early adolescence.[27]

By his mid-teens, however, Adebolajo was involved in local gangs, and was stealing phones, carrying a knife, as well as using and selling drugs. His worried parents moved the entire family a hundred miles away to Lincoln, a large country town and a much quieter environment. By the time Adebolajo returned to London aged nineteen, having scraped a single E grade in his A levels, he had 'calmed down', friends told reporters. Discipline was still an issue and, though he managed to get a place first on a building-surveying degree at Greenwich University and then on a politics course, he dropped out entirely in 2005.[28] There is no evidence that he was involved in any kind of activism at university, where few students appeared interested by hard-line ideologies.

It is unclear when, why or how he converted to Islam, but there were plenty of outreach efforts by Islamic activists in the neighbourhood, and soon after leaving university, Adebolajo became involved with a series of groups which were all eventually banned by British authorities. One was al-Muhajiroun, named after those who had accompanied the Prophet Mohammed on his flight from Mecca to Medina, which had a long history of provocation and protest.[29] The group gained notoriety with a celebration of the 'magnificent nineteen', as they described the 9/11 hijackers, in London shortly after the attacks in the US. The group's founder was Omar Bakri Mohammed, a Syrian-born cleric who had fled to the UK in the mid-1990s and was well known to the British media. (I once sat next to him on the sofa of a morning TV talk show in a surreal debate about the causes of Islamic militancy. Bakri Mohammed, citing the words and deeds of the Prophet, argued that because the UK had taken in refugees like him, a covenant forbade him from any attacks on Britons.) He later told reporters that Adebolajo had become a Muslim after attending al-Muhajiroun's meetings in south London. This is unconfirmed. Adebolajo offered another explanation. 'It was the Iraq war that affected me the most,' he told the jury in Court 2 of the Old Bailey.

Soon Adebolajo was one of the most active and vocal of al-Muhajiroun's members, taking part in demonstrations in 2006 against the publication of cartoons depicting the Prophet Mohammed in a Danish newspaper and finally being arrested after scuffles with police outside the Old Bailey following the trial of another al-Muhajiroun member who had been sentenced to four years in jail for inciting racial hatred. Adebolajo received a 51-day jail sentence for assaulting a police officer, but continued to attend protests and meetings on his release.[30] By 2008, the activist, now twenty-four years old, was well known to police and was being investigated by MI5.

Such individuals were of increasing interest to security services who, though still focused on the more predictable threat from small groups of young British Muslims from the South Asian community who somehow managed to connect with al-Qaeda, were beginning to understand the new danger from these 'lone wolves'. One of the first such attackers was a young convert who in May 2007 got on a bus in the northern English town of Rotherham carrying a plastic bag containing bags of sugar connected to an alarm clock and wrapped with wiring. Police found bomb-making equipment in his home, and a large poster of Abu Musab al-Zarqawi.[31] A year later, another convert with a history of mental illness blew himself up in a cafe toilet in the western city of Exeter. Both were described as 'peripheral' to Islamic militancy in the UK by officials at the time but, as the months passed and further evidence of a pattern accumulated, it became harder to dismiss such attackers quite so easily.[32]

In July 2009, Isa Ibrahim, a nineteen-year-old 'disturbed and alienated adolescent', was convicted of terrorist offences. He had made viable explosives, manufactured a suicide vest and carried out reconnaissance on a Bristol shopping centre.[33] A turning point came in 2010 when a Member of Parliament was knifed in the stomach by a young British Pakistani woman angered by his support for the Iraq war. Roshanara Choudhry, a gifted 21-year-old university student, later told police that she had carried out the attack because 'as Muslims we're all brothers and sisters and we should all look out for each other and we shouldn't sit back and do nothing while others suffer'.[34] Choudhry had spent more than a hundred hours watching videos of lectures by al-Awlaki, the Yemen-based extremist preacher, over previous months before finally resolving to act. When she was sentenced to life imprisonment a group of men began shouting '*Allahu Akbar*', 'British go to hell' and 'Curse the judge' in the public gallery of the court. The next 'successful' attack was on Rigby.

Quite how Rigby's killers went from being vocal and committed but non-violent activists to becoming murderers is unclear. In 2008, Adebolajo had been in touch with someone thought to have connections to al-Qaeda in the Arabian Peninsula, but there is no indication he was influenced unduly by any single individual, let alone 'brainwashed' by some kind of senior overseas-based militant.[35] In 2009, he said during his trial, he had broken with al-Muhajiroun, though he did not explain why. One possibility is that he, like a number of others who later became involved in violence, found the group too moderate.[36] In 2010, an MI5 investigation of Adebolajo indicated that he was involved in drug dealing and assessed him as 'low-risk'. The criminal activity may have been to raise funds for an ambitious overseas trip, however, which proved his commitment to the cause rather than indicated a declining interest. In October 2010, Adebolajo set off for Somalia, with the intention of joining al-Shabaab. This backfired badly, and, betrayed to police, he ended up in court in Mombasa, Kenya. He may have been mistreated, even abused in prison there. Once back in the UK, he was soon seen again in Islamic activist circles.

It was around this time that he is thought to have met Michael Adebowale, six years his junior. Adebowale's path to extremism resembled that of the older man in some aspects, though his life had been significantly more chaotic and violent, marked by crime and mental illness. His parents, also Nigerian-born and devout Christians, were separated, and his schooling had been intermittent. In his early teens, Adebowale first became known to police in Greenwich for his involvement in petty crime, and then with local gangs. One was the largely Somali 'Woolwich Boys'. In 2008, he was wounded in a frenzied knife attack at a crack den in which a friend was killed.[37] Adebowale got a fifteen-month sentence for dealing drugs, which he served in the notorious Feltham Young Offenders Institution. The incident also triggered the onset of psychological illness, with the young man suffering post-traumatic stress disorder and periods of delusion. It was around this time, according to MI5, that he 'converted to Islam in order to move away from the crime gangs and drugs scene he was involved with in London'.[38] By 2011, Adebowale had come to the Security Service's attention as a result of his interest in online extremist material. Of particular concern was his reading of *Inspire* magazine, produced by al-Qaeda in the Arabian Peninsula. An internal MI5 assessment of *Inspire* in 2012 described how the magazine, which sought to promote home-grown 'lone actor' attacks, had been read by those involved in 'at least seven out of the ten attacks planned within the UK since its first issue [in 2010] and had significantly enhanced the capability of individuals in four of these ten attack plots'. Al-Awlaki, who had been key to its creation, was dead but the magazine he had founded was proving extremely effective in propagating the idea of leaderless jihad. Though formulated in the days before mass usage of the Internet, the strategy was ideally suited to an age where everyone could access the Web anywhere in the world. The cover of one booklet, published on the Internet by AQAP in 2013, asked: 'R U dreamin' of wagin' jihadi attacks against [the unbelievers]? . . . Well, there's no need to travel abroad, coz the frontline has come to you. Wanna know how? Just read 'n' apply the contents of this guide which has practical 'n' creative ways to please Allah by killing his enemies 'n' healing the believers' chests.'[39]

By mid-2012, Adebowale and Adebolajo were both involved with the networks of Islamic activists in south-east London. They spent days in small groups, watching videos, praying, preaching angrily on local high streets and going over and over their various grievances.

In September, Adebowale attended a protest outside the US Embassy in the centre of the capital in which protesters marched with a banner reading: 'The followers of Muhammed will conquer America.' It is possible that the two converts met there and, with such similar backgrounds, were drawn to one another. Phone records later revealed that they frequently exchanged forty or more texts in a day.

Yet the activism they had been involved in until this point, however offensive, was still non-violent. It is unclear when the two men decided that they wanted to go further, or when they decided to kill a soldier. Others had laid similar plans before, leading to repeated warnings over previous years to servicemen in the UK not to wear uniforms outside barracks. In early 2013, Adebolajo described graphically what he hoped to do on Facebook, and just over a week before the attack he was seen a mile away from the Artillery Barracks in Woolwich, manning a stall outside a community centre after Friday prayers and preaching as the congregation dispersed.[40] There, he spoke of how killing unbelievers was justified, and how there was no need to travel to kill the 'enemy's soldiers', as they were here. However, most of his speech, a witness later said, described the war in Syria which was beginning to move into a newly murderous phase. Then came the trip to buy the knives, the drive to Woolwich and the wait for a suitable victim to step out of the station.

What are the lessons from the stories of Adebolajo and Adebowale? To what extent was either of these men a 'lone wolf'? Had al-Suri and bin Laden been right? Had 'the awakening' finally started? Was this a new era of 'leaderless jihad'?

It was true that the vast majority of UK Muslims, like those elsewhere in Europe and beyond, had long remained resolutely opposed to violence. In July 2005, 85 per cent of respondents to one poll said that further suicide bombings against the UK would never be justified, while 88 per cent agreed that Muslims should denounce any terrorist plot to the police. These figures had remained broadly unchanged since 2002, and were not to alter greatly in the coming years either. Support for al-Qaeda or approval of bin Laden in Britain had been almost non-existent in the 1990s, not least because virtually no one had heard of either, and remained extremely limited in the following decade. In moments of significant anger, such as that prompted by the publication of cartoons of Mohammed in a Danish newspaper in late 2005, there were plenty of protests but no upsurge of violent activism. The greatest preoccupations of British Muslims throughout the decade following the 9/11 attacks remained those of their non-Muslim counterparts: health, jobs, even immigration. This was entirely unsurprising and something which anyone spending any time on the streets of Walthamstow, Bradford or Sparkhill would have known without needing expensive polls.[41] On the whole, one important Europe-wide survey revealed, Muslims' views on key questions such as homosexuality or pre-marital sexual relations appeared to be more influenced by the country in which they were living than any 'common' Muslim identity.[42] This testified not just to the diversity of the Muslim community, but also to quite how problematic the concept of a 'Muslim community' was at all.

So al-Suri, who had been captured by Pakistani security services shortly after publishing his celebration of the 7/7 bombings, had been mistaken.[43] His belief that the attacks of 2005 were the first strikes of a major wave of violence that would lead to a general uprising had no basis in the truth. The total number of arrests, let alone charges or convictions, for terrorist offences linked to Islamic militancy from 2005 to 2013 was no more than a thousand out of a population of Muslims in the UK which in 2011 was 2.7 million.[44] But if al-Suri had been very wrong about imminent mass mobilisation, there had been one development in the UK since his short stay in London in the mid-1990s that could still have encouraged him. Polls might have revealed a widespread rejection of violence throughout the decade, but they still showed that there was a significant number of people, from 2.5 per cent to 15 per cent, depending on the survey and the exact question, who believed that suicide attacks in the US or the UK might indeed be justified. Equally, there were always some, 9 per cent in 2009 according to one survey, who said they would not inform the police if they suspected al-Qaeda-inspired terrorism.[45] This was a fraction of the total, and may indeed have been over-represented by the polls, but was still a substantial number of people

If there was still nothing to indicate that al-Suri's predictions of a wave of 'leaderless' violence were premature, rather than simply wrong-headed, this was worrying nonetheless. For the spread of such views indicated how practices, ideas and values which had once been associated with only a tiny minority of mainly foreign extremists, such as al-Suri, in the UK a decade or so earlier were now much more frequently heard, and much more vocally expressed. In the late 1990s, to hear such views one would have to visit particular mosques such as the one in Finsbury Park in north London, or radical bookshops in Birmingham, or a handful of specific Islamic centres around the country run by hardliners well known to both MI5 and journalists. Almost the only people who had personal experience of actual militancy were a few foreign refugees, and a small subsection of the British Pakistani community with a particular interest in Kashmir. Groups such as Hizb ut-Tahrir or offshoots such as al-Muhajiroun were growing but still restricted to what was effectively considered a lunatic fringe, with a narrative and views that resonated with no more than a negligible number of British Muslims, or anyone else, at the time. Those who envisaged that the US, still less the UK, might be a legitimate target for violence were a fringe of the fringe.

Establishing quite how many people accepted at least some of the principal elements of the extremists' world view – the deep anti-Semitism and aggressive homophobia; the conviction that the West was decadent, immoral and had been set on the humiliation, division and subordination of the Islamic world since the seventh century; the belief that most Muslims were weak, hypocritical, who had left the true path – at the time of Rigby's murder was of course extremely difficult. But, even just purely anecdotally, there certainly appeared to be more of them than ever before. One indication of quite how widespread this poisonous mix of prejudice and misinformation had become is that within five years of 2001, a UK-born seventeen-year-old of Bangladeshi parents in east London could earnestly tell me that he had no problem with 'British people' because they were, like 'the Muslims all over the world', victims of 'the Jews and the Americans' too, and think his statement was sufficiently banal to establish some kind of common ground between us. Expressed, in a more militant form, in the online lectures by firebrand clerics and self-taught preachers, such ideas had become principal elements not just of speeches given in back rooms of mosques, front rooms of homes, on street corners, even in universities on occasion, but also of the daily conversations of significant numbers of, particularly young, people. 'None of the words we heard [from Adebolajo] were new,' said the killer's brother revealingly, shortly after the attack.[46] Many of those who joined the 2011 Birmingham plot met in a gym popular among local young men in the Sparkhill neighbourhood because it did not play music or allow women to enter, had a prayer room and sold halal bodybuilding supplements. On its website the gym explained that 'this centre was much needed in our local community, due to the disgraced state of the youth. They are losing their Islamic identity and moral foundations which is central to the teachings of Islam. We offer to educate the youth and let them know how far they have strayed away from Islam i.e. inappropriate attitude, swearing, wearing of earrings and chains, non-Islamic hair styles and dresscode.'[47] There were few such establishments in the 1990s.

One clear difference from the previous decade was the emergence of a youth subculture – with its own rituals, aesthetics and language – that simply had not existed before. Dubbed 'jihadi cool' by commentators, this had its own dress code – styles ranged from the traditional shalwar kameez of Pakistani communities, though worn high at the ankle in emulation of the Prophet and often paired with a many-pocketed combat-style waistcoat, to the pristine white robes of Gulf communities, often worn with lurid and expensive trainers. It had its own language, such as 'kufr' for 'kuffar', or unbelievers, with some words, such as 'crew' for a group, borrowed from gang culture. The influence flowed both ways, and the closeness between some gangs and some faith-based groups is underlined by the view of the police who investigated Adebowale that the young man's conversion to Islam was in some part due to his involvement with Somali gangs in Woolwich and was more about a desire to fit in with the gang's own mixture of criminal and religious identities. This was characterised by one officer as 'jihad meets The Sweeney meets gangsta'.[48]

The last reference was particularly pertinent. One high-profile element of this complex phenomenon was the genre that had become known as 'jihadi rap'. This had begun to attract significant attention from around 2004, when a clip entitled 'Dirty Kuffar' was posted online by activists. It featured images of US soldiers celebrating after shooting an Iraqi, the 9/11 attacks and Western leaders. Lyrics included 'Peace to Hamas and the Hizbollah, / OBL [bin Laden] pulled me like a shiny star, / Like the way we destroyed them two towers ha-ha, / The minister Tony Blair, there my dirty Kuffar, / The one Mr Bush, there my dirty Kuffar, / Throw them on the fire.' The clip, posted on the Internet by Mohammed al-Massari, a Saudi Arabian Islamist who had arrived in Britain a decade earlier, developed something of a cult following. 'I do not know of any young Muslim who has not either seen or got this video. It is selling everywhere. Everyone I meet at the mosque is asking for it,' al-Massari said.[49] A year later a videotape containing 'Dirty Kuffar' was found in the flat of the leader of a second wave of bombers, whose abortive attempt followed the 7/7 bombings by two weeks in July 2005.[50] Also popular, though of very poor quality, were clips recorded by Omar Hammami, an American recruit to al-Shabaab, who in 2006 uploaded a rap including the lines 'Bomb by bomb, blast by blast, / only going to bring back the glorious past', a revealing if inadvertent reminder of the importance of history, however imperfectly known or imagined, for Islamic extremists.[51] Over the coming years, the genre would proliferate, in many languages and, in some cases, blurring in tone and message with mainstream music.

Such music could, conceivably, help draw some people into extremism, though to suggest a central role would be absurd. Of far more relevance is what its apparent popularity says about the profile of the new generation of militants to appear in the last ten years. There were of course many exceptions, but by 2012 or 2013, Islamic extremist ideas were attracting people who were younger, less educated and poorer than, certainly, the majority of the militants of the late 1990s in the UK. Their knowledge of Islam, and indeed of Islamic extremism, was more superficial, and the attraction of militancy appeared to be much less ideological. If the similarity with gangs is striking, it should not be surprising. Militant groups offered a different form of gang-type community with a different narrative but with often similar benefits – purpose, companionship, status, excitement, adventure and the prospect, infrequently realised, of both material and sexual advantages. They also offered a way to mark a clear difference with the Islamic practices of an older generation, which had stressed the importance of avoiding political issues rather than engaging with them. Above all, there was a sense of empowerment, as was very clear from the music, in both its jihadi and its more conventional versions. Belgian researchers working for the nation's intelligence services noted that posts made by extremists on social media referred to Tupac Shakur, icon of American gangsta rap, shot dead in 1996. 'At least some . . . [militants] identify with his life and his rap lyrics, which indeed seem to fit well into the world outlook of this group,' the report said.[52] The rapper 50 Cent, whose 2003 album was called *Get Rich or Die Tryin'*, was also popular. This new generation of recruits was also much more likely not just to have previously been involved in criminal activities, but to continue to be involved even when active in militancy too.[53]

So, the Rigby killing revealed two critical developments among militants in the UK in the period following the 7/7 bombings. The first was fairly obvious: the apparently random, low-tech, less ambitious, more chaotic attacks which had been developing since around 2006 or 2007 had finally become a significant threat, albeit one that would coexist with, rather than supplant, the ongoing danger posed by extremists intent on mounting bigger mass-casualty attacks. The second point was that 'lone wolves' were not actually alone. Of course in terms of absolute numbers there were very few extremists like Adebolajo and Adebowale. Indeed, there were few extremists at all. MI5 officials said that in 2013 they were watching two networks believed to be an imminent and serious threat, several hundred people who posed a significant danger, around a thousand others who were only involved in 'marginal aspects of activities under investigation' and then many more who were sympathisers or fellow travellers who associated with actively violent militants. Even this remained a very small proportion of the British Muslim population.[54] But these few thousand people were part of something still bigger. Al-Suri had not been entirely mistaken when he had seen in the London bombings the vindication of his strategy. The mobilisation that had taken place was neither as extensive as he had hoped, nor did it involve the degree of extremism and violence they had wished to see. But that an ideology, a world view, a language and an identity rooted in a profoundly polarised, dogmatic, prejudiced and hate-filled vision of the world had spread significantly over the previous decade and a half was without doubt.[55]

Nor, sadly, was this only true for the UK. As we shall now see, this language and identity would flourish elsewhere too, and, combined with the inherently social nature of the activity, would give rise to what is perhaps the most dangerous phenomenon of all.

8

THE MOVEMENT

The first to die was an off-duty paratrooper, shot dead from feet away outside a gym in the south-western French city of Toulouse. Then two more soldiers, both also off-duty, were killed with a handgun as they waited at an ATM in the nearby town of Montauban. Of the three victims, two were Muslims, and one was a Catholic of Algerian and eastern French origins. A week went by before the gunman struck again. This time the target was a Jewish school. Rabbi Jonathan Sandler and his two boys, aged six and three, were shot dead in the street. The elder of the two children, badly wounded but still alive, had been killed as he tried to crawl to his father. Eight-year-old Miriam Monsonego hesitated for an instant when told by teachers to flee, stopping to pick up her schoolbag. Surveillance footage shows how the gunman chased her, caught her by the hair, put the muzzle of one weapon to her forehead, changed it for another when it jammed, put that gun too to the girl's temple and killed her.

Two days later, a TV channel received a call from a man who said he was part of al-Qaeda and had carried out the attacks to protest against France's recently passed law banning full-face coverings in public places, its involvement in Afghanistan, where French troops were still deployed as part of the International Security Assistance Force, and the killing of Palestinian children by the Israeli military. The caller was Mohamed Merah, a 23-year-old petty criminal who lived in Toulouse, close to where the first paratrooper had been killed. Armed police surrounded Merah's one-bedroom ground-floor apartment in a quiet pedestrian neighbourhood. Their first attempt to enter was met by a fusillade from a handgun so intense it was thought to be automatic fire. A stand-off followed during which various attempts at negotiation were made. Finally, after thirty-six hours, at 7 a.m. on

22 March 2012, Merah emerged shooting from his flat and was killed by a sniper.

Until Merah's ten-day rampage, France appeared to have been largely spared the violence that had been seen elsewhere in Europe. Numerically, the French Muslim population was the biggest on the Continent, estimated at around five million in 2012. No one knew the exact figure because strict laws designed to maintain the impartiality of the theoretically secular French republic in the face of religious difference forbid any collection of such data. In any case, the French Muslim population was extremely varied. The designation 'Muslim' included many who ate pork, had married non-Muslim partners, drank and never prayed. It also included a small but significant minority who, as in the UK, were part of the growing wave of extremist thought and activism that had coursed through the Islamic world and Europe over the previous decades.

Like other European nations, France had imported large numbers of migrant labourers from colonies in the immediate post-war period and had parked them in poorly served but cheap housing near their places of work, often on the periphery of major cities. The French experience of decolonisation had been very different from that of the British. Bitter, acrimonious and brutal, the process by which France had disengaged from North African colonies and territories left wounds that never healed. Algeria, the biggest source of Muslim immigrants, had been, at least administratively, part of France, not just a colony, and its loss was more fraught as a result: the North African nation's struggle for independence between 1954 and 1962 had been horrendously violent, with all protagonists involved in appalling human rights abuses and most convinced by the end of the conflict they had been betrayed, traduced or denied what was rightfully theirs. Barely any of this was discussed openly in France for several decades.

It was an unpromising starting point for what was always going to be a painful and hesitant process of assimilation. From the beginning, the rigid certainties of the French secularism known as 'laïcité', meaning the total separation of governance and religion, left little room for migrant communities to find a sustainable compromise between what was demanded of them by the state and what they sought to preserve of their original distinctive identities. La République française did indeed welcome everybody equally as brothers, as its famous slogan demanded, but only as long as they were prepared to assume its values, norms and traditions. This contrasted with the more supple pragmatism of British 'multiculturalism', which made fewer such demands. As in Britain, what happened 'over there', in the freshly created states that the early Arab and Muslim immigrants to France had left behind, made itself felt in their new homes. Successive French administrations looked for interlocutors who might represent or influence the nation's Muslims, but their efforts were often stymied by rivalries between Algerian, Moroccan and other communities which mirrored those between their countries of origin. Militancy in these states too inevitably had an impact in France itself. Of all the violent campaigns launched by militants across the Islamic world in the early 1990s, that in Algeria was the most intense and by far the most murderous, killing perhaps between 50,000 and 150,000 people over the decade. The struggle led to intermittent violence linked to Algerian militant support networks within France itself, with bombings in Paris and elsewhere as well as the evolution of a particular mixture of armed robbery and militancy which was to resurface a couple of decades later in spectacular fashion. A few hundred Frenchmen, many of them converts, made their way to training camps in Afghanistan and at least one was killed during the final battles of 2001 as the US-led offensive cleared the Taliban, temporarily, from the country.[1]

Throughout the decade that followed, there were no bombings like those in Madrid or London, or even plots of the ambition seen elsewhere. One reason for this was the efficacy of intelligence services that had been quicker than their Anglo-Saxon counterparts in developing an understanding of the real nature of the threat posed by Islamic militancy. French agencies and investigating judges did not need to learn through investigating near misses or actual attacks that the threat was predominantly 'home-grown'. They already knew. The experience of the 1990s, and the nature of French policing more generally, also meant French security authorities already had legal powers of arrest and detention that were far greater than those of their counterparts in other European countries. A further reason for the lack of violence in France was the success of its political class in distancing the country from the US-led war on terror, its often vocal criticism of Israel and its almost universal opposition to the war in Iraq. The urban riots in France of 2005, though portrayed as a Muslim 'rising' by right-wing commentators overseas, were nothing of the sort. In weeks of reporting throughout these disturbances and hundreds of interviews with angry young Frenchmen, I never once heard Islamist rhetoric or slogans, simply the hardy perennials of urban unrest, while violence was exclusively directed at symbols of the state, such as the police and schools. Equally, though some French citizens continued to make their way to Afghanistan or Iraq to fight, and sometimes die, they were still fewer proportionate to the Muslim population of the country than citizens of other European nations. The popularity of revivalist, if quietist and apolitical, groups such as the Tablighi Jamaat as well as a steady flow of young French Muslims to Egypt or Gulf States to study in religious schools were a serious concern, but major protests in 2006 following the publication of cartoons supposedly ridiculing Mohammed were entirely peaceful. In both riots and demonstrations, France's Muslims were showing the strength of their integration rather than exclusion. Throwing stones at police and marching across Paris were quintessentially French activities, after all. Polls in France showed apparently contradictory trends. Young French second- or third-generation Muslims were increasingly integrated in terms of drinking alcohol or marriage with non-Muslims, but were also more likely to attend mosque or wear the veil. The latter trend, however, could hardly be described as a threat to security. French officials in 2009 or 2010 were confident of their ability to handle any internal threat, and had begun looking at new dangers beyond the nation's frontiers. One adviser to President Nicolas Sarkozy told me that his principal concern was 'classic' state-sponsored terrorism, perhaps involving Iran.

Mohamed Merah was one of these second-generation immigrants and his story shows how, if the overall context was complex but generally encouraging, a significant problem was nonetheless emerging. Merah was born in 1988 in Toulouse to parents who had emigrated from Algeria a few years before. His childhood was not a happy one.[2] Merah's parents were not particularly religiously observant, but if, as one family member later claimed, they 'just wanted to integrate' they were not without hostility to France, or at least the French, either. After the shootings Merah's father said that he had encouraged his children to pray – by giving them extra pocket money – to 'protect them from the bad life led by French people'. The casual prejudice against 'Arabs' that the family encountered outside the home was mirrored by the casual prejudice against Jews inside it. Merah's father often expressed anti-Semitic or racist views if not 'radicalism as such', one son later wrote, but after the authorities in Algeria cancelled an election in 1992 that the Islamists appeared set to win, thus triggering the horrific civil war of the 1990s, he began to speak 'more politically'.[3] The housing estates where many French Muslims live had been built in a way that made integration physically as well as culturally difficult. In Paris, most were constructed beyond a six-lane ring road which had few bridges and acted as a latter-day rampart separating what is still known as the 'intra-muros' parts of the capital from those that are 'extra-muros'.[4] In Toulouse, the situation was little better. The Cité des Izards, where Merah had spent much of his child-hood, is a small housing complex of around 4,000 mainly Muslim residents, distant from the city in every way. Youth unemployment in the neighbourhood touches 50 per cent, according to some reports.[5] Successive administrations in Toulouse have made efforts to integrate local Muslim communities, but are always going to be at a disadvan-tage when the most celebrated local product is cured pork and the patron saint of the city is a twelfth-century Catholic bishop.

Mohamed Merah showed no sign of any interest in extremist Islam until 2008 when, aged nineteen, he was imprisoned for snatching a bag. Previously, his main focus had been joyriding in stolen cars, girls, clubbing, horror films, video games and hip hop.[6] Jails in France – and they are far from alone in this regard – have a well-deserved reputa-tion for being environments favouring radicalisation. In the absence of other statistics about the faith identity of inmates, the number of halal meals ordered has long been used as a useful indication of the extreme over-representation of nominal Muslims within the prison system. Segregation of extremists and ordinary criminals is difficult in overcrowded facilities, and hard-line ideologies and strands of obser-vance easily spread, whatever the attempts of prison imams to counter them. More potent perhaps is the debased, popular subculture of jihad with its rap, violence, half-understood theology and juvenile geopol-itics. In a letter to a family member from jail in early 2009, Merah praised God and the Prophet, and said he knew 'very, very precisely' what his duty was when he was finally free.

When released in November 2009, Merah appeared to have slipped back into a familiar routine of violent videos, computer games and petty crime. In fact, he had changed considerably. 'He was moralising, intolerant and didn't hide his fascination with Holy War,' his brother Abdel-Gani later wrote.[7] Merah seems to have made a conscious effort to avoid any mosques or centres associated with local extremists, possibly on the advice of more experienced men he met in jail. He made one abortive bid to link up with militants in Algeria – a logical starting place given his origins but entirely impractical as anyone with a working knowledge of the situation there would have known – and then cooked up a plan to join the Foreign Legion to get sent to Afghanistan where he would turn his weapon on his fellow soldiers. This did not work out either, unsurprisingly. In 2010, he sold a car he had bought cheaply and refurbished, and used the money to fund a long trip around the Middle East. Travelling on his Algerian rather than his French passport, his aim was to join a militant group, or at least find some kind of extremist mentor. A first attempt to reach Iraq from Syria failed, as did a second bid from Turkey, and so Merah returned to France.[8] Several months later, he tried again. He entered Afghanistan via Tajikistan, thus avoiding applying for an Afghan visa at the embassy in Paris, and took a shared taxi south to Kabul. His plan, it appears, had been to get himself kidnapped by the Taliban, and then fight for them. This did not work out either. After a little over a week in the country, he was detained by local police near Kandahar, the south-eastern Afghan city, handed over to US military authorities and sent back home.

Nine months later, in August 2011, Merah was back in South Asia, flying this time from Paris to Pakistan's eastern city of Lahore, close to the Indian border. The city had long been a favourite destination for young men seeking an entry into Islamic militancy and a centre of extremist activism.[9] One of the best-known local groups, based in a sprawling complex just south of the city, was Lashkar-e-Toiba, which had carried out the 2008 attacks on luxury hotels, a Jewish centre, a tourist cafe and commuters in Mumbai, India's commercial capital. Another was Harkat ul-Mujahideen (HUM). The two groups, which had their origins in the long conflict between India and Pakistan over Kashmir, both had significant training facilities and a history of recruiting foreigners. Elements of both had become significantly closer to al-Qaeda and similar international or transnational groups based in

Pakistan since 2001. It is possible that Merah made contact with someone from one of these two organisations who dispatched him 180 miles across country to Islamabad, the capital, with an introduction to a mosque in the capital well known for its extremist sympathies.[10] This has never been confirmed, but whatever happened, Merah did reach Islamabad, did send emails home from a hotel very close to the radical mosque and was, within days of arriving in the Pakistani capital, on his way towards the tribal zones along Pakistan's frontier with Afghanistan, which had been the biggest single centre for Islamic militant activity anywhere in the world for more than thirty years.[11]

Quite who trained Merah in a house somewhere near Miranshah, a rough-edged town in the tribal agency of north Waziristan, in September 2011 also remains unclear. Literally dozens of different militant groups operate in and around the settlement. These include al-Qaeda and organisations such as the 'Haqqani network', named after the veteran extremist cleric Jalaluddin Haqqani, who is its head, as well as a range of lesser-known outfits from central Asia, south-western China and beyond. Here, too, were the Pakistani Taliban, the rough coalition of groups drawn from local Pashtun tribes, and factions of almost all those various organisations that Pakistan's security services had tried to use as proxies over the previous decades, in Afghanistan as well as Pakistan. There were also, still, some foreign volunteers, from Europe and elsewhere. It was far from unusual for a young European Muslim to turn up with a sketchy recommendation looking to fulfil his personal ambitions of jihad. 'They asked me if I wanted to join the Afghan Taliban, or the Pakistan Taliban or . . . al-Qaeda. They told me I should join al-Qaeda because I spoke Arabic,' Merah told the police during the final stand-off.[12]

Merah was made to wait for more than a week by his contacts while they verified his bona fides and later said he saw 'French, Chinese, Tajiks, Afghans, Pakistanis, Americans, Germans and Spaniards' while waiting to be cleared for training.[13] When he was finally accepted, his hosts suggested a number of possible ways in which he could contribute to the cause. But Merah had his own ideas. He refused a suicide operation in the US, pointing out that as a convicted criminal he would have trouble getting visas, and made it clear he was unenthusiastic about returning to France simply to await further orders that would come at some unspecified future date. He was keener on assassinating a senior journalist or a diplomat but ruled out bombs in his homeland because the necessary ingredients were very difficult to obtain. Finally, his own suggestion to go out shooting soldiers or policemen, with a handgun rather than an assault rifle, which he would not be able to procure at home, was accepted. He bought a weapon, received two or three days' training in its use from a local man associated with a Taliban faction, and then, after gifting the group his camcorder, left for Islamabad and eventually reached France in November. Four months later, he procured several handguns, ammunition and a flak jacket from criminal contacts, stole a scooter, bought a helmet and started killing. Following his death, a group calling itself Jund ul-Khalifat (the Army of the Caliphate) claimed responsibility for his attacks, saying that they had trained 'Abu Youssef al-Fransi' in Waziristan.[14] French officials initially scoffed at the claim but now believe it, identifying the group as that of a well-known Tunisian-born Belgian militant called Moez Garsallaoui who, since reaching Waziristan in 2007, had been a key contact for European volunteers and implicated in a number of attacks targeting the West. Garsallaoui was killed by a drone strike in October 2012.[15]

Even during the stand-off that led to his death, Merah was being described as a 'classic lone wolf'. Bernard Squarcini, head of the Direction Centrale du Renseignement Intérieur (DCRI), told reporters that the attacker had no link to any established network or group, and had 'self-radicalised'. Merah incarnated the new operational techniques of al-Qaeda, Squarcini said, based on a 'lone-wolf strategy'. The minister of the interior, Claude Guéant, supported the claim, arguing that 'lone wolves' were 'redoubtable adversaries'. Merah himself told negotiators: 'Everything I did, I did of my own free will, without any influence by anyone who said to me one day "do this, do that". I did it all alone. I organised it all alone. No one was with me.'[16]

However, if Merah did his killing alone, and was in that sense a lone actor, the evidence that Merah did indeed connect with a militant outfit while in Pakistan is incontrovertible. Merah had regularly contacted his family by phone and email, which is what allowed US and French agencies to reconstitute much of his journey. The details he gave to police negotiators during the siege were also corroborated by the investigations of French and other secret services.

But both Merah and the French authorities had good reasons to claim that he acted without any outside assistance. The killer himself did not want to share any of the credit for what he no doubt viewed as one of the few accomplishments in his entire life of which, by his own twisted logic, he could be proud. For the authorities, the idea that the 23-year-old gunman who had evaded the dragnet for nearly two weeks and killed seven people was a 'lone wolf' helped explain their failures. The public appeared to understand the difficulty of detecting a random attacker, the proverbial needle in a haystack, but were much less forgiving when an attack appeared to be the work of a major group which was deemed to have outwitted the security forces. This was important in the highly politicised context of a presidential election campaign which saw Nicolas Sarkozy, the incumbent right-winger whose credentials were largely based on a reputation for assuring the security of his countrymen, against a lacklustre Socialist opponent who nonetheless was winning the economic debate.

Of course Merah was not a lone wolf, whatever narrative he or security officials tried to construct. In some ways, he was a throwback to an earlier period, when so many militants made their way to Pakistan and then returned to attack in Europe. His repeated efforts to reach an established group, and get training, underlines the ongoing importance of the tribal areas of Pakistan and other similar enclaves, if only as a psychological focus, to aspirant violent extremists. It is striking how Merah pursued his goal of finding a mentor and a group with a determination he had rarely showed in his years in Toulouse.

But the importance of the links he eventually established in Pakistan can be exaggerated too. Firstly, Merah's training was extremely cursory. There is little that can be taught in two days beyond basic weapons handling, which is all his training amounted to. He did not need to travel 4,000 miles to spend a few hours in a room practising how to hold and disassemble a handgun. This is in stark contrast to the months of instruction and psychological conditioning offered to European volunteers five or ten years earlier. Secondly, Merah only managed to contact a semi-autonomous group which was not formally part of al-Qaeda, not the actual hard core. Finally, a focus on Merah's operational ties to a network or established group overseas obscures something far more telling in his development as a violent extremist and, by extension, about the nature of the threat men like him pose today. For the principal environments in which Merah was exposed to extremist ideas were very far from the dusty hills along the Pakistani border with Afghanistan and considerably less picturesque. They were prison, and the homes of his family members. The key figures who appear to have been of huge influence were not extremist leaders in Toulouse who 'brainwashed' Merah, or online clerics who uploaded fiery lectures which convinced him of the need to act, or senior figures in distant militant outfits who ordered him to act. They were his cell-mates, and his family.

Prisons have played a prominent role in almost all of the militants' careers focused on thus far. From the major leaders such as Abu Bakr al-Baghdadi in Iraq, Abu Musab al-Zarqawi in Jordan, Ayman al-Zawahiri in Egypt, Nasir al-Wuhayshi in Yemen through to less significant figures such as the gang members in the Maldives or the killers of Lee Rigby, incarceration has played an obvious and important role in the process of radicalisation. Security officials around the world have long wrestled with the dilemma of whether to disperse hardened veteran extremists and thus risk allowing them to spread their views to 'ordinary criminals', or to concentrate them and risk creating a de facto cell of senior militants behind bars. Yet prison remains an anomalous environment removed, by definition, from the everyday life of a nation's citizens. The family, on the other hand, is everyday life in its most essential form. In this respect, the two figures who stand out in the story of Mohamed Merah are his older brother, Abdelkader, and his sister, Souad.

At first sight it would be Abdelkader who would seem to have had the most significant influence. Taciturn, introverted, Abdelkader had been interested in extremist Islam since the late 1990s, when he had spent months in Algeria. Calmer than the excitable Mohammed, his was a more intellectual commitment to extremist Islam, though he allegedly stabbed another brother who refused to give up his Jewish girlfriend. Abdelkader, a jobbing house painter, travelled in 2006 to Cairo to study at an Islamic institute favoured by Western converts which had just reopened after being closed by local authorities on suspicion of fostering extremism. He was known to police in Toulouse as 'salafiste' even before being linked in 2007 to a network sending recruits to fight with what was then the Islamic State in Iraq.[17] Vast amounts of jihadi and anti-Semitic texts were found on his computer, seized after the 2012 killings.

Though there is no hard evidence that Abdelkader knew of his younger brother's plans, Merah had told him that he wanted to 'avenge himself on the miscreant unbelievers', according to seized letters and the two men ate together the night before the attack on the Jewish school. French officials described him as 'at the origin of the radicalisation of his brother, supporting him logistically in his criminal enterprise and perhaps inspiring his actions'. Abdelkader denied any involvement and appears to have decided against active participation in violence himself.[18]

But the older brother was not the only influence. Another was the older sister, Souad, described as the 'pillar of the family'. Like Merah himself, Souad, who was thirty-four at the time of the shootings, had shown no interest in religion, extreme or otherwise, until her early twenties. Former friends described a young woman who wore short skirts and bikinis and had boyfriends. She lived, most of the time, with a local petty drug dealer, with whom she married and had two children. But a series of events – her father's incarceration for drug dealing in 1999, the jailing of her husband, a depression and a difficult pregnancy – appear to have led Souad towards rigorous and intolerant beliefs and practices.[19] She divorced her husband and married a man known to local police for his extreme views. Music was banned from their home as un-Islamic, unhappy children were told 'a holy warrior doesn't cry' and withdrawn from school, all watched 'mujahideen videos' for hours. Souad too travelled to Cairo to study Koranic texts at the same institute as Abdelkader. Merah joined her there for some time in 2010 or early 2011.[20] She helped finance his overseas voyages, gave him tapes of religious songs, told him to grow a beard and expressed her admiration for his acts after his death.[21] 'I am proud of [him]. He fought right to the end. I think well of bin Laden. Mohamed had the courage to act. I am proud, proud, proud ... Jews, all those who massacre Muslims, I detest them.'[22]

A final influence were local friends, friends of friends and contacts of Merah within a broader community of what police called 'salafistes' in and around Toulouse. These included several individuals who had already travelled to war zones in the Middle East, and others who would do so in the future. There is no suggestion that Merah himself was explicitly encouraged to kill by any of these people, nor by his sister or older brother, but at the traditional mourning reception after his death, there was celebration. 'Be proud,' those coming to pay their respects told the gunman's mother, remarried since 2010 to an active extremist whose own son was in prison for trying to reach Iraq. 'Your son brought France to its knees.'[23]

So to say Mohamed Merah was a lone wolf, who had undergone a process of 'self-radicalisation', is deeply misleading on two counts. There is the fact that he managed to establish contact with a group allied to al-Qaeda in Pakistan, but more important, clear evidence that he had been steeped in a subculture of extremism for almost a decade before his killings, one that had been steadily growing in France for years. It might well have been technically accurate to describe this man, who could chase, catch and kill a child single-handed, as a 'lone actor', but in acquiring the motivation and capability to do such a thing he was anything but alone.

A year and a month after the killings in France, two bombs concealed in rucksacks exploded at the annual marathon held on Patriots' Day in Boston, Massachusetts. Despite being basic devices made with explosives from fireworks packed into a pressure cooker, they killed three people and injured nearly three hundred, many very seriously. The dead included an eight-year-old boy who died in great pain after sustaining shrapnel wounds which exposed his intestines, shattered parts of his spine, almost severed an arm and broke two ribs. The bombs had been placed beside the stands from which spectators watched the finish of the race. Three days after the attack, police released photographs and videos of the two suspects: they were brothers, who had come to the US with their family a decade before. Tamerlan Tsarnaev was a 26-year-old unemployed former amateur boxer. He was killed very early on the morning of the fourth day after the bombings, when hit by a car following a firefight with police.[24] Dzhokhar 'Jahar' Tsarnaev was a nineteen-year-old student and cannabis dealer, who was detained eighteen hours later and eventually sentenced to death in May 2015.

The Tsarnaevs were not the first young men living in the US to be drawn to extremist Islam. Hundreds, possibly thousands, of US citizens and long-term residents had sought out Islamic militant groups since the 1980s and the days of the war against the Soviets in Afghanistan. Americans had fought in Bosnia and in the Afghan civil war, among other places, during the widespread campaigns of the 1990s. A handful of US citizens had established contacts with the Taliban as well as Pakistan-based groups such as Lashkar-e-Toiba later in the decade. But attacks in the US itself, or even on US interests overseas, had not seen any significant involvement of US citizens or residents. The 1993 attack on the World Trade Center was the work of a Pakistani who had arrived five months before and left immediately after the operation. The extremist networks uncovered in the subsequent investigation involved Americans but were centred around an Egyptian cleric and the Americans were not directly implicated in any violent attacks. An attempt to bomb Los Angeles airport in 1999 involved an Algerian living in Canada.

There was also a series of shootings, involving individual attackers, but none of these were US citizens or long-term residents either.[25] The 9/11 attacks of course had no US component whatsoever, with all nineteen hijackers, from Saudi Arabia, Egypt, Lebanon and the United Arab Emirates, flying in from overseas, after being recruited in Afghanistan.

In the decade after 9/11, this began to change. From 2003, an increasing number of American citizens, almost all recent immigrants, were detained after investigations into plots to attack within 'the homeland'. Some of these inquiries were controversial, with authorities accused of using entrapment tactics to lead individuals into violent extremism, but others exposed what was clearly a growing trend. These plots averaged four or five a year through the rest of the decade. There was a narrow escape in 2010 when a naturalised US citizen of Pakistani origin travelled to his native land, was briefly trained by militants there and managed on his return to get as far as parking an SUV full of explosive substances in Times Square. The bomb malfunctioned, but otherwise could have killed scores, even hundreds, in the heart of New York. A steady stream of US citizens joined a variety of militant groups around the Islamic world too, though numbers remained negligible compared with the overall population of around three million Muslims in 2011 in the US. A significant number travelled to Somalia, including the aspirant rapper Hammami, while others undertook the increasingly arduous journey to find al-Qaeda, which itself counted at least two US citizens among its middle ranks.[26]

The vast proportion of these plots, though, simply involved individuals or small groups deciding to strike locally.[27] Some of them were clearly lost individuals caught in something they barely understood. Others had ambitions that evidently exceeded their capabilities, such as the Moroccan illegal immigrant detained after seeking assistance from an undercover FBI agent to launch a one-man armed assault on the White House.[28] As for successful plots, there have been only four since 9/11 and there has been some debate as to whether all should be defined as terrorist acts. Certainly, the motives of the man who drove an SUV into a crowd of students in North Carolina in 2006 are unclear. But less equivocal are those of the young convert who shot two soldiers outside an army recruitment office in Little Rock, Arkansas, in 2009, or of the psychologically unstable army officer who killed thirteen colleagues the same year. The fourth incident was the attack on the Boston Marathon.

The Tsarnaev family had their origins in the northern Caucasus but their lives had been full of wanderings long before they came to the US. Zubeidat, the mother of the two bombers, was born in Dagestan, the volatile and ethnically diverse Russian republic, though had met her husband, Anzor, when studying in the city of Novosibirsk, located 2,000 miles east of Moscow in south-western Siberia.[29] To complicate matters further, Anzor was a Chechen but had been raised in Kyrgyzstan, then a republic of the Soviet Union.[30] Tamerlan Tsarnaev, the couple's first child, was born in 1986, when his parents were barely out of their teens. They moved repeatedly, searching for opportunities to make a living and better their prospects. In 1992, they left Kyrgyzstan, newly independent following the collapse of the Soviet Union, and made a home in Chechnya. Two years later they were back in the central Asian republic, having narrowly avoided being caught up in the first of two major conflicts to take place that decade in Anzor Tsarnaev's ancestral homeland. In 2000, they were on the move again, this time to Dagestan, Zubeidat's birthplace. This was an odd choice. The conflict in Chechnya had spilled over the borders and the state was plunged into a vicious battle between insurgents and federal Russian forces. Their ambitions checked once again, this time Anzor and Zubeidat decided to do what many in poor, anarchic parts of the world only talk about, and sought asylum in the US, ending up, in 2002, in Cambridge, a small city of around 100,000 outside Boston and home to Harvard University and MIT.[31]

Anzor, taciturn and wiry, and Zubeidat came first, with Dzhokhar, then aged eight. The couple's elder son and two daughters joined them after a year. The family, noisy but apparently happy to be in America and hopeful of making a better life, rented a three-bedroom apartment on the second floor of a clapboard house. The two boys had a bunk bed in a small room, the two girls a mattress.[32] They all went to the local government school, which had a self-consciously progressive ethos and mediocre academic results. Both parents were popular in the small local Chechen community. Zubeidat, striking and vivacious, found work in a beauty salon – which made sense to everyone as she was known for her glamorous dresses and permanent heavy make-up. Her husband made a little money as a mechanic. Cambridge is a mixed town, with many diverse ethnicities and wealthy and poor neighbourhoods close by one another. There was no obvious reason for the Tsarnaevs not to make a better life.

For several years, the family survived, even if they did not prosper. Life was not easy and cash was short. The daughters married young, one at only sixteen, in matches arranged by their parents. When one of the girls had dated a local boy considered unsuitable by her father, Tamerlan ended the relationship by hitting his sister's suitor in the face. The older brother, six foot three, powerfully built and unafraid to use his fists, had done well at the various schools he had attended before coming to the US but had trouble adapting to his new environment. He dropped out of a college course, and made few friends. He did, however, have significant talent as a boxer, training hard at a local gym and winning successive local championships. Dzhokhar, laid-back, wry and charming, with a shock of curly brown hair and a quizzical smile, was popular and captained the school wrestling team. A decent student, despite a tendency to chaos and the consumption of considerable quantities of cannabis, he would eventually win a scholarship to study at the University of Massachusetts Dartmouth, an unexceptional college sixty miles from Cambridge which nonetheless offered the prospect of a useful qualification.

Yet within five years of their arrival in the US, the dreams of the Tsarnaevs began to disintegrate. The marriages of their two daughters failed and both young women moved back into the small crowded apartment with their babies. Anzor, a hard drinker and heavy smoker, began suffering chronic headaches and stomach pains, and gave up work. Tamerlan had been charged with assaulting a girlfriend, and this may have contributed to his continued failure to obtain US citizenship. In itself this was not too much of a problem, but having missed out on winning a national championship one year due to a controversial decision by match judges, it meant that he was disqualified from a second attempt following a rule change twelve months later. Dzhokar, who had become a US citizen, was focused more on an expanding drug-dealing business than his studies. Money at home, meanwhile, was increasingly tight, with the family on food stamps and welfare payments.[33] Zubeidat, who had previously been uninterested in religion or politics, began to develop a strong interest in conservative, contemporary Islam. Her glamorous dresses were replaced by loose black robes and a headscarf and she started reading the Koran. Her husband did not approve. 'Why are you dressing like that? We are in America!' Anzor reportedly shouted at her.[34] In 2008, Zubeidat lost her job, possibly let go because the economic slump meant she was no longer needed at the small beauty salon, possibly because her new beliefs had led her to refuse to work with male clients.[35]

The decline continued. Tamerlan had given up boxing after being disqualified from the championship and stayed at the family home with a baby daughter while his new wife, a convert, worked ten-hour days as a community nurse. Dzhokar's grades were slipping to the point where he risked losing his scholarship and expulsion.[36] He was also increasingly in debt, despite the revenue from the dealing. Anzor was increasingly sick, while his wife plunged deeper into strict religious observance, wearing gloves to avoid contact with male strangers and praying assiduously five times a day. Their marriage was effectively over. Worried about her elder son, perhaps after he complained to her about hearing 'voices', Zubeidat encouraged Tamerlan to read the Koran, attend mosque, be a 'true Muslim'. The 9/11 attacks, she was heard to say, had been the work of the US government, part of a wide-ranging plan to foment hostility to Muslims.[37] 'I told Tamerlan that we are Muslim, and we are not practicing our religion, and how can we call ourselves Muslims?' Zubeidat later told a reporter from the *Wall Street Journal*. 'And that's how Tamerlan started reading about Islam, and he started praying, and he got more and more and more into his religion.'[38] In January 2012, her elder son flew to Moscow, and then on to Dagestan, where his mother had grown up.

Exactly what Tamerlan did in Dagestan is contested. As in neighbouring Chechnya, a history of conflict, extreme inequality, venal and incapable authorities, and the influence of Wahhabi proselytisation had combined to sustain an ongoing, if intermittent, campaign by violent extremist groups to expel Russian forces and establish some kind of Islamic state. Early reports went as far as to suggest that he had contacted some of these militant organisations, and been radicalised and trained by them.[39] The most thorough investigations, by journalists Masha Gessen and Alan Cullison, have shown that this is not the case. Tamerlan's activities in Dagestan were restricted to protracted contact over months with a non-violent, legal group, which campaigned on 'human rights issues'. The group, called the Union of the Just, had a loose link to the Hizb ut-Tahrir organisation and the international pro-caliphate movement. Its agenda certainly focused on the undoubted abuses perpetrated by local authorities and Russian federal forces in Dagestan but also involved a broader vision familiar from many other such groups elsewhere in the world, of a West committed to violence against Muslims, with its attendant anti-Semitism, homophobia and social conservatism. Tamerlan spent hours with the group, reading holy texts and discussing the grievances of the *umma*. He does not actually appear to have made any real efforts to contact active violent militants, though he did frequently attend a mosque associated with extremists.[40] But if Tamerlan had not actually got in touch with militants, he was very deeply involved with people who shared much of their world view.

This showed on his return to Boston in July 2012. The ostentatiously dressed boxer, who wore white silk shirts and drove a Mercedes, had already disappeared, replaced by a house husband in shabby jogging pants and a T-shirt. This latest incarnation of Tamerlan Tsarnaev had a beard the regulation 'width of a man's hand', as the Prophet was supposed to have specified, and wore a white prayer cap and a long-tailed shirt of a type adopted by many Western Islamists. He argued publicly with the moderate imam of the mosque he had been attending in Cambridge over the celebration of secular national anniversaries such as the Fourth of July, and shouted down a local halal grocer who was selling Thanksgiving turkeys. He was, a friend of his brother said, 'intense'.[41]

It is at this point, in the autumn of 2012, that events appear to have accelerated. Zubeidat Tsarnaev was charged with shoplifting designer dresses and left the US, joining her estranged husband, now also in Dagestan. (She maintains her innocence.) Dzhokhar was still supposedly studying, though his grades were terrible, and he was rarely at home. The rent on the family apartment went unpaid, bringing threats of eviction. Tamerlan spent much time on the Internet, surfing extremist and conspiracy theory websites. He also created a YouTube playlist featuring extremist propaganda including the popular fifteen-minute video 'The Emergence of Prophecy: The Black Flags From Khorasan', which explains how the present conflict between Islam and unbelief is a sign of the imminent coming of the Messiah with armies bearing black flags from the east, and some videos from Caucasian militant groups. Images of the apartment reveal what appears to be a black flag, like those used by ISIS and some al-Qaeda affiliates, hanging on the wall.[42] Tamerlan downloaded, and presumably read, core extremist texts including works by Abdullah Azzam, the leader of the Afghan Arabs of the 1980s, and Anwar al-Awlaki. He also downloaded *Inspire*, the magazine produced by al-Qaeda in the Arabian Peninsula. In its first issue, which was found on the computer Tamerlan used, are instructions for making a home-made bomb. Tamerlan also accumulated a collection of publications specialising in conspiracy theories, particularly about the 9/11 attacks, works explaining the supposed economic success of Jews through racial theories, and a copy of the *Protocols of the Elders of Zion*, the fraudulent 1903 anti-Semitic text supposedly exposing a Jewish plan for global domination.[43]

In February 2013, Tamerlan bought $200 worth of fireworks, from which he extracted eight pounds of low explosives. He and his brother also went shooting with rented handguns. Quite when and how Dzhokhar was drawn into the extremist projects of his brother is unclear. Right up until the attack, the nineteen-year-old continued making plans to visit New York, spending days playing video games and dealing cannabis. He did, however, stop smoking the drug himself and skipped a spring break, a byword for drunken debauchery, in Florida organised by his friends. No one is entirely certain where the bombs were actually made, though investigators believe it was at home, where they found a jar of nails, rolls of tape and wire, tools including a soldering iron, lengths of fuse and parts of at least one pressure cooker. They did not find any trace of the black gunpowder from the fireworks, though. It is possible that the brothers originally intended to attack Fourth of July parades, but their explosive devices were quicker to manufacture than they had anticipated, leading them to search for a new target. The Boston Marathon, on 15 April, fitted the timetable. They placed their bombs on the pavement by the spectator stands at exactly 2.40 p.m. Eight minutes later, Dzhokhar called his brother. At 2.49, the two bombs detonated almost simultaneously.[44] The FBI first identified the two men from surveillance videos because they were the only people who did not react when the bombs exploded, walking without expression away from the explosions among the chaos.

The younger Tsarnaev had a Twitter account, @J_tsar, which was for friends and family and was full of comments about cars, TV shows, girls, breakfast and the sort of jokes – 'studying is just a combination of the words student and dying' – teenagers make all over the world. There were also darker elements. 'If you have the knowledge and the inspiration all that's left is to take action,' Dzhokhar messaged eight days before the bombing.

At his trial, the FBI disclosed the existence of a second account they believed was used by Dzhokhar or possibly his brother, or both men, with the handle @Al_firdausiA, a version of the Arabic for Paradise.[45] This had only been opened a month before the bombings and the first message read: 'I want the highest levels of Jannah [Heaven], I want to be able to see Allah every single day for that is the best of pleasures.' The last, sent on the day of the bombings, read: 'It's our responsibility my brothers & sisters to ask Allah to ease the hardships of the oppressed and give us victory over kufr.'

Dzhokhar Tsarnaev continued to use Twitter after the bombing. One message, sent seven hours after the attack, said: 'There are people that know the truth but stay silent & there are people that speak the truth but we don't hear them cuz they're the minority.' Dzhokhar sent a message from the @J_tsar account at 10.43 p.m. the following day. 'I'm a stress free kind of guy,' it read.[46]

So what do these three cases, and others in the West between 2005 and 2013 or 2014, tell us?

The first conclusion is obvious: simple, low-tech attacks with minimal logistics and limited ambitions succeeded over this period while complex ones involving large bombs and targets such as planes or mass transit systems did not.[47] Several operations which would undoubtedly have killed large numbers of people – especially in the US – came close to success but did ultimately fail. The most lethal attack in the West since 2005 involved a lone right-wing extremist, Anders Breivik, in Norway in 2012 in which seventy-seven people died.

The second conclusion is that the absence of 'spectaculars' did not mean that the danger of mass-casualty attacks of the type seen a decade earlier in Europe had passed entirely. Almost all those that had been successfully executed hitherto had involved a militant group overseas in some way. There were many people who remained clearly interested in such strikes if they had been feasible. The veteran extremists who, briefly, hosted Mohamed Merah in north Waziristan hoped to use him in an ambitious plot in the US or the UK, for example. But militant planners were also aware of the extreme difficulty of such operations and the huge investment of resources they implied, as well as the risks of massive retaliation by a Western state if they caused significant destruction or a backlash from potential supporters if the strike was seen as unjustified, gratuitous, disproportionate or misdirected. The two groups most committed to targeting the Far Enemy, al-Qaeda and al-Qaeda in the Arabian Peninsula, both repeatedly reminded aspirant recruits from the West that they would do more good remaining at home, launching their own local attacks, than travelling to Pakistan or Yemen to learn how to execute massive transnational ones. The logic, by 2013 or 2014, was fairly straightforward: there was little point in extremist groups going to all the trouble of trying to organise a major spectacular when it was perfectly possible to cause massive disruption, if not massive destruction, through other, less ambitious operations.

For this is the third conclusion. Even if the death toll was a fraction of the major strikes of the previous decade – a thousandth in the case of the Boston bombing compared to the 9/11 attacks – the low-tech, DIY violence still generated the intense media interest that remained the principal aim of many of the extremist groups and strategists. The combination of twenty-four-hour rolling news and an ongoing security 'situation' was an immensely potent one. The world's cameras had been focused on Mumbai in 2008 throughout the three days it took security forces to overcome a small team of gunmen who had raided luxury hotels and a range of other targets. The five days it took for the Boston bombers to be tracked down were marked by attention which bordered on the hysterical. The ten-day hunt for Mohamed Merah held France, and much of the West, captivated. Merah and the Boston bombers planned further attacks, aiming to prolong the drama as long as possible. This was the 'theatre of terror' as an ongoing series, not as a one-off production.

A final conclusion was less immediately obvious, but could be drawn from an analysis of the many elements these apparently varied attacks shared. One was the perpetrators' expectation that the violence would end in their own deaths. Suicide attacking, and particularly suicide bombing, is now so deeply associated with Islamic militancy that it is often forgotten that this was once far from the case. In the mid-1970s, as Europe and the Middle East were hit by a wave of violent extremism, one security official confidently told journalist Colin Smith that 'Arabs don't blow themselves up, only the Japanese do that'.[48] The first suicide bombings occurred in the Middle East in the early 1980s, primarily in Lebanon, and then became more numerous in the 1990s with a high-profile campaign in Israel which was very influential on extremists around the world. However, suicide bombings were still rare in overall terms. The hugely violent campaigns by extremists returning from Afghanistan to countries such as Egypt and Algeria in the early 1990s did not feature suicide tactics, and attackers in the West at the time, such as the men who first struck the World Trade Center in 1993 or shot up the CIA headquarters the same year, made careful plans to escape to sanctuaries overseas. Since then, however, martyrdom has become an integral part of Islamic extremist terrorism, with the average annual number of suicide attacks rising from fewer than twenty in the last half of the nineties, to 156 between 2000 and 2005, and nearly four hundred over the last decade.[49] The tactic saw its first recorded use in Afghanistan in 2003, in Somalia in 2009, and in Nigeria in 2011. Its proliferation has been accompanied by the spread of the cult of martyrdom. Though clearly linked, the one does not necessarily lead to the other, and of course there have always been martyrs of various types in Islam, as in every major faith, or indeed secular tradition. But the idea that deliberately seeking to die for the faith, let alone killing other unarmed individuals while doing so, appears more widespread now than at any time in living memory. If the Tsarnaevs did not carry out a suicide attack, they could not have expected any end other than either 'death by cop', or almost certain execution if taken alive. The killers of Lee Rigby had tapes about martyrdom in their car and appear to have been set also on being killed by the policemen who arrived at the scene of the murder. Merah barely considered giving himself up when surrounded in his apartment. 'Right from the moment I started with the attacks, I knew how it was going to finish: either I'd be gunned down in the street, or I'd be killed in my home, or someone else's . . . Given a choice between fighting or surrendering, the mujahideen fight to the death, you see,' he told a negotiator.[50] Even Roshanara Choudhry, who stabbed the MP in 2010, told police after her arrest that she wanted to die a martyr, though quite how she expected to achieve this was not immediately obvious. Most of the abortive spectacular mass-casualty terrorist operations planned since 2001 have involved the death of the attackers.

By 2014, from Toulouse to Boston, as from Kabul to Raqqa, it was taken as a given among militants that, as Merah put it, being killed is a duty and that the murder of unarmed civilians is legitimate. Clearly both of these ideas are not just controversial, but are emphatically rejected by the vast majority of Muslims and Islamic scholars. However, the argument that civilians in democracies are as culpable as soldiers because they have voted for governments which are themselves responsible for violence to Muslims, or at least accept a democratic system which allows those governments to remain in power, had become a standard part of the extremist ideological lexicon. The phrase 'we love death more than you love life', often wrongly attributed to bin Laden, was quoted so often by extremists that it became a cliché. Mohammad Sidique Khan said it in his 'martyrdom' video recorded somewhere in Pakistan before the 7/7 attacks in London in 2005. Even Dzhokhar Tsnarnaev, the laid-back, pot-smoking college kid, scrawled it on the wall of the boat in which he lay, wounded, as the police closed in, along with his version of the argument justifying the killing of civilians, even though, he said, this was something he did not 'like' doing.

Another striking theme is the resemblance of these attacks to the horrific executions that feature in the videos of the Islamic State. The murder of Rigby with knives, the attempt at decapitation, the speech afterwards, was clearly an execution of this sort. Merah, who shot his defenceless victims in the head at point-blank range, actually described his killings as 'executions' to police. One reason for this is the limited means of the attackers: the weapons they had available required a more personal, intimate form of killing. Another was, of course, the influence of the videos themselves. The pioneers of the genre were the Chechen militants in the late 1990s, but the first such production to come to wider attention was the execution of US journalist Daniel Pearl in Karachi in 2002, posted on the Internet by Pakistani militants led by Khaled Sheikh Mohammed. Then came the terrible productions of Abu Musab al-Zarqawi in Iraq between 2004 and 2006. Many more have since emerged from Syria and other theatres of extremist violence. Adebolajo, Adebowale, Merah and Tamerlan Tsarnaev had all watched violent videos including executions. Merah had even faced a police complaint from a relative after effectively abducting an adolescent and forcing him to watch horrific films. Like a suicide bombing, an execution too communicates a message in the choreography of its violence. Twenty years ago such events were extremely rare. Now they are part of the mainstream of violent militant activism.[51]

A further common element between the attacks described in the last two chapters is their choice of target. These were selected because they were vulnerable, but also because each had some symbolic significance. Merah pointed out to negotiators, correctly, that if he had shot random people in the street he would simply have been labelled a madman, so it was necessary to kill soldiers and Jews. Rigby was a soldier, albeit off-duty. The Tsarnaevs could have bombed a mall, or a busy street, or any number of weekend sporting events. Instead they chose a race held in the centre of a historic American city as part of Patriots' Day celebrations which commemorate the first battles of the American Revolutionary War. That all of these attackers made such choices without receiving direct instructions from any veteran extremist or authority – Merah's shootings were his own suggestion, not that of the men he spent a few days with in Pakistan – demon-strates that all had integrated a common set of principles. This was surely a vindication of the vision elaborated by thinkers such as Abu Musab al-Suri, the man who had formulated the idea of a 'leaderless jihad' a decade before. Al-Suri had envisaged a movement without organisation but held together instead by a commonly understood set of guidelines. This is exactly what evolved.

As al-Suri had foreseen, pretty much anyone with a computer, or, latterly, a phone, and an Internet data connection could, with a little effort, learn what targets were preferable for Islamic militants to attack. These were explicitly laid out in texts such as his own work and publi-cations like *Inspire*, but they were implicit in much else too. There were the simple historical pseudo-documentaries reframing the history of early Islam as a war of resistance against a violent and aggressive West and the much-viewed apocalyptic material that Tamerlan Tsnarnaev apparently enjoyed; the audio versions of the *Protocols of the Elders of Zion* and the jihadi raps; the huge variety of texts and clips expounding an immense range of conspiracy theories; the online lectures by a host of extremist clerics.[52] All of this had an impact, clearly identifying those responsible for the many ills afflicting the *umma*.

For what is especially striking about the Rigby killers, Merah and the Tsarnaevs is the similarity of their public statements. The angry rant of Adebolajo over the body of the dying soldier, the arguments of Merah as he fenced intellectually with a Muslim police officer in his final hours, and the sentences Dzhokhar Tsarnaev scrawled on the internal wall of the dry-docked boat in which he had taken shelter, all use identical phrases, despite their very different lives and locations. Extremists I have interviewed over the last two decades, in safe houses in Algeria and compounds in Pakistan's Khyber pass, in madrassas in Bangladeshi slums and kebab shops in east London, in the capital of the Maldives and in Gaza City during the war of 2014, all use this same vocabulary. Whether in Arabic, Urdu, Dhivehi, Bangla, English or Pashto, they voice the same set of imprecations, complaints, justi-fications and invocations which together constitute the international lingua franca of Islamic extremism. If a shared language is the defining characteristic of a community, then there can be no doubt that this particular global community exists, extending far beyond the particular circumstances of these five killers. These men were formed, conditioned and prepared for their ultimate acts over years, if not decades, by an entire culture of extremist activism. The words that they spoke after killing were not their own, but words that they had heard from others many, many times.

The killers of Rigby learned some of this language from the other activists they had spent so much time with over the years before they acted, even if their fellow campaigners often did not actually endorse or encourage violence. They had learned it too from immigrant gangs that mixed jihadism with gangsta criminality. Merah had certainly learned it from fellow prisoners in Toulouse jail, but also in a home where prejudice was as much a part of the environment as the dirty cutlery in the sink. Tamerlan Tsarnaev learned the language, or perhaps simply perfected his mastery of it, from the Union of the Just in Dagestan, a group which was not violent but committed nonetheless to a world view many would see as extremist. For Dzhokhar, there was Tamerlan as a tutor. For both brothers, there was a mother who had begun to speak a language of anger, alienation and hurt which they heard and never questioned and reinforced in their turn. For all of these men, there were the anonymous, distant, virtual authors, tweeters, posters, forum managers, password dispensers, bloggers and forwarders encountered through social media. Together these multiple contacts, whether virtual or real, meant the five eventual killers were, day after day, month after month, year after year, exposed to a culture of extremism. Perhaps most importantly of all, this environment in which they lived made them feel part of a shared endeavour involving very large numbers of people.

Yet despite this, officials and analysts have continued to talk of such men as 'lone wolves'. One explanation for this lies in a mistaken view of how people become violent extremists. 'Radicalisation' is seen as a specific event or, even more misguidedly, as a conscious act. By this same logic, people 'are radicalised', a term which implies they are voluntary but passive objects of a designed process, or that they are involuntarily 'brainwashed' despite themselves, or even that they somehow 'self-radicalise' in total isolation. This is reassuring as it implies that the responsibility for an individual's violent extremism lies solely with the individual themselves or with some other individual or group, all of which could theoretically be eliminated. But the truth is that terrorism is not something you do by yourself. It is, like any activism, highly social. Only its consequences are exceptional. It makes as much sense to talk about the 'radicalisation' of a sixteen-year-old who becomes involved in Islamic militancy, as it does of a sixteen-year-old who becomes involved in gangs, or in taking psychotropic drugs, or even in extreme sports, particular video games or a certain type of music and dress. People become interested in ideas, ideologies and activities, even abhorrent and immoral ones, because other people are interested in them. No one describes a young adult who suddenly takes up an activity such as rock-climbing or fly-fishing or campaigning against global warming as 'self-activising', even if that enthusiasm has been nurtured and developed largely through their own initiative, social media and exploitation of resources on the Internet. The psychological and social barriers to involvement in violence are certainly higher than in other less nefarious activities, but the mechanics of the process that draws people into them are the same. If lone wolves do exist, they are extremely rare. Even those individuals who do fulfil the commonly understood definition of the term, and operate entirely without contact or support from anyone else, still feel themselves to be part of a broader community. Nor, as should by now be clear, is this sense of belonging unfounded. These attackers are indeed, as they believe, part of something bigger.

So the final lesson to be drawn from the stories of Adebolajo, Adebowale, Merah and the Tsarnaevs is that the most important developments in Islamic militancy over the last three decades do not involve the achievements or failure of a major organisation, nor the creation or destruction of an enclave in a distant country, nor the seizure of a city, or the loss of a battle, but the emergence, consolidation and expansion of what can be called the movement of Islamic militancy. This movement, the last of the three broad categories identified in the introduction which constitute the phenomenon of Islamic militancy today, simply did not exist in the 1970s and 80s on anything like the present scale. Then, the language of extremism and violent action was restricted to a tiny fringe of Muslims, largely in the Middle East and South Asia. Today, if actual violence is still limited to a negligible proportion of the world's Muslims, the language is spoken by a much larger number. This is a phenomenon that is much more pervasive than the few scattered incidents of death and destruction that have occurred over recent years would suggest. If such killers had indeed been lone wolves, the problem of Islamic militancy would have been resolved long ago.[53]

A year after the bombings in Boston and the killing of Lee Rigby, two years after Merah's rampage in the south-west of France, there came a new attack, this time in Brussels. The target was wearily familiar – a Jewish museum in the Belgian capital. Two middle-aged Israeli tourists, a 65-year-old retired publisher and a 25-year-old man were killed. The alleged gunman also appeared to be of a type well known to security forces in Europe. Mehdi Nemmouche (who denies the charges) was a 29-year-old Frenchman, of Algerian origins, with a long criminal record who came from the run-down northern city of Roubaix, famous among security officials for a gang of militants based there in the mid-1990s and for activism, both violent and pacific, ever since. There was one aspect of Nemmouche's story that was new, though. According to prosecutors, on 31 December 2012, shortly after being released from prison having completed his latest sentence for armed robbery, Nemmouche left France for Brussels, London, Beirut, Istanbul and finally Syria, where he spent eleven months training with the organisation which was to become the Islamic State.[54]

Nemmouche was one of the thousands of Europeans, and a handful of US citizens, who had made their way to Syria to fight alongside extremist factions since the uprising against the Assad regime had gathered momentum from mid-2011. By late 2013, most Western foreigners were fighting with ISIS. The capture of Mosul and the creation of the Islamic State in June of 2014 prompted a renewed surge of volunteers. By early 2015, around 3,000 Europeans were estimated to have fought at one time or another in Syria or Iraq, most with extremist factions. At the time of writing, around half that number are still active in one or other of the two countries.[55]

Who were they? The British contingent, of around seven hundred, was representative of the whole.[56] It included men like Kabir Ahmed, who died at the wheel of an Islamic State car bomb near Baiji, the refinery town in north-west Iraq, in November 2014.[57] A thirty-year-old care worker and father of three from Derby, Ahmed had already been convicted in the UK of calling for homosexuals to be stoned or burned to death, the first person to be prosecuted in Britain under new laws against incitement of hatred on the basis of sexual orientation. 'I did it to protect our religion, and our people from oppression. I used to pray a little, and observe Ramadan, and my mother used to tell me stories about Islam . . . But I wouldn't say I was very religious . . . Islam had begun to reveal itself to me. I began to propagate my own vision of what Islam is, and I was arrested for the propagation of my religion,' was his explanation.[58] Another was Mohammed Nahin Ahmed from Birmingham, who bought *Islam for Dummies* before travelling to Syria to join one of the minor extremist factions. The British contingent also included six men from Portsmouth, all in their late teens and early twenties, whose complex identity issues were entirely apparent from the name they gave themselves, the 'al-Britanni Brigade Bangladeshi Bad Boys'.[59] There were some like Abdul Waheed Majeed, who was forty-one and thus much older than most of the volunteers and whose motivation appears rather different from that of the bulk of the other British volunteers. A lorry driver and father of three from Crawley in West Sussex, he died in a suicide bomb attack on a prison in Aleppo in February 2014. Before becoming involved with the al-Qaeda-affiliated Jabhat al-Nusra, he had spent months in Syria building relief camps for the displaced.[60] But for the most part the profile of the men who travelled to Syria to take part in the fighting there is almost identical to those who became involved in violence at home. They were young, nominally Muslim, largely ignorant of the faith or Islamic history, heavily influenced by propaganda videos and steeped in jihadi subculture on the Internet and in the real world.

What drew them to the war? Unlike other conflicts over the previous decade, which could be seen as pitting Islam against the West, the war in Syria was less clear-cut as a cause. Nonetheless, to a would-be militant it still offered many attractions. Indeed, as mentioned in chapter six, participation would be significantly less arduous than it had been for fighters in Afghanistan, Iraq or Somalia. Passages published in spring 2015 in *Dabiq*, the Islamic State propaganda magazine, emphasised the prospect for hopeful fighters of empowerment and the restoration of dignity: 'The modern day slavery of employment, work hours, wages, etc., is one that leaves the Muslim in a constant feeling of subjugation to a kafir master. He does not live the might and honour that every

Muslim should live and experience. Dedication of one's life towards employment, if the employer is a kafir, only leads to humiliation that could possibly over time lead to concessions followed by an inferiority complex,' the magazine announced.[61] To young, alienated, bored men from the UK as much as their counterparts in Morocco, Turkey or Pakistan, the conflict offered sexual opportunity, status and adventure – opportunities that could be seen, at least in the eyes of a particularly naive and ignorant young person, as more inspiring than trying to scratch together fifty pounds for a night out in a run-down British port city before another week's work of flipping burgers or studying for a low-grade, low-utility degree. For young men in the UK, it also offered an apparent respite from the challenge of reconciling a new sense of Muslim identity with being British, and from daily, casual xenophobia. An unexceptional school-leaver from an unexceptional provincial town might become Abu Sayyaf al-Britanni, named after the Prophet's own sword-bearer, with his British origins transformed from a source of difficulty into a source of pride. He could talk of the ultimate sacrifice – 'You only die once, why not make it martyrdom?' asked one recruitment video for the Islamic State – without actually following through. If one was prepared to ignore the reality of the systematic rape of Yazidi women, the massacres of the Shia, the torture of hostages, the execution of doctors, the cause in the abstract could be portrayed as a noble one. Some were no doubt genuinely moved by the plight of fellow Muslims in distress – new videos of horrific atrocities perpetrated by the Assad regime were being broadcast on the Internet every day – but the interests of others may have been less elevated. Imran Khwaja, a bodybuilder from Southall, told a friend he needed 'cocoa butter, soap and condoms for the "war booty"'. In the many videos they recorded and uploaded, and in their tweets and Facebook posts, the fighters self-consciously pose as champions of the global *umma*, fulfilling a mission and a duty of importance and consequence. They posted more pictures of landscapes, cats and swimming pools than severed heads, though these did feature too.

The mechanics of 'recruitment', or the processes by which these largely young men found their way from homes in the UK to the battlefronts in Iraq and Syria, were also familiar. Once again, it was a fundamentally social activity. Almost all of those who travelled from the UK had been involved with networks of Islamic activists before their departure, and few left for war alone. Mohammed Nahin Ahmed, reader of *Islam for Dummies*, went with a childhood friend. Kabir Ahmed, who had been jailed for his homophobic rants, had been part of a small and aggressively vocal band of extremists in the north of England. Ifthekar Jaman, from Portsmouth, convinced five friends from his Islamic study group and an existing street-preaching network in his home town and another three from Manchester to join him in Aleppo.[62] (These were the al-Britanni Brigade Bangladeshi Bad Boys.) Mohammed Emwazi, an IT graduate from north London, was part of an informal group, all from immigrant origins and similar backgrounds who were involved in various kinds of militant activism; they had met at school and during five-a-side football matches, not at mosques, Islamic centres or rallies. Emwazi, twenty-six in 2015, was eventually named by the media as the masked executioner in the horrific IS videos, though this identification has never been confirmed and has been denied by his parents.[63]

In other cases, the family, that most fundamental social unit of all, played an important role. There were several examples of siblings travelling or fighting together, most spectacularly three brothers from East Sussex, two of whom were dead by spring 2015. Abdel-Majed Abdel Bary, an aspirant rapper turned suspected Islamic State fighter, was the son of a well-known Egyptian militant who had come to the UK in the first wave of extremist arrivals in the 1990s and had subsequently been arrested on terrorism charges and extradited to the US.[64] Many siblings and, more rarely, parents of militants were detained and some charged with terrorist offences.[65] Security officials had long pointed at familial ties to active or past militants as predictors of involvement, so this was little surprise. However, the prominent role of women was new. Though there had been some female militant activists a decade or so before, they were extremely rare. By 2014, they were much more common, particularly in networks linked to Syria. There was no consistent profile: a pair of sixteen-year-old twins, three school friends from east London, a band of medical students and a 45-year-old former punk rocker who had converted all reached the new Islamic State's territory.[66] They came from all European nations, too, especially France. They included Souad Merah, the Toulouse gunman's elder sister, who tried to reach Syria in March 2015.[67]

One important trend in the new volunteers' rhetoric, particularly on social media once they arrived in Syria, was the inclusion of much of the Islamic State's representation of Shia Muslims as apostates, who were to be treated more harshly than the unbeliever. This sectarian emphasis, with its additional strand of hate and prejudice, had been absent from most previous calls to arms. On the whole, though, all of those who travelled to the Islamic State, male and female, young and old, from the UK and elsewhere, repeated the same stock phrases: about the legitimacy of the caliphate, the historic confrontation between Muslims and the West, the decadence of European society, Muslim solidarity, their desires for martyrdom, and the legitimacy of executions of captured 'spies'. They quoted the same ideologues, such as Syed Qutb and Abdullah Azzam, though it was extremely unlikely they had ever actually read their works even in English let alone in Arabic, which almost none spoke. They cited al-Awlaki's sermons and bin Laden's justification for attacks on civilians. They repeated the stale glorification of a violent death. 'I will sacrifice my children a hundred times for the sake of Allah,' said Kabir, the homophobic bomber from Derby. 'Jihad is obligatory,' said Aseel Muthana, a seventeen-year-old schoolboy who travelled with his elder brother, a medical student, to join IS.[68] 'We are trying to establish the law of God, the law of Allah. This is the duty on me . . . all these people are suffering. Muslims are being slaughtered,' said Iftekhar Jaman, the former Sky call-centre worker who coined the term 'five-star jihad' and eventually died when a tank shell severed both his legs.

Taken together, this flood of rote-learned rhetoric, the 'boilerplate' of jihadist discourse, was further evidence, if any were needed, of the sheer number of people in the autumn of 2014 and spring of 2015 who appeared to speak the language of contemporary Islamic militancy fluently. It underlined once again the lesson of the killers of Lee Rigby, Merah and the Tsarnaevs. The departure of British, European and even US volunteers to Syria and Iraq was not the consequence of some radical new development or a dramatic change in direction in the evolution of Islamic militancy but the climax of a process that had been under way for over forty or more years across the Islamic world and, latterly, in the West too. The new conflicts in the Middle East certainly brought a new focus and energy to Islamic militant activism, but this simply intensified and accelerated a process that had been ongoing for decades.

Of course, when the killing starts, another dynamic takes over. There is a frontier then which has been crossed and from which no return is possible. Even within the movement, only a very few are directly responsible for the death of others. For them violence brings only more violence in a savage escalation that can only have one issue.

'The day when I did it, I mean, the day when I killed [the first soldier], that morning when I woke up I didn't think I was going to attack that day, you know,' Mohamed Merah remembered as he spoke to police negotiators outside his apartment in Toulouse. 'It happened very quickly. And I had to do it all, all alone, to shoot, get back on my bike, get away, you know. And, well, so, the moment when, the second time, I saw that I had killed three of them, at that moment then, I felt my heart lighter, relieved, calm. And, you know, because it felt lighter, I wanted to do it again, and so every time I reoffended, and with each operation, I felt better and better.'[69]

9

THE NEW THREAT

Walk down a street or the steps to a subway in London, New York, Paris or Sydney. Sit on a cafe terrace in Copenhagen, Amsterdam, Madrid or Los Angeles, if the weather permits, and read a book, a novel perhaps, or even a recently published tome on current affairs. Order another coffee, or beer, or glass of wine, or fizzy water. Call a friend, worry about your career, ponder your favourite sports team's championship prospects, look forward to dinner with the family, plan a holiday with a loved one. Look at those around you, all doing much the same thing.

Nothing you see will tell you that you are facing any particular threat. There may be a policeman or two more than usual – their weapons only remarkable if you are in the UK – or perhaps some additional security evident when you take the train or bus or drive home. You will almost certainly no longer notice the barriers, metal detectors and security guards outside certain buildings in the city where you live or work. All have been part of the landscape for a decade or more, like the reports of violent conflict in distant, dusty countries. You notice them only when there is an 'incident', a seemingly random attack on a soft target somewhere in Europe or the US or against foreign tourists visiting a museum or a beach resort somewhere hot and Islamic. Then, with al-Qaeda, the Islamic State, lone wolves and extremism back in the headlines, you may, suddenly, feel a sharp, if fleeting, sense of vulnerability. At that instant, you have just become a victim of terrorism.

There are many definitions of terrorism, and no clear consensus has ever emerged on which one should be adopted in international law and by policymakers, let alone in the media or by the general public. One study found 109 different definitions suggested by academics and others between 1936 and 1981. The US government alone has used dozens of different definitions over the decades.[1] If knowledge of terrorism has increased enormously since 2001, the debate about its nature and causes is as divided and heated as ever. In this work, and my previous books, I have preferred to use the terms militant or violent extremist to describe, however imperfectly, those who are often called terrorists. This is not to downplay their atrocities, or suggest in any way that their acts of violence might be justified, but is simply an effort to avoid the distracting controversy which goes with the word. In fact, terrorism can be defined relatively easily. In its broadest sense, terrorism is a tactic which involves the use of violence against civilian targets to achieve political, social or religiously conceived aims through the provocation of fear. Lots of different actors do this – state and non-state, local and international. Plenty combine terrorism with other tactics or strategies too. Few, however, willingly accept what is, to almost everyone, a powerfully pejorative description.[2]

Of course, the simplest and most significant point about terrorism, shared by many (though not all) definitions of the term, is that its aim is to terrorise: to cause extreme fear of the kind that might even lead us to act irrationally, to behave without thinking, to panic, in short. Some terrorists never physically harm anyone or destroy anything, but simply threaten to do so. They exploit both the natural human instinct of self-preservation and our sense of collective solidarity to prompt the fear that they seek. The modern concept of terrorism has its origins in the late eighteenth century and 'La Terreur', a bid by the French revolutionary government to defend their radical project by intimidating all potential opponents through spectacular public violence, largely executions. It was the fear that the guillotine inspired, rather than the number of heads in baskets on what was to become the Place de la Concorde, that was important. Terrorism's greatest effects are thus achieved indirectly, through the reaction it inspires rather than the actual destruction of life and property. This is why, in that moment when, having read of an attack or the threat of an attack, you experience a sudden pang of fear, you become a victim yourself.

The fact that the number of people to have been killed in Britain in terrorist attacks by Islamic militants – fifty-three – is statistically negligible is irrelevant.[3] We know the actual chances of being hurt in even a sustained terrorist campaign are minimal, but when scrolling down headlines on your phone or tablet, and you come across news of a major road accident, outbreak of disease or simply the mortality rates of heart disease or cancer, you do not feel the same anxiety, or dread fascination, as you do when reading of a bomb blast or shooting, even though any of these scourges of modern life is infinitely more likely to cause harm to you or your loved ones. The reason, obviously, is that it appears utterly impossible to know when and where such an event might take place. The violence appears utterly unpredictable. Many of the places where we usually feel safe – trains, airports, schools – suddenly become danger zones. We extrapolate from the individual attack, and turn it into a general rule. A gunman has attacked a museum, so no museum is safe. A classroom, thousands of miles away, has been bombed, and we cannot help but wonder if that could, might, happen here. Our faith in the institutions we have built to protect us is shaken. Terrorism undermines the legitimacy of the state by demonstrating its inability to fulfil its fundamental function of protecting its citizens as they go about their daily lives. It threatens too the state's all-important monopoly on the legitimate use of violence.[4] We all recognise this instinctively. A single bomb on a bus is manageable for policymakers. Two is a serious problem. Three can bring about the fall of a government, simply because there is a general consensus, among officials, policymakers and voters, that those in charge are no longer doing their job. We may understand that the threat is not immediate, but it appears present, everywhere and at all times, and this makes us feel deeply vulnerable. Life or death, injury or health, seems a lottery. This sense of perpetual menace is what the terrorists seek above all, for this is what will mobilise pressure on policymakers to change policies, weaken economies, or simply influence the way millions of people see themselves and the world. It is also what inspires us to raise the drawbridge, shun the foreign or the different, narrow the channels of communication and exchange, and return to the comforting certainties of what we think is sure and familiar.

If the terrorists' aim is to appear ubiquitous, unknowable, entirely unforeseeable, then it follows that our aim must be to try to identify and assess the reality of the overall threat they pose. And this is what the remaining pages of this book seek to do.

Over the previous chapters I have outlined the principal components of Islamic militancy today. These are the two major groups which are currently operational – the Islamic State and al-Qaeda; there are the networks of affiliates that both have established as well as other independent groups that may or may not pose a danger to the West; and there is the movement of Islamic militancy. Each currently poses different threats in different ways, but the last decade or so has taught us that it is when elements of one or other category combine forces that we should be most concerned.

One clear threat at the time of writing remains al-Qaeda. Though the group is undoubtedly much weaker than it was a decade ago, it is still committed to pursuing broadly the same strategy formulated by bin Laden during the 1990s. Al-Qaeda still aims to inflict damage and fear on the West to dissuade intervention in the Islamic world as well as to mobilise and radicalise the *umma* through acts of spectacular violence. It aims to construct a caliphate, though as a long-term aspiration, not an immediate goal. It has increasingly localised its operations, but has retained an interest in developing the capacity to strike in the West.

Al-Qaeda's ongoing rivalry with the Islamic State will no doubt spur the group to make greater efforts to execute a spectacular international operation like those which established its pre-eminence in the world of Islamic militancy fifteen or so years ago. To do this the group may well leverage the resources of its network of affiliates which, though battered, still exists. Most of these affiliates appear primarily focused on local or regional targets for the moment, so the most likely candidate for close collaboration on or subcontracting of such a project would be al-Qaeda in the Arabian Peninsula. However, with the energies of the latter currently largely devoted to exploiting, or surviving, recent upheavals in Yemen, and its capable leader, Nasir al-Wuhayshi, killed in a US missile strike in June 2015, the al-Qaeda senior commanders in Pakistan may be forced to seek alternatives. The affiliate in Syria, Jabhat al-Nusra, is still struggling to hold off IS and it seems unlikely that its commanders on the ground would be enthusiastic about diverting resources to open a front against the Far Enemy. Al-Shabaab, if it is still an affiliate, is also clearly focused on its local campaign, and what is left of al-Qaeda in the Maghreb appears unlikely to be of much assistance either. The group may have to call on any remaining assets in South Asia to fill the gap.

The second major danger is that the Islamic State escalates its current carefully calibrated strategy of calling for individuals to mount their own strikes in the West to direct involvement in a campaign of terrorist violence within European nations or across the Atlantic. There are already signs of such an escalation. From a position of eschewing all international targets, IS first shifted to calls for leaderless jihad in the West, then, using local affiliates, to attacks on Western targets in the Islamic world such as tourists in Tunisia. The next stage of this fairly typical progression is obvious: to attempt to strike hard in the West itself.

But though this might also fit with the rhetoric and world view of many of the IS leaders, particularly those of a more apocalyptic cast of mind, there are reasons to believe it will not occur immediately. First, the more pragmatic of the senior commanders may see such a campaign as counter-productive. It would prompt a powerful response from the West which, even if it did not involve ground troops, would be unwelcome, as it would distract from the state-building project of IS and it would drain resources from the battle against the Shia in the region. It could also jeopardise local support from tribes and factions uninterested in global campaigns but which might well be worst hit by Western reprisals. Much will depend on the degree to which Abu Bakr al-Baghdadi, the self-appointed caliph, and the former Ba'ath Party officials and military men who exercise significant power within the organisation agree on strategy. The former appears to genuinely believe he is a protagonist, chosen by God, to play a key role in the final and imminent battle between good and evil. The latter appear more prag-matic. The future direction of the movement may depend on who exercises the greatest influence, and, of course, who remains alive.

For it is likely the IS leader, who has repeatedly been reported to have been seriously injured, will be killed eventually. What might then happen is entirely unclear. Could the group agree on another leader? Could they find one with the same capabilities and apparent authority? Would he become caliph? Would the loss sufficiently weaken IS for other rival militant groups in Syria, the Iraqi government, so-called 'moderate' factions or even the Assad regime to roll back its advances?[5]

The answer to these questions would lie in the evolution of the environment in which IS operates as much as the internal dynamics of the group. IS emerged through exploiting opportunities created by the multiple weaknesses of local and, to a lesser extent, international powers. As long as these remain, so too will the group, in one form or another. It has thrived also on the increasingly sectarian nature of the conflict in the region, which is likely to intensify as regional powers, primarily Iran, and organisations, such as Hezbollah and a variety of hard-line Shia paramilitary groups, seek to bolster Assad in Syria and the government in Baghdad. In late spring 2015, there were suggestions that a stalemate had set in. IS had been pushed out of some marginal territories, and even out of the solidly Sunni city of Tikrit. Yet in May IS enjoyed perhaps its most successful week since the campaigns of June 2014, taking Ramadi, an important city in western Iraq an hour's drive from Baghdad, and Palmyra, the desert town famous for its Roman-era ruins 120 miles east of Damascus. The best-case scenario over the next two to five years is that IS is somehow pushed out of all the territory in Iraq over which its hold is tenuous at the moment, including Mosul, and if, and it's a very big if, events in Syria take some kind of marginally more positive turn, then IS could also be worn down there to a fragmented, tenacious but significantly less dangerous remnant. The worst-case scenario, sadly more likely, is that those fighting IS remain disunited, committed to narrow sectarian or other agendas, blinded by a short-term vision of their own interests, and weak, and the group itself becomes more entrenched in the areas it currently controls, able to pick off targets of opportunity as they arise to capture new territory.

A major consideration, though, must be what capability IS actually has to strike the West. Though it has significantly more conventional arms and many more fighters than any other Islamic militant movement has ever possessed, this does not necessarily translate into the power to launch attacks overseas. In today's security environment, for IS as for al-Qaeda, sending teams of Syrian or Iraqi bombers into France or Germany or the US is extremely difficult and any such effort would at the very least require them first to have established a local presence in the target country. IS needs to create those critical connections outside its own organisation, as al-Qaeda has done, if it is to pose a genuine threat. Its outreach effort may not be much use in this regard. Of the various 'governorates' established around the Islamic world, perhaps only the groups in Libya and Tunisia might be able to reach into Europe. Certainly Boko Haram or a handful of disaffected Afghan commanders will not provide that capability.

The obvious candidates to fill the gap would be European veterans of the wars in Syria and Iraq who fought with IS and either maintained contact with the group after returning home, or who could be sent home with orders to prepare a campaign of terrorist violence. But no one is entirely certain how likely, or even feasible, this might be. One historical parallel to the role the Syrian conflict is currently playing in the general landscape of contemporary Islamic militancy is the role Afghanistan played, with a few short breaks, for around three decades from the early 1980s. From then until only a few years ago, the country, and of course the adjacent strip of largely ungoverned land over the border in Pakistan, drew somewhere between 25,000 and 30,000 foreign volunteers, and perhaps more. Some, maybe several thousand, came from the West. This is similar to the number and composition of the 'foreign fighters' today in Syria. Life in contemporary training camps run by IS resembles that in earlier Afghan counterparts, though it is of course considerably more comfortable. There is the same mixture of physical and psychological conditioning – especially important for 'soft' Europeans unused to any hardship – the same basic training in light weapons and the same process of selecting certain volunteers for more advanced missions, whether local suicide attacks or, potentially, something more far-ranging.[6] There are reports of at least one camp being called 'al-Farouq', in homage either to the second caliph, or to the famous al-Qaeda camp near Kandahar where the 9/11 hijackers were first selected for their mission, or indeed both.[7] There is also the same initiation for some volunteers into greater and greater violence, and advancement into leadership roles for others, just as was the case among Afghan trainees. Few, it is fair to suppose, left for Syria attracted by the idea of taking part in beheadings, but in a brutalising environment of conflict, surrounded by fellow believers and others who have already been hardened to horrific levels of cruelty, outlook and behaviour can change. Afghan veterans were at the forefront of successive waves of violence around the Islamic world throughout the late 1980s and early 1990s. Many played a significant role until very recently. Some still do. It seems likely, or at least very possible, that Syrian veterans will play a similar role in years to come.

However, it is still very unclear quite how useful the historic lessons of Afghanistan might be. Many of those Europeans who travelled to Afghanistan, and other conflict zones, over previous decades ended up dead, maimed, disillusioned with the whole militant project, or, even if they did return, were no more enthused by the idea of killing people in their native lands than when they left home.[8] For some, such experiences were certainly a gateway into more active violence. Omar Saeed Sheikh, the LSE graduate who became infamous for his role in Pakistan-based groups in the 1990s, was one. The transformative experience for him was charity work during the conflict in Bosnia. But at the same time, hundreds of young British men were fighting in Kashmir, some making the journey from Pakistan into the disputed territory to battle Indian security forces several times. I knew a few, and though most described the experience as hugely important to them, none had even contemplated violence in the UK on their return. Admittedly, this was before the culture of contemporary transnational militancy had begun to spread more widely among young Muslim men born in the West, but even a decade later, in 2006, a London-based businessman remembered his own journey via Pakistan to Afghanistan as 'a bitter experience'. The sight of wounded foreign volunteers who had sought to fight for the Taliban leaving an assault in the back of a pickup truck convinced him that he was there as 'cannon fodder, nothing more', and on his return he set up a small NGO working to stop others repeating his experience.

Then there is the precedent of Iraq. Hundreds of men from the West went to Iraq between 2003 and 2008, primarily to fight the US occupying forces. Though it was widely predicted that they would come back and launch terrorist attacks at home, few actually did. And if there are signs that many Europeans who travel to the territory held by IS are drawn into greater and greater radicalism, there is evidence too that some are profoundly disappointed by the gulf between their expectations and the reality. Recent studies looking at the phenomenon of 'foreign fighters' over decades have suggested that between one in seven and one in forty individuals who return from such conflict zones become involved in violence once back home.[9]

The truth is that with this particular component of the overall threat to the West, we are in uncharted territory. In 2014, police officers in the UK made 165 arrests for offences linked to Syria, including terrorist financing, commission, preparation or instigation of acts of terrorism, and attending a terrorist training camp. This was more than six times the total of 2013 and constituted almost exactly half of all terrorist-related arrests in Britain over the year.[10] In Europe, there were also worrying signs. Beyond the attack by Mehdi Nemmouche, the gunman who shot four dead in the Jewish museum in Brussels in May 2014, there was a young Frenchman arrested in Cannes with explosives six months later shortly after returning from Syria, and a group of Syrian veterans who were detained after a firefight in Belgium in January 2015. They had been planning a shooting spree in Brussels. Yet of the fifty to two hundred US citizens who are thought to have actually travelled to Syria in recent years,[11] senior officials said only a 'relatively small number' had joined IS, even fewer had returned to the US, and none had so far been identified as 'engaged in attack plotting.'

A further concern is that one of the many independent groups that are currently uninterested in attacks in the West might conceivably become so in the future. A substantial number of these are based in South Asia – an area which this book has not covered in the depth it deserves and one which is entering a period of some instability as almost all remaining US troops pull out of Afghanistan and seek to put a definitive end to the international involvement there. The three of most concern are the Afghan Taliban, the Pakistani Taliban and Lashkar-e-Toiba, the Pakistan-based group responsible for the 2008 attacks in Mumbai. There are several key differences between them. The Afghan Taliban, a movement with numerous sub-factions and strands, has always stuck to a nominally nationalist agenda and shunned international terrorism. Even back in the 1990s, many within the Taliban saw the global agenda of the largely Arab extremists living in Afghanistan as an irritant, even a threat to their regime. Since, relations have evolved, but though personal associations developed between senior al-Qaeda militants and Taliban leaders during the decade after the 2001 war, these by no means indicated a convergence of organisation, method or aims. The Afghan Taliban by 2015 was divided between more hard-line ground commanders and an apparently more moderate senior leadership based mainly in Pakistan which had been involved in an intermittent peace process for several years. It had also, in a precedent useful when looking at IS and the trouble it is likely to have expanding beyond Sunni-dominated areas, been unable to spread far beyond rural areas dominated by the Pashtun ethnicity, who constitute around 40 to 45 per cent of the total population and had always been its core constituency. There was certainly no immediate indication that the movement would lurch suddenly towards either launching terrorist attacks on the West anywhere outside Afghanistan, or permitting others to do so from the territory they controlled.

As for the Pakistani Taliban (Tehreek-e Taliban Pakistan, TTP), any cohesion among its varied factions and commanders had largely collapsed by the spring of 2015. This was not necessarily a good thing for the West, as the rare previous occasions when the TTP had been linked to international terrorism had been the result of individual commanders within the movement seeking some kind of internal advantage over rivals, or simply going 'off-message' and ignoring the orders of more senior leaders to prioritise the local battle against Pakistani security forces. The TTP had been badly hit by a series of offensives launched by the Pakistani Army in 2013 and 2014, which was one reason for the horrific attack on a school patronised by military families in Peshawar in December 2014 in which more than 130 children died. Fragmented, disorganised and, in some cases, desperate, the TTP posed a threat because of its weakness, rather than its strength. In such a state, it is always possible that one of its commanders will come across an opportunity, like a group of young British or American volunteers, to cause serious harm. But this scenario, though plausible, is nonetheless improbable. As with their Afghan counterparts, it is hard to imagine a serious threat from the TTP to the West in the immediate future.

Finally there is Lashkar-e-Toiba (LeT), which, despite claims to the contrary, does not have, and has never had, links to al-Qaeda. Its leaders have, in part because of their close relationship with the Pakistani security agencies, always maintained a focus on the local region, India and particularly Kashmir. LeT does have, however, a long history of factions breaking away to join forces with extremists who are committed to a more international agenda. LeT's effective and organised global support network has never previously been exploited for any kind of long-range terrorist operation but would be a very significant asset should the leadership of the group, for whatever reason, decide that they wanted to launch one.[12]

Beyond the established groups, and the affiliates and the independents, there is of course the movement, which is the primary concern of the last two chapters of this book. Swelling the ranks of the its members is an explicit focus of both al-Qaeda and IS. 'To my Muslim brothers residing in the states of the Zionist–Crusader alliance . . . know that Jihad is your duty as well . . . You have an opportunity to strike the leaders of unbelief and retaliate against them on their own soil,' Adam Gadahn, a US convert who regularly offered media advice to bin Laden and al-Zawahiri, said in a broadcast tape as early as 2010.[13] 'Strike the soldiers, patrons, and troops of the [tyrants]. Strike their police, security . . . as well as their treacherous agents. Destroy their repose. Embitter their lives for them and busy them with themselves. If you can kill a disbelieving American or European – especially the spiteful and filthy French – or an Australian, or a Canadian, or any other disbeliever from the disbelievers waging war . . . against the Islamic State, then rely upon Allah, and kill him in any manner or way however it may be,' said Adnani, the former mason turned IS main spokesman, in September 2014.[14] And exhortations such as this from IS are having an effect: individual attackers in Australia, the US and Denmark in the first half of 2015 all claimed to be acting on behalf of IS. A shooting at a Prophet Mohammed cartoon contest in Texas in May was actually claimed by IS itself.[15] In Canada, an attack took place when an aspirant IS volunteer was *prevented* from travelling to Syria. More generally, though few around the world may react to the repeated calls that al-Qaeda and IS broadcast, there is little reason to imagine that the movement and the violent activism it fosters will weaken any time soon. It is simply too well established.

Within this context, one real threat from Syria and other conflicts may not be a direct physical one but rather a less tangible but potentially more significant danger: that of returning veterans who do not get involved in any terrorist violence themselves but who help propagate extremist ideas among others. The role of these more experienced men, with the spurious credibility derived from seeing combat, as a vector for violent extremist ideologies has been demonstrated again and again over recent years.

None of this is particularly heartening, but then few threat assessments ever are. This has induced a form of 'threat fatigue' in Western publics. Security officials tend to see this as a problem, but it could equally be seen as the healthy result of a much greater general understanding of the danger Islamic militancy actually poses. Over the last decade, an astonishing amount of information about Islamic militancy has become available. In 1995, there were around a thousand books with terrorism in the title; by 2011, there were ten times as many.[16] In 1997, no one outside specialist circles had heard of al-Qaeda. Now there is barely a day without a news story somewhere in the world mentioning the group. There are lots of articulate and perceptive analysts working in the field, and a huge body of academic research on everything from pre-Islamic poetry in the Arabian peninsula (essential for understanding the meanings of the vocabulary used in the Koran) to the network analysis of the social dynamics of recruitment among contemporary extremist groups. Many of the more dubious commentators who were so prolific in the immediate aftermath of the 9/11 attacks have been marginalised. The publics in the UK, US and Europe are both increasingly informed and increasingly sceptical of claims of officials and politicians about if, why and how they should worry.

This scepticism is often justified. Knowledge may mean power, but power does not necessarily mean knowledge. Even when the facts are known, decisions may be based on other concerns. Security services have strong professional and institutional motives for erring on the side of caution, particularly when discussing a domestic threat. 'We'd be daft to say it's all under control, we'd just get our budgets cut,' one MI5 officer admitted in a moment of unexpected frankness over a drink in a Whitehall pub at the end of the last decade.[17] Policymakers are now aware that exaggerated claims of threats can be counterproductive, damaging their own credibility but also that of agencies like the police or security services who need the public's confidence in order to keep them safe. This is weighed against a need to remind the public to be vigilant and, more nefariously, to convince them that yet another increase in the security services' powers is justified. The difficulty that legislators face when arguing for more surveillance or greater powers of detention is usually countered with dire warnings of what might happen if Parliament does not acquiesce. There is also the simple truth that none will risk the accusation of having been complacent in the aftermath of an attack. The penalty of publicly underestimating a threat is considerably higher than overestimating it. The oft-cited mantras of anti-terrorist officials are 'it only takes one to slip through' and 'they have to be lucky once, we have to be lucky all the time'. Such statements are accurate but entirely unhelpful when it comes to policymaking.

Of course, the greater the uncertainty, the more vulnerable any assessment of danger is to exaggeration and exploitation, and in this case it is the very rarity of such attacks that makes them so especially hard to predict. Take the risk of a major attack using some kind of biological or chemical agent. Between 1998 and 2001, bin Laden did describe the obtaining of chemical weapons as a religious duty and even claimed to have stockpiled such arms as a 'deterrent'. Al-Qaeda also made desultory efforts to build laboratories in Afghanistan. I visited the biggest such facility, in a camp near the eastern Afghan city of Jalalabad, just days after it had been vacated by extremists in November 2001 and saw quite how basic the operations were: a small hut crammed with sacks of chemicals and apparatus found in most school science laboratories. In 2002 in London, a supposed plot to create ricin, a poison, from castor beans turned out to be largely bogus, the work of an Algerian agent provocateur.[18] In 2003, Saudi and US intelligence services claimed to have learned of a plot to release cyanide gas on the New York subway system, though no one was ever arrested nor evidence released to the public. One of the main sources for US claims that Saddam Hussein had a substantial biological weapons programme before the invasion of Iraq later confessed he had fabricated his entire story to bring down a hated, repressive regime.[19] A few simple questions I put to a captive militant held in northern Iraq who had supplied information to Western intelligence services about Saddam Hussein's supposed supply of chemical weapons to al-Qaeda immediately established that he was lying: he had never been to Afghanistan, or met bin Laden, as he claimed. The 'factories' in northern Iraq run by Islamic militants who had carved out an enclave there before the conflict turned out to be basic in the extreme too. In 2004, Jordanian authorities claimed Abu Musab al-Zarqawi had planned a strike with chemical weapons on the US

Embassy in Amman and a range of other targets. Al-Zarqawi denied the planned use of chemicals, though was happy to admit the existence of the plot. No evidence was offered to contradict him. Little has emerged in recent years to counter the conclusion that all these various examples encourage: that the fear of chemical or biological weapons is unjustified.

Such arms are, after all, extremely difficult to produce, store, weaponise and use effectively. They are almost certainly beyond the capabilities of any extant Islamic militant group. Some commentators point to the example of the Aum Shinrikyo sect in Japan, which was able to manufacture sarin gas and release it on the metro in Tokyo in 1995. But the sect had a billion dollars in assets, access to state-of-the-art scientific facilities, highly qualified and capable experts, a degree of toleration from authorities, and political connections within the Japanese establishment.[20] Even IS has nothing approaching these resources today.[21] The group has reportedly inserted chlorine into mortar bombs to make chlorine gas, which is prohibited by the 1997 Chemical Weapons Convention.[22] But this First World War technology is of limited lethality and very far from being a weapon of mass destruction. On the other hand, the Syrian regime, though almost all of its nastiest weapons have been destroyed, has repeatedly used chemical arms, killing hundreds at least and neatly demonstrating that it is really only states that have the wherewithal to manufacture and deploy even basic versions of these arms locally, let alone thousands of miles away. True, a state may one day pass such a weapon to a militant group, but this brings us back to the original problem: if all policy decisions were made on the basis of what could conceivably occur, rather than what will probably occur, government would be impossible. No state has previously transferred such technology to terrorists, nor does any state appear likely to in the short or mid-term. There is much that can be done, and should be done, to reduce that possibility but it should be seen for what it is: extremely unlikely.

Perhaps the most familiar doomsday scenario involves fanatical terrorists in possession of a nuclear device. This is equally implausible. Bin Laden vetoed a suggestion to target a nuclear power plant with one of the planes on 9/11. A supposed plot to use a 'dirty bomb' – a low-tech device which spreads mildly radioactive material through conventional means – in the US in 2002, much publicised by the Bush administration at the time, was based on a spoof article about how to make an 'H-bomb', which a US convert who had trained in an Afghan camp and then returned to the US might have read and, just possibly, might have taken seriously.[23] Bin Laden held some kind of discussions in August 2001 with a Pakistani nuclear scientist who had extremist views, but otherwise there is no evidence that al-Qaeda or any other Islamic militant group have even begun to look for such arms. One scenario that is occasionally suggested is that Islamic militants somehow raid Pakistani nuclear facilities. But the nuclear arsenal in Pakistan is kept in numerous locations, with weapons disassembled and spread across various sites. So a militant group would have to have exact intelligence about the location of each component of a weapon, then be able to find them, seize them and finally assemble them. All this would seem, by any stretch of the imagination, an almost impossible task for groups which so far have relied on little more sophisticated than assault rifles, grenades, box cutters, fairly banal commercial or home-made explosives and ingenuity. If the egregious manipulation of public opinion or media sensationalism seen in the early part of the last decade is rarer now, old habits die hard. In the aftermath of the Islamic State's seizure of Mosul in 2014, British newspapers reported that forty kilograms of uranium stolen from science laboratories in the city's university had been used by IS to make a dirty bomb.[24] The source was a boast by supposed militants in Syria on Twitter and was entirely uncorroborated. Almost a year later, the Australian foreign minister made a similar claim, raising the prospect of a 'large and devastating' attack.[25]

So where does this leave us? The Islamic State has dramatically changed the landscape of extremism but so far has not altered the threat to the West in the same way. There remains the possibility of mass-casualty attacks, probably closer in form to those seen in Madrid and London in 2004 and 2005 than to the 9/11 attacks or the abortive bid to bring down half a dozen transatlantic planes in 2006, but only if the major groups manage to lever the capabilities of their affiliates or successfully find volunteers in Western countries. There is also a greater likelihood of low-tech, DIY attacks by individuals and small groups which emerge from the potent movement of extremism. Taken together, this is enough to be worrying, but is not a threat that can realistically be termed 'existential'.[26] It is no reason to be relaxed, of course, but our communities, societies and nations have weathered far worse. The real impact of Islamic militancy will not be felt in the places where this book is likely to be read. It is in the Islamic world where the monthly death toll frequently exceeds the total in the West over the last decade.

This is not to minimise the costs of such terrorism to the West, however, nor of the effort to counter the threat it poses. Though less obvious than a blast in a Tube train or a shooting at a synagogue, the indirect impact of Islamic militancy on our lives is significant. The cost in civil liberties has been high. In every country in the West over the last decade and a half, citizens have given up substantial rights in the name of security. We have also spent, and continue to spend, an enormous amount of money in the effort to keep ourselves safe. There has been the vast expense of the controversial wars fought in Afghanistan, Iraq and elsewhere, estimated in the trillions of dollars.[27] By June 2015, the US had spent $2.7 billion on its bombing campaign against IS, with the overall cost of its military operations in Iraq and Syria running at more than $9 million a day.[28] The budget for the US National Intelligence Program, which includes the CIA, military intelligence agencies and several others, has been around $50 billion each year for the last eight, while that for the Department of Homeland Security is around $40 billion. The single intelligence account from which GCHQ, MI5 and MI6 are funded in the UK receives more than £2 billion every year of public funds.[29] These are huge sums, particularly at a time of economic hardship for all Western nations. Then there is private sector expenditure on 'security', which is considerable and unquantified but has helped create and sustain an industry that has become a powerful and influential actor itself. This is not a positive development.

Added to these costs are those caused indirectly by the ongoing instability in the Middle East, to which extremism evidently contributes significantly. The new surge of Islamic militancy, and particularly the growing sectarian divide throughout the Muslim world that it exacerbates, impacts on the price of oil and gas, for example, having massive consequences on economies across the globe. A constant security threat means that countries like Pakistan, Libya, Egypt, even the giant Nigeria, remain unable to address all the other problems of development that afflict them. Trade deals languish; important reforms are postponed; neighbourly relations deteriorate; counter-productive strategic decisions are taken based on the apparently urgent, short-term need to eliminate a physical threat; terrorist violence is used to justify the state's violence; the security establishment and the military is reinforced; crime flourishes. All this makes the world a less safe place for everyone. Problems with indirect effects on our lives have an unwelcome habit of becoming direct ones. The sudden surge of migrants across the Mediterranean from Libya in the summer of 2015 was, at least in part, a consequence of extremism. Who, having made the hellish journey from sub-Saharan or eastern Africa, both areas racked by militant violence, to the North African shore, would now want to remain in a region where men can not only execute a dozen or more people on a beach, but release a video of their acts that is seen by huge numbers of people around the world and escape any kind of sanction? There are other costs too, incalculable for the moment. In a few decades we may well look back on the effort and resources committed over the last decade or two to countering terrorism, and try hard to remember why we decided this was a greater priority than mitigating the growing threat posed by climate change.

But perhaps the greatest damage done so far – beyond the sheer loss of human life and the physical destruction that has resulted from the phenomenon of Islamic militancy and the efforts of the West and its allies to eradicate it – is to relations between communities at a global and a local level.

Surveys of the attitudes of populations in the Arab or Islamic world towards their Western counterparts make almost as depressing reading as threat assessments. The US-based Pew Center has completed a series of surveys over the post-9/11 era. These revealed the rapid decline of support for al-Qaeda and its methods from around 2004 onwards and, especially important, the correlation between that decline in any one country and the advent of a campaign of violence there. Pew's surveys between 2011 and 2014 found much that was heartening. A vast poll of Muslims across the world in 2013 revealed that support for suicide bombing still remained limited, concerns about extremism were high, and levels of support for al-Qaeda remained low. But the same survey also found that at least half of respondents in the majority of countries surveyed believed Western popular culture was harmful to morality, that relatively few Muslims found the idea of intermarriage acceptable, and that a substantial

minority of Muslims in twenty-four of the twenty-six countries said
'most' or 'many' Muslims and Christians were hostile towards one
another.[30] There was also little to suggest that the findings of two
earlier surveys, between 2003 and 2011, were no longer valid either.
These had examined Muslims' views of non-Muslims and vice versa
across the world. They had revealed a deeply worrying trend. The
proportion of people in the West who said they viewed Muslims
'favourably' or 'somewhat favourably' had remained more or less
steady, at between around two-thirds in the US, UK and France over
the period, and had risen from around one-third to closer to a half
in Germany and Spain. But almost everywhere in the Islamic world
the view of Christians and Jews had become more negative. In
Indonesia and Jordan, the decline was limited, with around half the
Muslim populations of each country still saying they saw Christians
favourably in 2011. But elsewhere it was dramatic. In Turkey, 31 per
cent of people had said they saw Christians favourably in 2003, only
21 per cent in 2005, and only 6 per cent five years later. In Pakistan,
the level was just over 25 per cent in 2006 but had dropped to 16 per
cent in 2011. In no state surveyed did more than 17 per cent of
respondents say they felt favourably towards Jews, with the level down
to 2 or 3 per cent in most countries by 2011.[31]

Even less encouraging were responses to questions about the qualities
associated by Muslims with the West. Around two-thirds in 2011 said
they thought people in the West were selfish, greedy and violent, while
more than a half thought they were immoral, arrogant and fanatical.
These were higher levels than five years before. The proportion of people
in the Islamic world believing that Arabs had carried out the 9/11 attacks
was under 30 per cent everywhere, 9 per cent in Turkey, and dropped
below its level in 2006 in many places. Those believing that the West
was fundamentally hostile to Muslims were in a solid majority pretty
much everywhere, more than 70 per cent in places, with the proportion
again increasing over the years.[32]

And though Pew had found that the Western view of Muslims and
the Islamic world was more positive, and had improved marginally over
the period, other pollsters, particularly in the US, did not. In October
2001, one survey found that 47 per cent of Americans viewed Islam
favourably. This had declined to 37 per cent by 2010, and to only 27 per
cent in 2014.[33] Significantly, the survey also showed much depended on

age, with younger respondents consistently more favourable towards Muslim Americans – largely, it was presumed, because they are more likely to actually come into contact with any.

This was encouraging in that it indicated some hope of improvement in the future, but underlined too why extremists are so committed to driving communities apart, physically as well as emotionally and politically. To reiterate a point made several times already in this book, the aims of terrorist violence are threefold. The first is to terrorise enemies, and thus, through the functioning of democracy, to force the leaders of those democracies to make decisions that they would not otherwise have made. The second is to mobilise supporters by inspiring them into action. The third aim is perhaps the most important. Here, the violence is addressed to the uncommitted, the swing voters in the global struggle between right and wrong, belief and unbelief. These are the people within a terrorist's own community, or a particular constituency of significance in their campaign, who need to be convinced of the righteousness of a cause, the efficacy of a strategy, and the ability or vision of a leader. But they are also those who have so far resisted the urge to hate, to retaliate, to use violence themselves among the community which is being targeted. The aim, then, is to polarise.

Al-Qaeda leaders and extremist thinkers more generally have often described their desire to force Muslims around the world to make a choice and to deepen divisions within and between communities. Bin Laden repeatedly spoke of the importance of reducing the immensely complex matrix of identities that each of us is composed of – one's social origins, gender, education, nationality, city, favourite sports team, sexual proclivity, language and so on – to a single marker of faith. Abu Musab al-Zarqawi frequently explained how he sought to use violence to turn communities against each other. In early 2015, in a chilling if lucid editorial in its magazine *Dabiq*, IS laid out its own strategy to eliminate what the writer, or writers, called 'the Gray Zone'.[34] This Gray Zone was, according to IS, what lay between belief and unbelief, good and evil, the righteous and the damned, and home to all those who had yet to commit to the forces of either side too.

The Gray Zone, IS claimed, had been 'critically endangered [since] the blessed operations of September 11th, as these operations manifested two camps before the world for mankind to choose between, a camp of Islam and a camp of kufr'. The magazine even quoted bin Laden, in line with the IS belief that it, rather than the current al-Qaeda, is the true inheritor of his legacy: 'The world today is divided. [President George] Bush spoke the truth when he said, "Either you are with us or you are with the terrorists." Meaning, either you are with the crusade or you are with Islam. Eventually, the Gray Zone will become extinct and there will be no place for grayish calls and movements. There will only be the camp of [the caliphate] versus the camp of kufr.'

Over the years, the anonymous author of the ten-page article claimed, successive violent acts had narrowed the Gray Zone and by the end of 2014 'the time had come for another event to . . . bring division to the world and destroy the Gray Zone everywhere'.

This event, apparently, was the attack on the offices of the satirical magazine *Charlie Hebdo*, in Paris, in January 2015.

The park of Buttes-Chaumont lies in the north-east of Paris. It is not one of the most fashionable neighbourhoods of the French capital, with a very different look and atmosphere from the *beaux quartiers* in the city's west, but it is steadily being gentrified. There is still much public housing and streets dominated by communities of immigrant origins, with lots of halal butchers and busy back-room mosques. There are lots of restaurants and organic food shops serving the new middle classes too.

The park itself commands one of the best views over Paris, and is enjoyed from dawn to dusk by an eclectic collection of elderly and very young locals, occasional tourists, students from nearby schools, aspirant landscape artists, office workers and joggers. Among the last, for a short time in the middle of the last decade, were several young men whose parents were born in Algeria, Tunisia and elsewhere in Africa, but who had all grown up in France. They were part of several interlocking networks spreading across the nation which all supported organisations in Iraq fighting the US occupying forces. They had decided they needed to get fit before joining the mujahideen in Iraq themselves. The training was hardly rigorous: a few sessions of light exercise on the well-clipped grass among the daffodils and chrysanthemums, and a fifteen-minute explanation of how a Kalashnikov worked from a man who had once fired one.[35]

The members of the 'Buttes-Chaumont network', as it became known to police, were young, poor, with few educational qualifications or skills, and from broken homes or chaotic families. None had much knowledge of politics, or religion, or of much at all beyond a life of fast food, hip hop, badly paid temporary jobs, overcrowded apartments in undermaintained housing blocks, cheap cannabis and petty crime. They had been to the same schools, played for the same sports teams and had come together once again to listen to a young and charismatic preacher who had set up his own study circle after publicly arguing with a series of established clerics in the neighbourhood. In 2004 and 2005, eight set off to join the mujahideen. Three were killed, two badly injured and one imprisoned. In court, the survivors described how they had made their decision to travel to Iraq after watching videos of the fighting there, news reports of abuse of prisoners by US soldiers, clips from other conflicts, and after listening to the preacher's argument that jihad was an obligation on all Muslims if one was attacked anywhere in the world. Among those convicted for their roles in the network was a pizza-delivery boy called Chérif Kouachi, twenty-two years old in 2005, who was arrested days before he was due to leave for Iraq.[36]

Kouachi had grown up in care homes in west and central France and had come to Paris in his late teens. For several years, he had done odd jobs and slept on friends' sofas. Before eventually being sentenced to three months in prison for his bid to reach Iraq, Kouachi had been held on remand for more than a year and a half in the huge Fleury-Mérogis prison, Europe's largest, in the southern suburbs of Paris.[37] The prison was known for acute overcrowding, and authorities struggled to keep veteran Islamic militants and ordinary criminals apart in an institution where 3,800 inmates were crammed into space designed for half that number. One of the veterans was Djamel Beghal, a French Algerian and one of those senior extremists active in the violent campaigns of the early 1990s across the Middle East who had fled to the West when local authorities began to gain the upper hand. Beghal had split his time between France and the UK, and had been detained in France in 2001 shortly before the 9/11 attacks while returning to Europe from Afghanistan. Charged with planning to bomb the US Embassy in Paris, he had been jailed for ten years, which gave him the opportunity to preach, organise and convince. He became a mentor to Kouachi.

Beghal's reputation and charisma had drawn other men too. Also in Fleury-Mérogis was Amedy Coulibaly, a serial armed robber whose parents had come from Mali in the 1960s. Small, muscular, energetic, almost febrile, Coulibaly was born in 1982, the only boy among ten children, and had grown up on one of the toughest public housing developments in France. He was no stranger to incarceration and had been robbing shops with guns when still at school. In Fleury-Mérogis, where prisoners were able to mix in the vast recreation yards almost without supervision, Coulibaly had become a close friend of Chérif Kouachi and another follower of Beghal.[38]

Coulibaly and Kouachi continued to see each other on their release. They also sought out Beghal, who had been moved out of Fleury-Mérogis and into house arrest in a small rural village. Surveillance from French security authorities initially turned up little of interest, however. Kouachi got a job in a supermarket, married a young woman who had come to France from Morocco ten years earlier, and had a child. For a honeymoon, the couple travelled to Mecca. On their return, Kouachi's wife gave up her job as a kindergarten teacher and began wearing the full veil. Coulibaly, who had earlier been described by a court-appointed psychiatrist as 'immature' with 'psychopathic tendencies', found employment at a Coca-Cola bottling factory and as a coach in a gym.[39]

He too had a steady partner: a young French woman called Hayat Boumeddiene, whom he had met in 2007. Boumeddiene also had a troubled background, having grown up in care homes after her Algerian mother died and her father remarried, though she had never been in trouble with the law. The couple were hardly observant Muslims, taking holidays in Malaysia and Crete, where Boumeddiene was photographed on a beach in a bikini with her arms around her lover. Coulibaly kept up with his contacts and friends in the underworld, played Internet poker and went clubbing.

Of the two it appears that Boumeddiene was the first to move towards a more rigorous practice of Islam. Just a year or so after the holidays in the sun, in 2010, she gave up her job as a supermarket cashier when it became illegal to wear the full-face veil, or niqab, in public places in France. Quite what Coulibaly made of this is unknown. When police heard the former armed robber's name mentioned in a plan being formulated by Beghal, his mentor in

Fleury-Mérogis, to break a well-known Algerian militant out of prison, they raided the apartment he shared with Boumeddiene and found ammunition for an assault rifle. Coulibaly said he was merely hoping to sell the cartridges but received a four-year sentence. Interviewed by police at the time, his girlfriend denied being an extremist and condemned al-Qaeda attacks. Phone records showed the content of most of the hundreds of text messages that the young woman sent and received every month was phrases from the Koran or other religious texts. She also told the police her boyfriend was less than pious. 'He likes having fun, probably goes to mosque once every two or three weeks, he condemns [al-Qaeda attacks] as well,' she said. 'But he keeps in mind . . . well, the bad things that are done to innocent people in occupied countries, and that it's normal that people who suffer injustices defend themselves and take up arms against their oppressors.'[40]

Quite when Kouachi became interested by extremist Islam is also unclear. At his trial in 2008, Kouachi's lawyers had argued he was a reluctant, or at least naive, member of the Buttes-Chaumont network. This may not have been entirely true. Kouachi had told French security services on his arrest that he had been 'ready to die fighting' in Iraq and co-defendants remembered the young aspirant rapper as at least talking the language of militancy long before their abortive effort to go to war. 'Chérif spoke to me about smashing Jews' shops, or grabbing them in the street to beat them. He spoke about nothing else; that and doing some [attacks] in France before going,' one told investigators. Interviewed by police, the preacher who had formed the group described Kouachi's desire to 'burn synagogues and terrorise Jews'.[41] Any nascent militancy was certainly hardened during his time in Fleury-Mérogis. At the hearing in 2008, after twenty months on remand in the prison, Kouachi refused to stand for a woman judge. In 2010, he too was detained in the dragnet prompted by the discovery of the prison break-out plan but, for lack of evidence of any direct involvement, was released after four months without charge.[42]

So far, there is little very extraordinary in the story of Kouachi, or Coulibaly. Their marginal background, youth and profound ignorance of Islam or the world in general were characteristic of an increasing number of European extremists during the period and are even more so today. So too is the role of prison, of older, more experienced extremists and of an interlinked network of dozens of individuals in their 'radicalisation'. All that is missing is the lack of any great activity online, which suggests that the role of the Internet in extremism today may be sometimes exaggerated. Adhering faithfully to the pattern of other such militants, in August 2011 Kouachi and his older brother Saïd travelled to Yemen where they successfully made contact with elements within, or close to, al-Qaeda's affiliate there.

The contact was fleeting but appears nonetheless to have been very significant. AQAP had occupied the southern coastal towns of Zinjibar eight months before and were downplaying their global jihad in favour of a local one. This was a period where they did not launch any significant attacks on the West. Yet the Kouachi brothers seem to have made contact with Anwar al-Awlaki, the high-profile preacher killed a year later in a US drone attack. Al-Awlaki was not part of the official AQAP hierarchy and so had more liberty of action. According to Chérif Kouachi's public claims, and those of AQAP senior leaders, al-Awlaki both inspired the brothers to launch an attack on *Charlie Hebdo* and provided some funding for it. The pair also received some basic weapons training, an experience of mainly psychological and symbolic importance. It is not hard to learn how to handle an AK-47 – it takes about a day or so – but it is difficult to take the final step to becoming someone who is prepared to kill in cold blood. That the Kouachi brothers could now claim to be 'mujahideen' fighting for 'al-Qaeda' allowed them to frame any attack as a legitimate part of an ongoing war: the murder of unarmed civilians became a military act. They were no longer 'terrorists', they were soldiers of faith. It also allowed AQAP, however tendentiously, to claim their attacks afterwards.

The Kouachi brothers stayed out of trouble on their return to France in the autumn of 2011. Saïd Kouachi had never really been considered a threat by authorities, despite a tangential involvement in the Buttes-Chaumont network and several trips to the Middle East.[43] Steadier and more cautious than his brother, Saïd lived with his wife and child in Reims, a small city east of Paris, where he ran a Koranic bookshop.[44] He was able to bolster his brother's ill-informed extremism with a certain amount of knowledge and argument. Their sister later described how the two men were 'sectarian' in outlook. 'They had an intolerant vision of Islam, certainly. They were very racist towards anyone who wasn't a Muslim or Arab,' she told police.[45]

Though intermittently watched, surveillance on the pair was dropped in early autumn 2014 around the same time as Amédy Coulibaly was released from prison. Coulibaly, now thirty-two, almost immediately married his long-term partner, Boumeddiene. If there had been any doubts over his commitment to extremist Islam before his latest incarceration, there were none after it. Over the following weeks, the couple bought cars on credit using fraudulent papers and then sold them to raise tens of thousands of euros. On 5 January 2015, Coulibaly travelled to Belgium to swap a Mini Cooper for assault rifles, handguns and ammunition. On the 6th, he met Chérif Kouachi late in the evening. On the 7th, at 10.19 a.m. the two men exchanged text messages. Kouachi had left his home in Gennevilliers in the north-western suburbs of Paris a short time before, having told his wife he was going shopping in the city and would be back in the evening or the next morning. An hour and a half later, the Kouachi brothers reached the offices of *Charlie Hebdo* in an anonymous office building on the eastern side of central Paris and the killings began.

The satirical magazine had been a target of Islamic extremists around the world since reprinting caricatures of the Prophet Mohammed in 2006 in the middle of what became known as the Cartoon Crisis. The images in question had been drawn for a Danish newspaper which itself had subsequently been the target of a series of extremist attacks. The outrage they prompted was far from spontaneous, being largely provoked by a group of northern European Islamic clerics who mobilised followers, then lobbied successive governments in the Muslim world to publicly condemn the images. The clerics also included more offensive pictures among those they claimed had been published. Once sufficient anger had been generated, with demonstrations in Afghanistan, Pakistan, Syria, Iran and elsewhere, all government-sanctioned or -organised, the row took on a momentum of its own.[46] *Charlie Hebdo*, which had existed in various forms since 1960 and was part of a long tradition of irreverent and anti-clerical French satire, reprinted the original cartoons alongside similar contributions from their own team of artists. Five years later, the *Charlie Hebdo* offices were destroyed in an arson attack on the eve of publication of a 'sharia' special edition and further cartoons of the Prophet. In 2013, the magazine's editor, Stéphane Charbonnier, was listed in AQAP's *Inspire* magazine alongside Salman Rushdie and Geert Wilders, a Dutch far-right politician, as 'wanted dead or alive for crimes against Islam' with the headline 'A bullet a day keeps the infidel away'.

When the Kouachi brothers entered the *Charlie Hebdo* offices, they first shot a maintenance worker who was sitting at his desk, then sought out Charbonnier. They killed him and then ten others, all members of the editorial team except for one policeman, who had been guarding the editor, and a visiting travel writer. They then left, shouting, '*Allahu Akbar*, God is Great.' Outside, a second policeman tried to stop them, was shot and wounded and begged the advancing gunmen for his life. They ignored his pleas, shooting him again as he lay on the pavement.[47] Then they drove away, changing cars in the north of Paris. Sleeping out in woods, the brothers somehow evaded a vast dragnet for nearly forty-eight hours. Early on 10 January, they stole another car but were recognised and chased by police. After an exchange of fire outside the town of Dammartin-en-Goele, twenty miles north-east of Paris, the two men dumped the vehicle and ran into a small printworks in a light industrial zone. They shook hands with the owner and told a visiting salesman there to leave, explaining 'we don't kill civilians'. When police assault specialists landed on the roof of the works at around five in the afternoon, the brothers emerged shooting, and were killed.

Coulibaly died at almost exactly the same moment. He does not seem to have selected his targets in advance, though his actions were clearly coordinated with those of the Kouachis.[48] Hours after the attack at *Charlie Hebdo* he shot and wounded a jogger in a park near his home in a suburb of south-west Paris. The next day he killed an unarmed policewoman and seriously injured a local authority street cleaner. At around lunchtime on the 10th, probably after somehow communicating with the cornered gunmen in Dammartin-en-Goele, he entered a kosher supermarket in the east of Paris. Coulibaly was wearing body armour and armed with a sub-machine gun, an assault rifle and two handguns. He killed four people and took the remaining customers and staff hostage. He talked to some, threatened others, and made himself a sandwich from food on the shelves. Armed police stormed the shop minutes after receiving word that the siege in Dammartin-en-Goele had ended. Coulibaly did not survive the assault.

If the profiles of the attackers in Paris were familiar, so too was the form of their attacks. Coulibaly had wired the supermarket with explosives according to some reports but killed with firearms, not big bombs. These were the most effective weapons men like the former armed robber and the Kouachis could practically lay their hands on and an indication of the continuing pragmatism of violent extremists in the West.[49] At the offices of *Charlie Hebdo* in particular, the killings resembled executions, with the gunmen shooting unarmed victims from very close range.[50] We do not know if the Kouachis had been watching videos of executions over previous months or years, but it seems likely. As others had frequently done before them, the attackers made efforts to explain their acts. Coulibaly called a TV station from the supermarket; Chérif Kouachi spoke from the printworks when a journalist called a fixed line there.[51] Both justified their violence with the standard arguments, heard so often over a decade or more. All three knew that their actions would almost certainly end in their own deaths. The Kouachi brothers reportedly told police negotiators they wanted to die as martyrs. Certainly none appeared to have any escape plans.

What made the Paris attacks of January 2015 notable were three things. The first was the target. One of the most significant problems facing al-Qaeda over the previous decade or so had been that of preventing others, such as Abu Musab al-Zarqawi in Iraq or al-Shabaab in Somalia, from conducting indiscriminate attacks in the name of al-Qaeda against targets that most Muslims which would consider illegitimate or in which the 'collateral damage' was seen as unjustified. This was particularly the case when the dead were Muslims. Bin Laden and al-Zawahiri had repeatedly tried to mitigate al-Zarqawi's savagery for this reason and both men had repeatedly urged extremists to avoid causing such casualties over subsequent years. The strategy of 'leaderless jihad' magnified this risk. But there was no such danger posed by the choice of *Charlie Hebdo* as a target. Punishing those who had insulted the Prophet was seen as a legitimate objective by many who could not realistically ever be described as extremist. A poll found that 27 per cent of British Muslims said they had some sympathy with the motives of the *Charlie Hebdo* attackers, while a quarter disagreed with the statement that acts of violence against those who publish images of the Prophet can never be justified.[52] The attack was also guaranteed to attract massive attention across the world. The staff of *Charlie Hebdo*, whether one agreed with their views or not, represented certain values that are central to Western traditions of thought and politics – specifically, the belief in freedom of speech. The number who died in the attack on their office was identical to the toll of Merah's rampage, but because of the symbolism of the target the impact was immeasurably greater.

During the attacks, the Kouachis would say they had been sent by al-Qaeda in the Arabian Peninsula. Coulibaly, however, would claim that he was acting for the Islamic State. In the video he prepared before the attacks, which was uploaded in its aftermath by a still unknown third party, the black flag of the group is visible behind him as he speaks. That the Kouachis, with a decade or more of involvement in the movement of Islamic extremism, were loyal to the older group does not seem surprising. Nor does the attraction of IS for Coulibaly, whose involvement was much more recent. This is the second notable lesson to be drawn from the attack: with its newer, fresher, more immediate message and with its more accessible, less austere tone, IS holds an appeal for a new generation of extremists in a way that al-Qaeda increasingly appears to lack. A video from al-Qaeda in the Arabian Peninsula was uploaded within days of the attack, claiming responsibility for the killings at the *Charlie Hebdo* office, but it took care to distance itself from Coulibaly, who it said was acting independently. The Islamic State never explicitly claimed the supermarket attack as their own but did by implication when Boumeddiene surfaced in Syria a month later and gave an interview to *Dabiq*, the organisation's English-language magazine. She had fled France a few days before the operation. In March, she appeared again, without speaking, in an IS video entitled 'Blow Up France II'.

In the turmoil surrounding the Paris attacks, one detail went largely unnoticed. In the car abandoned by the Kouachi brothers during their flight from the site of the shootings in Paris, police discovered two

GoPro cameras. Such devices can be fixed to a helmet or clothing and are often used by practitioners of extreme sports to provide startlingly immediate images of their activities. The third lesson from the attacks in Paris is that extremists will continue to exploit, and be influenced by, developments in media technology and that their use of the media will continue to present us with difficult choices.

This was not the first appearance of such cameras in terrorist acts. Mohamed Merah, the Toulouse and Montauban gunman, had a GoPro camera fixed to his body armour throughout every one of his twelve killings. He filmed his approach to the site of the murders, the deaths themselves, and his escape. Merah spent much of the last thirty-six hours of his life editing these images into a twenty-four-minute clip. He told police he had made arrangements for it to be broadcast. Quite what these were is still unclear but one USB key containing the clip was sent to Al Jazeera. Merah was confident that the network would broadcast the short film because it was always showing 'massacres and bombs and suchlike'. In fact, Al Jazeera, after appeals from victims' relatives and President Nicolas Sarkozy, showed none of the clip because Merah's images revealed 'nothing not already in the public domain'. Mehdi Nemmouche, who will stand trial for the killing of four at the Jewish museum in Brussels in May 2014, also had a GoPro camera but appears to have made some kind of programming error which meant it failed to capture images of his attack. The two GoPro cameras that the Kouachis had purchased a few weeks before the massacre were still in their packaging when they were found in the abandoned car. The one that Coulibaly had bought was not: it was fixed to his body armour throughout the hostage-taking in the supermarket. At least one witness remembered seeing the gunman with a laptop computer, apparently downloading images from the device, with his weapons beside him.[53] No one is entirely sure what happened to the images Coulibaly recorded during the siege of the supermarket, where they are, or what might be done with them. But the next step for the terrorists is obvious and inevitable. It is a live stream of a terrorist attack, the ultimate combination of terrorism and media. The question all of us will face is: will we watch?

There were vast demonstrations of solidarity in France in the days that followed the January attacks. Dozens of world leaders flew into the French capital, including a handful from Muslim-majority states. Saudi Arabia issued a statement condemning a 'cowardly terrorist attack that was rejected by the true Islamic religion'. A 'survivors' edition' of *Charlie Hebdo* sold nearly seven million copies, with generous assistance from the French government and others. The words 'Je suis Charlie' were worn on T-shirts and hats, projected onto buildings, and posted on Twitter and Web pages across the world. 'It is not the prophet who was avenged, it is our religion, our values and Islamic principles that have been betrayed and tainted,' Tariq Ramadan, the high-profile and often controversial commentator and thinker, said.[54] Many other Islamic clerics and leaders expressed similar sentiments, as did large numbers of ordinary Muslims in Europe and beyond. So too did the killers' families. The Muslim policeman who was shot dead outside the *Charlie Hebdo* offices and the Muslim shop assistant who helped his Jewish customers escape from the supermarket were feted as heroes.

On the other hand, there were isolated instances in France of schoolchildren refusing to take part in a minute's silence in memory of the victims, and some #jesuiskouachi hashtags appeared online. In many countries there were protests by Muslims against *Charlie Hebdo*, and particularly the survivors' issue, which was felt to have compounded the magazine's original offence.[55] There was a 500 per cent rise in Islamophobic attacks on mosques in France in the first quarter of 2015, while one survey in the UK three months after the attack suggested that more than half of people felt there was a fundamental clash between Islam and the values of British society.[56] Overall, however, it was clear that the prediction by the Islamic State that the Gray Zone would soon disappear entirely had not come to pass, and nor was it likely to do so any time soon, either in France or anywhere else.

This, amid all the fear, pain and alarm, was good news. The Gray Zone is where all that is best about the world we have created for ourselves exists: it is where there is diversity, tolerance, understanding, discussion and debate. It is where there is exchange and enquiry and curiosity. This is no doubt why it is detested with so much vehemence by extremists, who cannot abide it. The rest of us cannot live without it. The Gray Zone is worth protecting, with all the resources and courage we have, which means with moderation, sense and, of course, with as accurate and impartial an understanding of those who threaten it as possible. The principal aim of terrorism is to 'terrorise', to provoke irrational fear that forces policymakers or populations to alter their thinking or behaviour. To be afraid of terrorism is normal, to be concerned is natural. But it is better to be so in measure and in reason, not in panicked ignorance, and thus win one immediate and important victory.

SELECT BIBLIOGRAPHY

This is a short selection of the books I found useful, or simply enjoyed reading or re-reading, while writing this one. Some are academic and specialist, many are not. They are included here primarily as a guide for anyone interested in pursuing particular themes or topics in greater depth.

Tamim Ansary, *Destiny Disrupted: A History of the World Through Islamic Eyes*, PublicAffairs, 2009

Karen Armstrong, *Fields of Blood: Religion and the History of Violence*, The Bodley Head, 2014

Scott Atran, *Talking to the Enemy: Violent Extremism, Sacred Values, and What It Means to Be Human*, Penguin, 2011

Michael Axworthy, *Revolutionary Iran: A History of the Islamic Republic*, Penguin, 2013

Peter Bergen, *The Osama bin Laden I Know: An Oral History of al-Qaeda's Leader*, Simon & Schuster, 2006

—*Manhunt: The Ten-Year Search for Bin Laden from 9/11 to Abbottabad*, Broadway Books, 2013

Jason Burke, *Al-Qaeda: The True Story of Radical Islam*, Penguin, 2003

—*The 9/11 Wars*, Penguin, 2011

Peter Chilson, *We Never Knew Exactly Where: Dispatches from the Lost Country of Mali*, Foreign Policy, 2013

Patrick Cockburn, *The Rise of Islamic State: ISIS and the New Sunni Revolution*, Verso, 2015

—*Muqtada al-Sadr and the Shia Insurgency in Iraq*, Faber and Faber, 2008

Toby Dodge, *Iraq: From War to a New Authoritarianism*, International Institute for Strategic Studies, 2013

John L. Esposito and Emad El-Din Shahin, eds, *The Oxford Handbook of Islam and Politics*, Oxford University Press, 2013

Jean-Pierre Filiu, *Apocalypse in Islam*, University of California Press, 2012

Fawaz Gerges, *The Rise and Fall of Al-Qaeda*, Oxford University Press, 2011

Masha Gessen, *The Brothers: The Road to an American Tragedy*, Riverhead Books, 2015

Mary Habeck, *Knowing the Enemy: Jihadist Ideology and the War on Terror*, Yale University Press, 2006

Fred Halliday, *Arabia Without Sultans*, Saqi Books, 2001

Mustafa Hamid and Leah Farrall, *The Arabs at War in Afghanistan*, Hurst, 2015

Stig Jarle Hansen, *Al-Shabaab in Somalia: The History and Ideology of a Militant Islamist Group, 2005–2012*, Hurst, 2014

Mohammed Heikal, *Autumn of Fury: The Assassination of President Sadat*, Andre Deutsch, 1983

Bruce Hoffman, *Inside Terrorism*, Columbia University Press, 2nd rev. edn, 2006

Bruce Hoffman and Fernando Reinares, eds, *The Evolution of the Global Terrorist Threat: From 9/11 to Osama bin Laden's Death*, Columbia University Press, 2014

Tom Holland, *In the Shadow of the Sword*, Abacus, 2013

Robert Hoyland, *In God's Path: The Arab Conquests and the Creation of an Islamic Empire*, Oxford University Press, 2015

Andrew Hussey, *The French Intifada: The Long War Between France and its Arabs*, Granta, 2014

Saad Eddin Ibrahim, *Egypt, Islam and Democracy: Critical Essays*, American University in Cairo Press, 2002

Ayesha Jalal, *Partisans of Allah: Jihad in South Asia*, Orient Blackswan, 2008

Dominic Janes and Alex Houen, eds, *Martyrdom and Terrorism: Pre-Modern to Contemporary Perspectives*, Oxford University Press, 2014

Gregory D. Johnsen, *The Last Refuge: Yemen, al-Qaeda, and America's War in Arabia*, Norton, 2012

Hugh Kennedy, *The Great Arab Conquests: How the Spread of Islam Changed the World We Live In*, Da Capo, 2007

Gilles Kepel, *Jihad: The Trail of Political Islam*, I.B. Tauris, 2004

—*Muslim Extremism in Egypt: The Prophet and Pharaoh*, University of California Press, 2003

Gilles Kepel and Jean-Pierre Milelli, *Al-Qaeda in Its Own Words*, Harvard University Press, 2009

Robert Lacey, *Inside the Kingdom: Kings, Clerics, Modernists, Terrorists, and the Struggle for Saudi Arabia*, Penguin, 2010

David Levering Lewis, *God's Crucible: Islam and the Making of Europe, 570–1215*, Norton, 2008

Terry McDermott, *Perfect Soldiers: The 9/11 Hijackers*, HarperCollins, 2005

Peter Mansfield and Nicholas Pelham, *A History of the Middle East*, 4th edn, Penguin, 2013

Justin Marozzi, *Baghdad: City of Peace, City of Blood*, Allen Lane, 2014

Abdelghani Merah and Mohammed Sifaoui, *Mon frère, ce terroriste*, Calmann-Lévy, 2012

Beverly Milton-Edwards and Stephen Farrell, *Hamas: The Islamic Resistance Movement*, Polity, 2010

David Motadel, ed., *Islam and the European Empires*, Oxford University Press, 2014

Vali Nasr, *The Shia Revival: How Conflicts in Islam will Shape the Future*, Norton, 2006

Peter Neumann, *Old and New Terrorism*, Polity, 2009

Raffaello Pantucci, *We Love Death as You Love Life: Britain's Suburban Mujahedeen*, Columbia University Press, 2015

Eric Pelletier and Jean-Marie Pontaut, *Affaire Merah: l'enquete*, Michel Lafon, 2012

Malise Ruthven, *A Fury for God: The Islamist Attack on America*, Granta, 2002

Adam Silverstein, *Islamic History: A Very Short Introduction*, Oxford University Press, 2010

Mike Smith, *Boko Haram: Inside Nigeria's Unholy War*, I.B. Tauris, 2015

Jessica Stern and J.M. Berger, *ISIS: The State of Terror*, HarperCollins, 2015

Devin R. Springer, James L. Regens and David N. Edger, *Islamic Radicalism and Global Jihad*, Georgetown University Press, 2009

Morten Storm, with Paul Cruickshank and Tim Lister, *Agent Storm: My Life Inside al-Qaeda and the CIA*, Atlantic, 2014

Michael Weiss and Hassan Hassan, *ISIS: Inside the Army of Terror*, Regan Arts, 2015

Mark Weston, *Prophets and Princes: Saudi Arabia from Muhammad to the Present*, Wiley, 2008

Lawrence Wright, *The Looming Tower: Al-Qaeda and the Road to 9/11*, Vintage, 2007

As ever when writing about very current topics, much useful material can be found in reports published by think tanks or independent analysts. I particularly recommend those of the Combating Terrorism Center at West Point, the Rand Corporation, the Institute for the Study of War, the Washington Institute for Near East Policy and the Soufan Group in the US; the Quilliam Foundation and the International Centre for the Study of Radicalisation at King's College in the UK; and the Brookings Institution in Qatar. The work of the International Crisis Group is always rigorous and reliable too. There is also of course a range of very useful websites and blogs.

Finally, there is a rich stream of reporting by my many colleagues in the world of news media, both international and local. Modern technology allows readers to follow not just publications but specific journalists too. Anyone whose name is either cited in the previous pages or in the endnotes is worth adding to whatever feed you choose to use to sort through the vast amount of material produced daily.

NOTES

INTRODUCTION

1. Deputy Assistant Secretary Brett McGurk, Statement for the Record before the US Senate Foreign Relations Committee, Hearing: Iraq at a Crossroads: Options for US Policy, 24 July 2014. • 2. 'How Mosul fell – An Iraqi general disputes Baghdad's story', Ned Parker, Isabel Coles and Raheem Salman, Reuters Special Report, 14 October 2014. • 3. Patrick Cockburn gives the figure of 1,500. Reuters says 2,000. Patrick Cockburn, *The Rise of Islamic State: ISIS and the New Sunni Revolution*, Verso, 2015. • 4. There are various estimates. Cockburn gives the higher one. Cockburn, ibid., p. 9. • 5. 'Mosul falls to militants, Iraqi forces flee northern city', Reuters, 10 June 2014. • 6. 'Islamic State Executions in Tikrit', Human Rights Watch, 2 September 2014. Al-Sham is an Arabic word meaning, in this context, most of present-day Syria, plus much of Jordan, Israel, the occupied territories and Palestine. One possible translation is the Levant, which is arguably more accurate than 'Syria'. However, the latter is most commonly employed and so is used here for the sake of simplicity. • 7. Nobody actually knows how many, and estimates range from five to eight million. • 8. 'The New Jihadism: A Global Snapshot', ICSR, 8 December 2014; 'Jihadi attacks – the data behind November's 5,000 deaths', Michael Safi, *Guardian*, 11 December 2014. Sixty per cent of these deaths were caused by the militant groups Islamic State and Boko Haram but the death toll in Yemen, Somalia and Pakistan also stretched into the hundreds. Just over half of those killed in November's attacks were civilians – 1,653 were caused by bombings but 3,400-plus by shootings, ambushes and executions. • 9. See Jason Burke, *The 9/11 Wars*, Penguin, 2011, pp. 502–5. • 10. Up to 99 per cent of the attacks by al-Qaeda and its affiliates in 2013 were against local targets in North Africa, the Middle East and other regions outside of the West. For a useful statistical analysis see 'A Persistent Threat: The Evolution of al Qa'ida and Other Salafi Jihadists', Seth Jones, RAND Corporation, 2014. • 11. Remarks by the president at the National Defense University, Fort McNair, Washington DC, Office of the Press Secretary, White House, 23 May

2013. 'Global armed conflicts becoming more deadly, major study finds', Richard Norton Taylor, *Guardian*, 20 May 2015; 'Clapper, Kerry appear at odds on terror threat', Eric Bradner, CNN, 27 February 2015. • **12**. Obama has repeatedly made clear his view that to wage a 'boundless global war on terror' would be counter-productive and that carefully focused efforts involving a variety of tools – military, diplomatic and other – against specific extremist threats are much more effective. 'We must define the nature and scope of this struggle, or else it will define us . . . Neither I, nor any President can promise the total defeat of terror . . . But what we can do – what we must do – is dismantle networks that pose a direct danger to us and make it less likely for new groups to gain a foothold.' The White House House, Office of the Press Secretary, Remarks by the President at the National Defense University, 23 May 2013. • **13**. 'Lindsey Graham: We need troops to fight Islamic State "before we all get killed here at home"', Philip Bump, *Washington Post*, 14 September 2014. • **14**. 'Fox News apologises for terror pundit's "Birmingham totally Muslim" comments', *Guardian*/Press Association, 18 January 2015. Burke, *The 9/11 Wars*, pp. 220–1. • **15**. In July 2014, I had the bizarre experience of reporting from Gaza during the short war there, interviewing Hamas officials every day, and hearing Binyamin Netanyahu, the Israeli prime minister, describe their organisation and IS as identical. One of his predecessors, Ariel Sharon, had made similar statements, as had a variety of other leaders such as Vladimir Putin and Islam Karimov of Uzbekistan, in the immediate aftermath of the 9/11 attacks, all looking to exploit the tragedy in the US in different ways. • **16**. '"They will kill us all!" Critically assessing ISIS fear mongering by US politicians', Brian Glyn Williams, *Huffington Post*, 19 November 2014. Hamas is an acronym for Harakut al-Muqawama al-Islamiyah (Union of Islamic Resistance). • **17**. 'ISIS is not a terrorist group', Audrey Kurth Cronin, *Foreign Affairs*, March/April 2015. Obama had earlier, infelicitously, described IS as the Junior Varsity squad of international terrorism to David Remnick of the *New Yorker*. • **18**. Home Secretary Theresa May on counter-terrorism, 24 November 2014, transcript of the speech at Royal United Services Institute, Whitehall, London. • **19**. According to one estimate, between 2010 and 2013, there had been a 58 per cent increase in the number of 'Salafi-jihadist' groups, and the number of individuals engaged in violence over the period had increased to between 44,000 and 105,000. Jones, 'A Persistent Threat'. • **20**. These include David Cameron, Nick Clegg and John Kerry. • **21**. Afterword to *Networks and Netwars: The Future of Terror, Crime, and Militancy*, John Arquilla and David Ronfelt, RAND Corporation, 2001. • **22**. So, for example, terrorists started crowd-sourcing funds, or using digital media for propaganda, before most counter-terrorists had even begun understanding the capabilities the techno-logical transformation of the late 1990s had brought. Similarly, terrorists started hijacking planes in the 1960s, and using explosives in the nineteenth century.

CHAPTER 1

1. Statistic from the South Asian Terrorism Portal, www.satp.org. • **2.** 'Dynamic Stalemate: Surveying Syria's Military Landscape', Charles Lister, Brookings Institution, May 2014. • **3.** Various analysts have suggested different schema. In my first book I suggested three categories: hardcore, network and ideology. The Obama White House has described 'affiliates', 'adherents' and 'inspired', see the US Congressional Research Service's report, 'Al Qaeda-Affiliated Groups: Middle East and Africa', 10 October 2014, pp. 5–6. • **4.** Claiming in typically melodramatic language on 17 April 2014 that 'al-Qaeda is no longer a base of jihad [but] has become a hammer to break the project of an Islamic state [because its] leaders have deviated from the correct path'. See *Dabiq*, vol. 2, July 2014. • **5.** See the useful discussion in 'The War Between ISIS and al-Qaeda for Supremacy of the Global Jihadist Movement', Aaron Zelin, Washington Institute for Near East Policy, 26 June 2014. • **6.** So, arguably, does Jabhat al-Nusra, depending on what importance is given to pre-existing Islamist networks in Syria in its formation. • **7.** Burke, *The 9/11 Wars*, p. 159. • **8.** Author interviews, London, June 2014. • **9.** Remarks by the president at the United States Military Academy Commencement Ceremony, the White House, Office of the Press Secretary, 28 May 2014. • **10.** Quoted in Patrick Cockburn, *The Jihadis Return: Isil and the New Sunni Uprising*, OR Books, 2014, p. 18. • **11.** Bruce Hoffman, *Inside Terrorism*, Columbia University Press, 2006, pp. 83–4. Many would contest this definition, particularly of the Thugs. • **12.** See the excellent *Carlos: Portrait of a Terrorist* by Colin Smith, Penguin, 2012. • **13.** In *Holy War in China: The Muslim Rebellion and State in Chinese Central Asia, 1864–1867*, Hodong Kim, Stanford University Press, 2010. • **14.** 'An Islamic alternative in Egypt: The Muslim Brotherhood and Sadat', Saad Eddin Ibrahim, *Arab Studies Quarterly*, Vol. 4, No. 1/2, Spring 1982, pp. 75–93; Jason Burke, *Al-Qaeda: The True Story of Radical Islam*, Penguin, 2003, p. 151. • **15.** Mohamed Heikal, *Autumn of Fury: The Assassination of President Sadat*, Andre Deutsch, 1983, p. 211. • **16.** Ibid., p. 212. • **17.** Saad Eddin Ibrahim, 'The changing face of Egypt's Islamic activism', in *Egypt, Islam and Democracy: Critical Essays*, American University in Cairo Press, 2002. • **18.** Ibid. • **19.** Michael Axworthy, *Revolutionary Iran: A History of the Islamic Republic*, Penguin, 2013, pp. 73–5. • **20.** People in Saudi Arabia still remember this period with a mix of nostalgia and horror. A friend in Jeddah still regrets the bulldozing of old markets but smiles at the thought of the freewheeling, optimistic atmosphere of the time. For statistics and more analysis, see chapter 2 of Fred Halliday's classic *Arabia Without Sultans*, Saqi Books, 2001. Also Tim Niblock with Monica Malik, *The Political Economy of Saudi Arabia*, Routledge, 2007, pp. 54–6. Abdulaziz M. Aldukheil, *Saudi Government Revenues and Expenditures: A Financial Crisis in the*

Making, Palgrave Macmillan, 2013, pp. 28–9. For an accessible, informed account of the period, try Robert Lacey, *Inside the Kingdom: Kings, Clerics, Modernists, Terrorists, and the Struggle for Saudi Arabia*, Penguin, 2010. • **21**. Fawaz Gerges notes that 'The Neglected Obligation' was the 'operational manual for jihadis' in the 1980s and first half of the 1990s. • **22**. An Indian Islamic State volunteer described reading Qutb in or near Raqqa to Indian police interrogators in late 2014. Author interview, Indian security official, Delhi, October 2014. • **23**. Sayyid Qutb, *Milestones*, American Trust Publications, 1990, p. 49. Even closer is Maududi who said in 1926: 'Islam is a revolutionary ideology and program which seeks to alter the social order of the whole world and rebuild it in conformity with its tenets and ideals,' A.A. Maududi, *Jihad in Islam*, Holy Koran Publishing House, 1980, p. 5. • **24**. One of the reasons that Mohammed had been accepted in Medina when he fled there in 620 was that his teachings were far from unfamiliar, even among the Jews who lived in the city. Muslims believe Mohammed to be the last in a series of prophets that include Moses and Jesus. Certainly, the revelations he received, as well as his reported sayings and deeds, reveal the clear influence of both Judaism and Christianity. However, a variety of episodes from the life of Mohammed have also long fuelled anti-Semitism, particularly the massacre of a Jewish tribe by early Muslims and their helpers. • **25**. Qutb, *Milestones*, p. 6, cited in Burke, *Al-Qaeda*, p. 54. • **26**. Ibid. • **27**. The six men who killed Sadat were all in their mid-twenties. Farraj, aged twenty-seven in 1982, also rejected the requirement to gain the assent of one's parents before participating in jihad. This, too, fitted perfectly with the general spirit of the times. • **28**. Gilles Kepel, *Muslim Extremism in Egypt: The Prophet and Pharaoh*, University of California Press, 2003, pp. 73–8, 87. Mustafa, who was in his early thirties, had left the Muslim Brotherhood after six years in prison and concentration camps where he had read Qutb and other key thinkers. He started his own group while behind bars and began to expand it steadily after his release in 1971, beginning with former associates from jail and close relatives, including his brother, then later roaming the villages around Asyut, the upper Egyptian city, impressing young men and some women. In a precursor to many later militant Islamic groups, recruits were sucked into a hermetically sealed world in which all their social needs were catered for. Mustafa physically and psychologically distanced his nascent community from temptation, idolatry and wrongdoing, and when camping in caves palled his followers were installed in furnished flats in poor Cairo neighbourhoods. Some were married according to the group's own inter-pretation of religious rites, and this alone caused outrage. • **29**. Eleven died and twenty-seven were wounded in the attack. *Al-Ahram*, 20 April 1974; Montasser al-Zayat, *The Road to al-Qaeda*, pp. 36–7, quoting al-Zawahiri's confession before Higher State Security Court, 1981. • **30**. Fawaz Gerges, *The Rise and Fall of Al-Qaeda*, Oxford University Press, 2011, p. 32. • **31**. A series of groups in the post-9/11 era, operating in Lebanon, Gaza, Sinai, Pakistan and elsewhere, have named themselves after Abdullah Azzam, the foreign fighters' leader. One such group, formed in 2009, has been designated a terrorist entity by the US and has been a significant actor in Syria in recent years.

CHAPTER 2

1. Karen Armstrong, *Fields of Blood: Religion and the History of Violence*, The Bodley Head, 2014, p. 166. • 2. Many deal with very specific points about the administration of a seventh-century Arab community – touching on such matters as taxation, inheritance arrangements, marital relations and sanitation. In fact the Koran mentions community – using a word that distinctly does not designate ethnic origin or 'tribe' – more than sixty times. This is significantly more mentions than 'jihad' as other words are generally used to refer to war or fighting. Ayesha Jalal, *Partisans of Allah: Jihad in South Asia*, Orient Blackswan, 2008, pp. 7–8. • 3. See Jalal, *Partisans of Allah*, p. 14, and interesting discussion in Tom Holland, *In the Shadow of the Sword*, Abacus, 2013. • 4. In 2014, I travelled through an insurgency-ridden part of Kashmir with a local driver who listened on his car stereo almost exclusively to a series of sermons by a well-known extremist preacher entitled: 'It is your responsibility, and only yours, to bring about the true Islamic society.' • 5. Azzam's exact words were: 'Jihad under this condition becomes an individual obligation on the Muslims of the land which the unbelievers have attacked and upon the Muslims close by. If the Muslims of this land cannot expel the unbelievers because of lack of forces, because they slacken, are indolent or simply do not act, then the obligation spreads to the next nearest. If they too slacken or there is again a shortage of manpower, then it is upon the people behind them, and on the people behind them, to march forward. This process continues until it becomes [an obligation] upon the whole world.' • 6. The term 'Wahhabi' is rejected by those to whom it is usually applied, who, if anything, prefer Muhawiddun, or unitarian. • 7. One physical manifestation of this was the architecture of the new mosques which proliferated through villages, towns and cities across the Islamic world. Mosques had traditionally used local materials and incorporated local building styles, and thus reflected the pluralism of Islamic observance as it had evolved in different communities across the world. The new constructions were all identical boxy, whitewashed, charmless cement constructions resembling places of worship in poorer neighbourhoods in Gulf cities. There were none in northern Iraq or Pakistan in the early 1990s, when I travelled there. A decade later, they were ubiquitous. • 8. Not all tribes converted. Mohammed is not thought to have

demanded conversion to Islam as a condition of alliance. • **9**. As the Islamic State was destroying the shrine of Jonah near Mosul in the summer of 2014, clerics in Saudi Arabia even raised the possibility of razing the tomb of Mohammed himself in Medina. • **10**. Among the Palestinians, the sudden hope prompted by the peace process with Israel swung the initiative back to Yasser Arafat and the PLO and away from Hamas. An Islamist government in Turkey simply imploded. In Sudan, Islamists who had won huge influence following a military coup in 1989 were losing ground fast while in Pakistan the conservative Muslim League, close to Islamists, was forced to alternate in power with the progressive, more secular, pro-Western Pakistan People's Party of Benazir Bhutto. See Gilles Kepel, *Jihad: The Trail of Political Islam*, I.B. Tauris, 2004, pp. 200–2, 356. • **11**. The 'blind sheikh', an Egyptian cleric called Omar Abdel Rahman, was incarcerated in a US prison on terrorist charges in 1993. Rahman, a key religious authority for militants in Egypt in the 1980s, had designated the US and the West as a *priority* target well before bin Laden did. Peter Bergen, *The Osama bin Laden I Know: An Oral History of al Qaeda's Leader*, Simon & Schuster, 2006, pp. 204–5. • **12**. 'Behind the curve: Globalization and international terrorism', Audrey Kurth Cronin, *International Security*, vol. 27, issue 3, Winter 2002/03, pp. 30–58. • **13**. Quoted in Marc Sageman, *Understanding Terror Networks*, University of Pennsylvania Press, 2004, p. 21. • **14**. Terry McDermott, *Perfect Soldiers: The 9/11 Hijackers*, HarperCollins, 2005, p. 228. • **15**. Hoffman, *Inside Terrorism*, pp. 58, 177–83. • **16**. An exception was Hezbollah, the Shia Lebanese-based organisation which launched its own channel in 1991. • **17**. Transcript of statement aired on Al Jazeera, 10 June 1999. • **18**. Author interview, al-Qaeda courier, Peshawar, 2001. • **19**. Author interviews, Islamabad, 2002, and Qatar, 2005. • **20**. Much later, shortly before his death, bin Laden would write to an associate outlining his irritation at this constant failure to get his message out. His associate, Ayman al-Zawahiri, wrote in 2001 of the 'media siege' imposed on Muslims by states in the Middle East and cautioned against 'Muslim vanguards getting killed in silence'. • **21**. Burke, *The 9/11 Wars*, p. 24. • **22**. Bin Laden finally acknowledged that he had organised the attacks in 2004.

CHAPTER 3

1. His full name is Abu at-Tayyib Ahmad ibn al-Husayn al-Mutanabbi. • **2**. For a fuller description of Baghdad in the late 1990s, see Jason Burke, *The Road to Kandahar*, Penguin, 2006. Justin Marozzi, *Baghdad: City of Peace, City of Blood*, Allen Lane, 2014, p. 33–4. • **3**. The pioneering activism of Shia extremists in the early 1980s has largely now been forgotten, but for several years in the early 1980s it was the Iraqi al-Dawa organisation that was making headlines. This Shia organisation, drawing its leadership from newly educated middle classes in the expanding cities of south and central Iraq, was responsible for what can be considered the first suicide bombings of the modern militant era, against US, French and Iraqi government targets in Kuwait and a bid to assassinate Tariq Aziz, the Iraqi vice president. • **4.** Among Iraqi Shias, it was also the failure of the revolts in the aftermath of the Gulf War which prompted a return to the fundamentals of faith. • **5.** Marozzi, *Baghdad*, p. 355. • **6.** 'Saddam wields sword of Islam', Jason Burke, *Observer*, 19 December 1999. • **7.** Indeed, it was probably because they were in a minority, and thus vulnerable, that they appeared such good local partners. That certainly was one of the tactics employed by British administrators elsewhere. • **8.** Iraq's Kurds are predominantly Sunni. References in the text to Iraq's Sunni community mean the Sunni Arab community of Iraq. • **9.** Author interview, Baghdad, July 2004. • **10.** For further background, see Burke, *Al-Qaeda*, pp. 273–5. • **11.** There are various explanations for al-Zarqawi's turn to religion. Some report his mother sent him to classes at a mosque in Amman, the Jordanian capital; others mention the Tablighi Jamaat organisation as key to the process. It appears equally likely that he was drawn to Afghanistan, like so many others, for reasons that had little to do with faith and became more interested in radical strands of Islam there. • **12.** Gilles Kepel and Jean-Pierre Milelli, *Al Qaeda in Its Own Words*, Harvard University Press, 2009, p. 243. • **13.** 'The Group That Calls Itself a State', Combating Terrorism Centre (CTC), December 2014, p. 10. • **14.** Al-Zarqawi was here in Kurdistan, not in Baghdad, when Colin Powell, the US secretary of state, cited him as evidence of Saddam Hussein's links to Islamic militancy before the United Nations in his speech of February 2003 to rally support for the forthcoming US invasion. Nor had Saddam's surgeons treated al-Zarqawi, as Powell claimed. Nor did al-Zarqawi have any connections to an alleged plot to spread home-made biological poisons on the London Underground. • **15.** Author interviews with returned veterans, Riyadh, 2008. See Burke, *The 9/11 Wars*, pp. 168–72. • **16.** Kepel and Milelli, *Al Qaeda in Its Own Words*, p. 343. • **17.** Ibid., pp. 250–67. • **18.** Ibid., p. 251. • **19.** Saddam Hussein's father had authored a Ba'athist tract called 'Three whom God should not have created: Persians [i.e. Shia], Jews and Flies'. Marozzi, *Baghdad*, p. 341. • **20.** Al-Zawahiri letter to al-Zarqawi, Saturday, 2 Jumada al-Thani 1426/9 July 2005. • **21.** Even Abu Muhammad al-Maqdisi, a Jordanian radical cleric and perhaps the most important living extremist ideologue, weighed in. He was blunt in his criticism, even if he had known al-Zarqawi for a decade or more and had been a formative ideological influence on the younger man. 'The pure hands of jihad fighters must not be stained by shedding inviolable blood. There is no point in vengeful acts that terrify people, provoke the entire world against mujahideen, and prompt the world to fight them. This is, by God, the biggest catastrophe,' he wrote. Maqdisi's real name is Isam Mohammad Tahir al-Barqawi. 'The master plan', Lawrence Wright, *New Yorker*, 11 September 2006. • **22**. For more on this, see Burke, *The 9/11 Wars*, pp. 248–51. This was a practice which had caused great anger among locals in the war against the Soviets in Afghanistan in the 1980s but was seen as being sanctioned by reference to the holy texts • **23**. 'Widespread concerns about extremism in Muslim nations, and little support for it', Pew Center, 5 February 2015. Burke, *The 9/11 Wars*, p. 253. • **24**. Burke, *The 9/11 Wars*, p. 256. • **25**. US intelligence gathering, surveillance and other operations in Iraq itself also played a significant role. • **26**. Its leaders made an interesting attempt to reconcile conflicting global and local agendas by appointing two leaders, one from Iraq who was focused on the internal campaign and one from Egypt dedicated to the worldwide battle against unbelief, Crusaders, Zionists, etc. • **27**. Al-Maliki had been part of al-Dawa, the Islamist Shia organisation which pioneered suicide bombing in the early 1980s. • **28**. The reference to poor communications with Iraqi groups is in the second batch of files released by US authorities in May 2015. • **29**. Pentagon news briefing, June 2010. • **30**. 'Who is Isis leader Abu Bakr al-Baghdadi?', Janine Di Giovanni, *Newsweek*, 8 December 2014. • **31**. 'Is this the high school report card of the head of the Islamic State?', Loveday Morris, *Washington Post*, 19 February 2015. • **32**. Author interviews, UK and former Iraqi security officials, London, 2014. Detractors claim he studied education. This document can be found here: https://archive.org/stream/TheBiographyOfSheikhAbuBakrAlBaghdadi/ The%20biography%20of%20Sheikh%20Abu%20Bakr%20Al-Baghdadi_ djvu.txt. • **33**. 'How a talented footballer became world's most wanted man, Abu Bakr al-Baghdadi', Ruth Sherlock, *Daily Telegraph*, 11 November 2014. • **34**. Author interviews, UK and former Iraqi security officials, London, 2014. • **35**. Some have suggested it was because of his relative youth, others because he was seen as more malleable than alternative candidates by a key former Ba'athist officer now with ISI. 'Abu Bakr al-Baghdadi emerges from shadows to rally Islamist followers', Martin Chulov, *Guardian*, 7 July 2014. This was Samir Abd Muhammad al-Khlifawi, better known as Haji Bakr. 'The terror strategist: Secret files reveal the structure of Islamic State', Christoph Reuter, *Der Spiegel*, 18 April 2015. See also 'Military skill and terrorist technique fuel success of ISIS', Ben Hubbard and Eric Schmitt, *New York Times*, 27 August 2014, and 'Isis: the inside story', Martin Chulov, *Guardian*, 11 December 2014. • **36**. 'Isis: the inside story', Chulov. • **37**. Al-Baghdadi had grown up among such men too. Samarra, though a mixed city, is close to the heartland of Saddam Hussein's Ba'athist and tribal bases of support. There are unconfirmed reports that two of his close relatives may have worked for the security services of the Ba'ath Party. Al-Baghdadi appears to have avoided military service as well, something which, like his place at a prestigious university in the capital, would have needed contacts within the regime. See Michael Weiss and Hassan Hassan, *ISIS: Inside the Army of Terror*, Regan Arts, 2015, pp. 120–6, for a useful account of Al-Baghdadi's relations with the Ba'athists. • **38**. Weiss and Hassan, *ISIS*, p. 206. • **39**. Author interview, Iraqi security official, London, July 2014. Lister, 'Dynamic Stalemate', p. 10. 'A marriage of convenience: The many faces of Iraq's Sunni insurgency', *Terrorism Monitor*, vol. 12, issue 15, 25 July 2014. • **40**. 'The terror strategist', Reuter, *Der Speigel*. • **41**. The Islamists' rule in Egypt was short-lived, ending when the army removed the moderate president Mohamed Morsi in July 2013. • **42**. Radwan Mortada, *Al-Akhbar*, 10 January 2014. The defector, tweeting as @wikibaghdady, has remained unidentified but also suggests that the original impulse for setting up JAN was to avoid veteran operators from ISI and rank-and-file volunteers leaving the group to go and fight in Syria as the civil war there became more intense. • **43**. Author interviews, UK and former Iraqi security officials, London, July 2014; telephone interviews, international security officials, September 2014. • **44**. 'Arab Tribes Split Between Kurds and Jihadists', Carl Drott, Carnegie Endowment for Peace, 15 May 2014. See also the excellent chapter on IS and the tribes in Weiss and Hassan, *ISIS*, p. 200–9 • **45**. 'The Islamic State and the Arab Tribes in Eastern Syria', Haian Dukhan and Sinan Hawat, E-International Relations, 31 December 2014. • **46**. Vali Nasr, *The Shia Revival: How Conflicts in Islam will Shape the Future*, Norton, 2006.

CHAPTER 4

1. 'ISIS Abu Bakr al-Baghdadi first Friday sermon as so-called "Caliph", transcript, Al Arabiya, 5 July 2014. • **2**. 'Isis has reached new depths of depravity. But there is a brutal logic behind it', Hassan Hassan, *Observer*, 8 February 2015. • **3**. Abu Bakr Naji, *The Management of Savagery*, translated by William McCants, 2006. See also discussion in Devin R. Springer, James L. Regens and David N. Edger, *Islamic Radicalism and Global Jihad*, Georgetown University Press, 2009, p. 79. • **4**. 'The ancestors of Isis', David Motadel, *New York Times*, 23 September 2014. • **5**. Quoted in Springer, Regens and Edger, *Islamic Radicalism*, p. 82. • **6**. Hugh Kennedy, *The Great Arab Conquests: How the Spread of Islam Changed the World We Live In*, Da Capo, 2007, p. 58. • **7**. Ibid., pp. 6, 367. • **8**. The collective memory of the Shia is very different from that of the Sunnis, and much more pessimistic. On this whole topic, see the fascinating discussion of Islamic, Jewish and Christian law in Adam Silverstein, *Islamic History: A Very Short Introduction*, OUP, 2010, pp. 135–6; Kennedy, *The*

Great Arab Conquests, p. 48. • **9**. Tamim Ansary, *Destiny Disrupted: A History of the World Through Islamic Eyes*, PublicAffairs, 2009. • **10**. King Hussein of the Hijaz claimed succession but was defeated in 1925. • **11**. United Nations High Commission for Refugees, press briefing notes on ISIL/Iraq and Death penalty in South-East Asia, 20 January 2015. • **12**. 'Syrian extremists amputated a man's hand and live-tweeted it', Liz Sly and Ahmed Ramadan, *Washington Post*, 28 February 2014. • **13**. Isis members claim immolation, killing captives and throwing people off high buildings were either carried out, or approved, by the first Muslim caliph, Abu Bakr. • **14**. 'Isis releases "abhorrent" sex slaves pamphlet with 27 tips for militants on taking, punishing and raping female captives', Adam Withnall, *Independent*, 10 December 2014. See also Weiss and Hassan, *ISIS*, pp. x, xi. • **15**. 'ISIS destroys Prophet Sheth shrine in Mosul', Al Arabiya, 26 July 2014. • **16**. There were other clues too. Schools in Mosul, Raqqa and elsewhere had already been ordered to replace any reference to the republics of Iraq or Syria with 'Islamic State', while anthems and lyrics that encourage 'love of country' were decreed to be evidence of 'polytheism and blasphemy' and banned. When he had rejected al-Zawahiri's 2014 edict that he keep to Iraq and let Jabhat al-Nusra operate in Syria, al-Baghdadi had argued that he would not be restricted by frontiers created by colonial powers in 1916. Ironically, the Sykes–Picot agreement was never fully implemented. • **17**. 'A message to the Mujahideen and the Muslim Ummah in the month of Ramadan', Middle East Research Institute (MEMRI), 1 July 2014. • **18**. 'The terror strategist', Reuter, *Der Spiegel*. • **19**. Two obvious exceptions are Hamas, in Gaza, and Hezbollah, in Lebanon, both of which are far more than simply a violent extremist group. • **20**. 'You Can Still See Their Blood', Human Rights Watch, 10 October 2013. • **21**. Especially Ahrar al-Sham. How that donations, as that from private donors, led to the 'Islamisation' of the opposition as commanders competed to prove their religious credentials to attract donations is an important factor that is often overlooked. • **22**. Author interview, MI6, London, July 2014. • **23**. Author telephone interviews, senior US and UN officials, May 2015. 'The war in Syria: ISIS's most successful investment yet', Suhaib Anjarini, *Al-Akhbar*, 11 June 2014. Author interviews, Afghan and British officials, Kabul, June 2011. Of that sum around two-thirds actually reached the Taliban's leadership. Reuters, Michelle Nichols, United Nations, 11 September 2012. 'Drug cash turning Taliban into wealthy criminals', UN report, Andrew North, BBC, 19 June 2014. • **24**. 'Islamic State sets up "ministry of antiquities" to reap the profits of pillaging', Louisa Loveluck, *Daily Telegraph*, 30 May 2015. 'Islamic State group's war chest is growing daily', Ken Dilanian, 15 September 2014. 'How an arrest in Iraq revealed Isis's $2bn jihadist network', Martin Chulov, *Guardian*, 15 June 2014. • **25**. Zakat varies in terms of percentage taken, depending on the activity, but generally is between 2.5 and 20 per cent. • **26**. Author telephone interviews, senior US and UN officials, May 2015. • **27**. 'Insight – Islamic State's financial independence poses quandary for its foes', Raheem Salman and Yara Bayoumy, Reuters, 11 September 2014. 'Profiling the Islamic State', Charles Lister, Brookings Institution, 2014, p. 22. Also, McGurk testimony, see Introduction, n. 1. • **28**. 'Islamic State', Salman and Bayoumy. During the seizure of the city, the group were reported to have captured $435m from banks. 'U.S. strikes cut into ISIS oil revenues, Treasury official says', Julie Hirschfeld Davis, *New York Times*, 23 October 2014. 'Cutting off IS cash flow', Charles Lister, Brooking Institution blogpost, 24 October 2014. 'Islamic State issues fake tax receipts to keep trade flowing', Mitchell Prothero, McClatchy, 3 September 2014. • **29**. In Iraq, most of the poor have been fed through state-subsidised rations for decades, a relic of the UN sanctions regime introduced after the 1991 Gulf War and continued by the Iraqi government after the 2003 invasion. • **30**. 'ISIS Governance in Syria', Charles C. Caris and Samuel Reynolds, Institute for the Study of War, July 2014, p. 22. • **31**. If there were no complaints against the group's members, IS would not have established a 'Court of Grievances'. 'ISIS Governance in Syria', Caris and Reynolds, p. 19. • **32**. The central government still pay salaries worth $130m per month. 'IS: the rentier caliphate with no new ideas', Charles Tripp, Al Arabiya, 8 February 2015. • **33**. 'Mosul residents describe "hell" of Isis occupation as Kurdish fighters close in', Fazel Hawramy, *Guardian*, 22 January 2015 • **34**. 'Under Islamic State, life in Mosul, Iraq, turns grim', Molly Hennessy-Fiske and Nabih Bulos, *Los Angeles Times*, 26 January 2015. • **35**. 'Syria: Isis Tortured Kobani Child Hostages', Human Rights Watch, 4 November 2014. • **36**. 'U.S. official: 10,000-plus ISIS fighters killed in 9-month campaign', Laura Smith-Spark and Noisette Martel, CNN, 4 June 2015. • **37**. 'The Islamic State', Richard Barrett, Soufan Group, 3 October 2014, p. 9. 'Who Are the Soldiers of the Islamic State?' Aron Lund, blogpost for Carnegie Endowment for International Peace, 24 October 2014. 'The Motivations of Syrian Islamist Fighters', Vera Mironova, Loubna Mrie and Sam Whitt, CTC, 31 October 2014. • **38**. 'Arabian nightmare', Rahul Tripathi, *India Today*, 9 February 2015. Author interview, senior police officials, Mumbai, November 2014. • **39**. 'To Its Citizens, ISIS Also Shows a Softer Side', Vocativ, 20 March 2015. • **40**. This cost the group nothing, other than the minor inconvenience of the occasional off-message Facebook post or 'tweet'. ISIS leader Abu Bakr al-Baghdadi and the group's spokesman, Mohammad al-Adnani, said only four accounts were authorised to speak on their behalf with any future messages. 'ISIS leader warns unauthorized tweets don't speak for caliphate', Catherine Herridge, Fox News, 2 February 2015. • **41**. See useful account in Jessica Stern and J.M. Berger, *ISIS: The State of Terror*, HarperCollins, 2015, pp. 145–7. • **42**. 'Crowdsourcing Terror: ISIS Asks for Ideas on Killing Jordanian Pilot', Vocativ, 26 December 2014. • **43**. It is certainly not the first insurgent group to attempt to service the basic needs of a population while simultaneously employing terrorist tactics and committing horrific and systematic atrocities. According to one researcher, roughly a third of all insurgencies from 1945 to 2003 provided health care and education, with the total rising to nearly half among those which acquired territory. 'What's so new about the Islamic State's governance?', Megan A. Stewart, *Washington Post*, 7 October 2014. • **44**. 'IS: the rentier caliphate', Tripp, Al Arabiya. Also, on relations with tribes, see 'The Islamic State identity and legacies of Baath rule in Syria's northeast', Kevin Mazur, Project on Middle Eastern Political Science, 16 March 2015. See too 'How much of a state is the Islamic State?', Quinn Mecham, *Washington Post*, 5 February 2015. Also, Weiss and Hassan, pp. 122–4, discussion on the sectarian agenda of IS and the legacy of Ba'athism.

CHAPTER 5

1. Bin Laden had been living with two loyal retainers, three wives, around a dozen children and a handful of grandchildren. Information obtained through so-called coercive techniques, or torture, may possibly have expedited the search, may have slowed it due to being inherently unreliable, but appears not to have been critical either way. Nor is there any reliable evidence proving that the Pakistani authorities knew of bin Laden's location, though it remains entirely possible that at least some individuals were aware of his presence. The broad consensus among Western security services and many analysts, at least in the few years since the event, is that Inter-Services Intelligence (ISI), the country's main intelligence service, was unaware as an institution, and so too were the key policymakers. See Peter Bergen's *Manhunt: The Ten-Year Search for Bin Laden from 9/11 to Abbottabad*, Broadway Books, 2013, for the best account of the operation which led to bin Laden's death. For an alternative view, see Carlotta Gall, *The Wrong Enemy: America in Afghanistan, 2001–2014*, Houghton Mifflin, 2014. • **2**. Several of the senior militants preferred Saif al-Adel, another Egyptian veteran who had been appointed as interim leader following bin Laden's death. There were other candidates too, such as Atiyah Abd al-Rahman, a key Libyan who had been bin Laden's chief of staff. • **3**. Knights under the banner of the Prophet, 2002, author collection. In 'Join the Caravan' Azzam explained that 'the establishment of the *umma* on an area of land is a necessity, as vital as water or air'. For useful points see Gerges, *The Rise and Fall of Al-Qaeda*, pp. 44–50. • **4**. 'Bin Laden wanted to change al-Qaida's bloodied name', Jason Burke, *Guardian*, 24 June 2011. See also 'Letters from Abbottabad: Bin Ladin Sidelined?', CTC, May 2012. • **5**. 'Zawahiri discusses infighting in Syria, opposition to Egyptian government', Thomas Joscelyn, *Long War Journal*, 21 April 2014. • **6**. Some define the *salaf* as the first four generations, others the first six. • **7**. The price per barrel went from about $3.5 to $15 in eighteen months. Saudi Arabia's revenues went from less than a million dollars before the Second World War to $56m in 1950, and from $2.7bn in 1972 to $25bn in 1975. • **8**. Al-Wuhayshi had fled from Afghanistan in late 2001 to Iran, then been extradited to Yemen, where he had been incarcerated. He had been among the score or so of capable senior militants who escaped from prison in 2006. • **9**. For details on the prison break and al-Wuhayshi's refounding of AQAP, see Gregory D. Johnsen, *The Last Refuge: Yemen, al-Qaeda, and America's War in Arabia*, Norton, 2014, pp. 192–5. • **10**. 'Christmas Day bomber sentenced to life in prison', David Ariosto and Deborah Feyerick, CNN, 17 February 2012. Johnsen, *The Last Refuge*, pp. 262–3. • **11**. Anwar al-Awlaki obituary, Jason Burke, *Guardian*, 2 October 2011. • **12**. Morten Storm, *Agent Storm: My Life Inside al-Qaeda and the CIA*, Atlantic, 2014, p. 95. • **13**. One exception might arguably be bin Laden, who had relied on a rather different medium to communicate his message. • **14**. 'Being Bin Laden: al-Qaida leader's banal jihad business revealed', Jason Burke, *Guardian*, 3 May 2012. • **15**. Johnsen, *The Last Refuge*, p. 271. 'Bin Laden document trove reveals strain on al-Qaeda', Greg Miller, *Washington Post*, 1 July 2011. • **16**. 'AQAP's Resilience in Yemen', Andrew Michaels and Sakhr Ayyash, *CTC Sentinel*, vol. 6, issue 9, September 2013. • **17**. UNESCO data centre, http://www.uis.unesco.org/DataCentre/Pages/country-profile.aspx?code=YEM&regioncode=40525. • **18**. Storm, *Agent Storm*, pp. 280–3. • **19**. Gregory D. Johnsen, 'How We Lost Yemen', *Foreign Policy*, 6 August 2013. • **20**. 'Conflict in Yemen: Abyan's Darkest Hour', Amnesty International, 3 December 2012. • **21**. 'Yemen retakes ground in push on Islamist rebels', Reuters, 11 June 2013. • **22**. 'Yemen terror boss left blueprint for waging jihad', Rukmini Callimachi, Associated Press, 9 August 2013. • **23**. Author interviews, security officials, London, August 2014; telephone interviews, international officials, March, May 2015. 'Al-Qaeda leaks II: Baghdadi loses his shadow', Radwan Mortada, *Al-Akhbar*, 10 January 2014. 'The jihad next door: The Syrian roots of Iraq's newest civil war', Rania Abouzeid, *Politico*, 24 June 2014. Al Jazeera interview with Abu Muhammad al-Golani, broadcast 19 December 2013. 'Jabhat al-Nusra: a strategic briefing', Quilliam Foundation, 8 January 2013. • **24**. Parts of which have been occupied by Israel since 1967. • **25**. Author interviews, security officials, Islamabad, June 2013, London, July 2014. See also 'Al-Qaida's membership declining and leadership damaged, but threat remains', Jason Burke, *Guardian*, 5 August 2013. • **26**. 'Profiling the Islamic State', Lister. In particular, Jabhat al-Nusra had spearheaded the seizure of two major military facilities in northern Syria – the Hanano barracks in Aleppo in mid-September 2012 and the Taftanaz airbase in Idlib on 11 January 2013. • **27**. 'Dynamic Stalemate', Lister, p. 3. • **28**. 'A gathering force', Bourzou Daraghi, *Financial Times*, 12 February 2014. • **29**. 'Al-Shabaab joining al Qaeda, monitor group says', CNN, 10 February

2012. • **30**. 'Pentagon confirms death of Somalia terror leader', Associated Press, 5 September 2014. • **31**. See Burke, *The 9/11 Wars*, pp. 417–18, for more detail. • **32**. Similarly, al-Shabaab had made tens of millions of dollars annually from the illicit and immensely profitable trade in charcoal. • **33**. In December 2012, Belmoktar, the disgruntled former commander, swore allegiance to Ayman al-Zawahiri. • **34**. 'Jihadists Praise Paris Attacks', Caleb Weiss, *Long War Journal*, 12 January 2015. 'Seven U.N. peacekeepers wounded in Northern Mali attack', Reuters, 9 January 2015. • **35**. In what was probably his last letter, bin Laden indicated that al-Qaeda was receiving funds from affiliates, rather than the reverse. 'Letters from Abbottabad: Bin Laden Sidelined?' CTC, 3 May 2012, p. 40. • **36**. In the words of a senior British security official. Author interview, London, August 2012. • **37**. See Burke, *The 9/11 Wars*, pp. 293–4. • **38**. A new plot was uncovered in May 2012. 'CIA thwarts new al-Qaida underwear bomb plot', Adam Goldman and Matt Apuzzo, Associated Press, 7 May 2012. 'Foiled plot shows militants seek detection-proof bombs', Mark Hosenball and Tabassum Zakaria, Reuters, 8 May 2012. • **39**. Storm, *Agent Storm*, p. 251. • **40**. 'Qaeda branches urge unity against US-led "war on Islam"', Agence France-Presse, 16 September 2014. See useful discussion in 'The al Qaeda network: A new framework for defining the enemy', Katherine Zimmerman, American Enterprise Institute, 10 September 2013. • **41**. Author interviews, Indian police officers, Mumbai, November 2014. 'Al-Qaida's shadowy new "emir" in south Asia handed tough job', Reuters, 10 September 2014. • **42**. 'Al-Qaida leader announces formation of Indian branch', Jason Burke, *Guardian*, 4 September 2014. One IS video included footage from the cult video game *Grand Theft Auto*.

CHAPTER 6

1. Author interviews, Maldives, February 2014. 'Saudi Arabia's growing role in the Maldives', Charles Haviland, BBC, 24 March 2014. • **2**. Ali Jaleel, a Maldivian, carried out a suicide attack with large, bomb-laden truck to penetrate the perimeter of Pakistan's Inter-Services Intelligence agency in Lahore on 27 May 2009. • **3**. Author interviews, local security officials in Malé, UK officials in Sri Lanka, Indian officials in Delhi and Mumbai, November 2014 and February 2015. • **4**. 'Footage leaked of museum vandals destroying pre-Islamic artifacts', Ahmed Naish, Minivan News, 14 January 2013. 'Maldives mob smashes Buddhist statues in national museum', Agence France Presse, 8 February 2012. • **5**. Alongside a US citizen, a Syrian and a 'Turkestani'. 'Maldivian militant killed in Syrian suicide attack', claims online jihadist group, Ahmed Rilwan, Minivan News, 25 May 2014. • **6**. 'Jihadist media claims two more Maldivians killed in Syria', Minivan News, 2

September 2014. • **7**. 'Paradise jihadis: Maldives sees surge in young Muslims leaving for Syria', Jason Burke, *Guardian*, 26 February 2015. • **8**. At least one was linked to the murder of the cleric in 2012. • **9**. As ever, prison was an important vector of extremism. There is no segregation of inmates in the Maldives' overcrowded jails, allowing self-appointed preachers to run unofficial religious study groups for anyone who wants to attend, and the only permitted reading material in prison is religious texts, many of which are supplied by Gulf-based charities. 'In prison you have nothing to do but think about your life and read these books,' said one gang leader. Leaders and more junior members of the gangs all served repeated sentences. In the summer of 2014, around the time IS declared its caliphate, one particular leader was released and ordered the gang to cease trafficking in drugs and alcohol – key sources of income hitherto – because they were 'haram', forbidden. • **10**. Ibid. • **11**. 'Terror threat to India rising again six years after Mumbai attacks', Jason Burke, *Guardian*, 26 November 2014. Author interviews, security officials, Mumbai, Delhi, November 2014. • **12**. 'IS recruiting thousands in Pakistan, govt warned in "secret" report', Mubashir Zaidi, *Dawn*, 8 November 2014. 'Capital's Jamia Hafsa declares support for Islamic State', Amir Mir, *The News*, 8 December 2014. • **13**. 'Pakistan arrests local Islamic State commander – sources', Reuters, 21 January 2015. • **14**. See 'Foreign Fighters in Syria', Richard Barrett, Soufan Group, 2 June 2014. 'Foreign Fighters Trickle into the Syrian Rebellion', Aaron Y. Zelin, Washington Institute for Near East Policy, 11 June 2012. 'The Saudi Foreign Fighter Presence in Syria', Aaron Y. Zelin, *CTC Sentinel*, vol. 7, issue 4, April 2014. Author interview, UK officials, London 2014. Also see 'Foreign fighter total in Syria/Iraq now exceeds 20,000; surpasses Afghanistan conflict in the 1980s', ICSR blogpost, 26 January 2015. It gives the following totals: Tunisia 1,500–3,000, Jordan 1,500, Morocco 1,500, Russia 800–1,500, Saudi Arabia 1,500–2,500. • **15**. 'Deciphering the Jihadist Presence in Syria: An Analysis of Martyrdom Notices', Aaron Y. Zelin, *CTC Sentinel*, vol. 6, issue 2, February 2013. • **16**. One was identified as Maxime Hauchard, a Muslim convert from France. Others appeared to be from Western Europe, Australia, Indonesia, the Philippines, Central Asia and the Middle East. The exact number of victims or killers is unclear in the video but seems to be between sixteen and twenty-two. 'ISIS's brutal beheading video: Search for clues', Atika Shubert, CNN, 8 December 2014. • **17**. According to one survey by the Pew Research Center in 2013, a median of 67 per cent in eleven 'Muslim publics' say they are somewhat or very concerned about Islamic extremism. 'Muslim Publics Share Concerns About Extremist Groups', Pew Research Center, 10 September 2013. 'In many of the countries surveyed, clear majorities of Muslims oppose violence in the name of Islam. Indeed, about three-quarters or more in Pakistan (89%), Indonesia (81%), Nigeria (78%) and Tunisia (77%), say suicide bombings or other acts of violence that target civilians are *never* justified.' • **18**. 'Which countries don't like America and which do', Bruce Stokes, Pew Research Center, 26 July 2014. • **19**. 'The World's Muslims: Religion, Politics and Society, Chapter 7: Religion, Science and Popular Culture', Pew Research Center, 30 April 2013. • **20**. See 'Muslim–Western Tensions Persist', Pew Research Center, 21 July 2011. • **21**. 'The World's Muslims: Religion, Politics and Society', Pew. • **22**. See Jean-Pierre Filiu, *Apocalypse in Islam*, University of California Press, 2012. Also, Stern and Berger, *ISIS*, pp. 219–31; 'ISIS Fantasies of an Apocalyptic Showdown in Northern Syria', William McCants, Brookings Institution, 3 October 2014. • **23**. Patrick Cockburn, *Muqtada al-Sadr and the Shia Insurgency in Iraq*, Faber and Faber, 2008, pp. 70–94. • **24**. 'Islamic State: Where does jihadist group get its support?', Michael Stephens, BBC, 1 September 2014. See also Cockburn, *The Rise of Islamic State*, for a fuller discussion. • **25**. 'The Challenge of Youth Inclusion in Morocco', Arne Hoel, World Bank, 14 May 2012. • **26**. 'New freedoms in Tunisia drive support for Isis', David D. Kirkpatrick, *New York Times*, 21 October 2014. • **27**. See, for example, 'In stark transformation Egyptian rights activist dies fighting for Islamic State', Erin Cunningham, *Washington Post*, 5 November 2014. • **28**. 'To Its Citizens, ISIS Also Shows a Softer Side', Vocativ, 20 March 2015. Vocativ investigated over 570 videos between 21 January and 28 February. • **29**. 'Tunisian Jihadists Fighting In Syria', Nesrine Hamedi, Al-Monitor, 24 March 2013. 'Syria: 132 Tunisian Insurgents Killed in Aleppo, Tunisia Developing into Salafist Hot-Bed', nsnbc, 15 February 2015. 'Courts kept busy as Jordan works to crush support for Isis', Ian Black, *Guardian*, 27 November 2014. 'The Geography of Discontent: Tunisia's Syrian Fighter Dilemma', Dario Cristiani, Jamestown Foundation, *Terrorism Monitor*, vol. 12, issue 20, 24 October 2014. 'The Jihadi Factory', Christine Petré, *Foreign Policy*, 20 March 2015. 'ISIS draws a steady stream of recruits from Turkey', Ceylan Yeginsu, *New York Times*, 15 September 2014. • **30**. Author interview, Saudi security official, London, July 2014, by telephone, March 2015. 'ICG Red Alert in Jordan: Recurrent Unrest in Maan', *Middle East Briefing*, no. 5, 19 February 2003 • **31**. 'Tunisia becomes breeding ground for Islamic State fighters', Eileen Byrne, *Guardian*, 13 October 2014. • **32**. Author telephone interview, February, March 2015. • **33**. This may have encouraged the group to genuinely think about the controversial move of actually declaring a caliphate. There is evidence that IS floated the idea on social media to test the potential reaction among other extremists, and may have approached senior al-Qaeda commanders too. 'The Islamic State', Barrett, Soufan Group, p. 18. See also 'Al-Qaeda leaks II', Mortada, *Al-Akhbar*. A useful list can be found in 'ISIS's Global Messaging Strategy Fact Sheet', Jessica Lewis McFate and Harleen Gambhir with Evan Sterling, Institute for Understanding War, December 2014. • **34**. 'Islamic State franchising', Rivka Azoulay, Netherlands Institute of International Relations

Clingendael, April 2015, p. 10. • **35**. See 'Jihadi discourse in the wake of the Arab spring', Nelly Lahoud, CTC, 17 December 2013, pp. 82–4. • **36**. The first was in October 2004, when a series of car bomb blasts hit Sinai resorts, killing thirty-four. In July 2005, hotels and restaurants were attacked in Sharm El-Sheikh, the major Sinai tourist resort, killing and wounding two hundred people. A group calling itself the Abdullah Azzam Brigades (AAB) claimed responsibility. • **37**. Israeli services estimate there are around a thousand militants in Sinai, broken down into fifteen to twenty cells with varying ideologies and affiliations, but admit that their knowledge is patchy. Author interviews, former intelligence officials, Jerusalem, July 2014. • **38**. 'Sinai attackers were educated, not local Beduin', Joanna Paraszczuk and Yaakov Lappin, *Jerusalem Post*, 3 October 2012. • **39**. According to a report by expert Daveed Gartenstein-Ross, a senior ABM member travelled from the group's base to Raqqa. The envoy spent around three months there and eventually swore allegiance to al-Baghdadi. 'Ansar Bayt Al-Maqdis's Oath of Allegiance to the Islamic State', Daveed Gartenstein-Ross, Wikistrat, 2015. Others say envoys travelled from Raqqa to Sinai too. See Azoulay, Clingendael, pp. 25–6. • **40**. '31 Egyptian soldiers are killed as militants attack in Sinai', David D. Kirkpatrick, *New York Times*, 24 October 2014. • **41**. 'At least 32 killed in Egypt as militants attack army and police targets in Sinai', Patrick Kingsley and Manu Abdo, *Guardian*, 30 January 2015. • **42**. See 'Religious Revolts in Colonial North Africa', Knut S. Vikor, in David Motadel, ed., *Islam and the European Empires*, OUP, 2014. As elsewhere, those networks were largely Sufi. • **43**. See Burke, *The 9/11 Wars*, p. 422. • **44**. Author interviews, security officials, Islambad, June 2013, by telephone, senior UN official, September 2013. • **45**. 'Al-Qaeda in Libya: A Profile', Library of Congress, Federal Research Division, August 2012, citing Atiyah Al-Libi 'A-thawarat Al-Arabiyah Wa Mawsimu Al-Hasad' (The Arab Revolutions and the Season of Harvest). • **46**. 'A deadly mix in Benghazi', David D. Kirkpatrick, *New York Times*, 28 December 2013. • **47**. In September a senior associate called Abu Nabil al-Anbari may have visited the city with the aim of organising existing support to allow a declaration of a new *'wilayat'*. • **48**. 'Disenchanted militants in South Asia eye Islamic State with envy', Jibran Ahmad and Mohammad Stanekzai, Reuters, 21 January 2015 • **49**. A rivalry sparked by the death in a drone strike of the charismatic Hakimullah Mehsud a few months previously. 'The Shadows of "Islamic State" in Afghanistan: What threat does it hold?' Borhan Osman, Afghan Analysts Network, 12 February 2015. • **50**. Author interview, Delhi, March 2015. • **51**. Author interviews by telephone, Saudi officials, June 2015. • **52**. 'Que sait-on du groupe qui a revendiqué l'assassinat d'un Français en Algérie?', *Le Monde*, 23 September 2014. 'Algeria's Al-Qaeda defectors join IS group', Al Jazeera, 14 September 2014. 'Algérie: l'armée a tué l'assassin d'Hervé Gourdel', Amir Akef, *Le Monde*, 24 December 2014. • **53**. 'Pledging

Bay'a: a benefit or burden to the Islamic State', David Milton and Muhammed al-Ubaydi, *CTC Sentinel*, March 2015, p. 6. • **54**. Mike Smith, *Boko Haram: Inside Nigeria's Unholy War*, I.B. Tauris, 2015, pp. 184–8. '"Now I'm scared of everyone": fear and mistrust after Nigerian mass abduction', Monica Mark, *Guardian*, 2 May 2014. • **55**. 'Boko Haram Leader Abubakar Shekau's Latest Speech', Clement Ejiofor, Naij.com • **56**. 'Nigerian president: kidnapping will mark beginning of the end of terror', Monica Marks, *Guardian*, 8 May 2014. • **57**. The name Boko Haram is a pejorative one, given to the group first by local communities and then adopted by officials and finally the international community. • **58**. Particularly the Jamaat Izalat al-Bida wa Iqamat al-Sunnah (Society for the Eradication of Evil Innovations and the Re-establishment of the Sunna), better known as the Izala Movement. • **59**. There was also widespread sectarian violence elsewhere in the country, unconnected with Boko Haram. In 2008, religious clashes had left seven hundred dead. • **60**. '"Those Terrible Weeks in Their Camp", Boko Haram Violence against Women and Girls in Northeast Nigeria', Human Rights Watch, October 2014, p. 3. • **61**. 'Boko Haram leader speaks on global jihadists in video', *Vanguard*, 29 November 2012, http://www.vanguardngr.com/2012/11/boko-haram-leader-speaks-on-global-jihadists-in-video/#sthash.nVKmlh5J.dpuf. • **62**. A January 2012 United Nations report stated that seven members of Boko Haram 'were arrested while transiting through the Niger to Mali, in possession of documentation on manufacturing of explosives, propaganda leaflets and names and contact details of members of Al-Qaida in the Islamic Maghreb [AQIM] they were allegedly planning to meet'. 'Report of the assessment mission on the impact of the Libyan crisis on the Sahel region', Security Council, S/2012/42, 18 January 2012, p. 12 • **63**. 'Boko Haram generates uncertainty with pledge of allegiance to Islamic State', Rukmini Callimachi, *New York Times*, 7 March 2015 • **64**. Almost the entire remainder of the 27-minute speech was devoted to a vicious tirade against the Shia, and their treacherous alliance with the Crusaders.

CHAPTER 7

1. 'Aspects of all this were seen, as they were intended to be, by members of the public . . . in order to achieve maximum effect,' a trial judge pointed out. R v. Michael Adebolajo & Michael Adebowale, 26 February 2014, sentencing remarks of Mr Justice Sweeney. • **2**. 'Woolwich attack, the terrorist's rant', *Daily Telegraph*, 23 May 2013. Report on the intelligence relating to the murder of Fusilier Lee Rigby, Intelligence and Security Committee of Parliament, 25 November 2014. • **3**. In 1951, there were an estimated 23,000 Muslims in Britain. Raffaello Pantucci, *'We Love Death as You Love Life': Britain's*

Suburban Mujahedeen, Columbia University Press, 2015, p. 21. • **4**. Figures are notoriously difficult, and also obscure a huge variety of ways in which an individual can identify as a 'Muslim'. Pantucci, *'We Love Death'*, p. 21. Burke, *The 9/11 Wars*, pp. 187, 556. • **5**. 'I was of a generation that did not think of itself as Muslim or Hindi or Sikh or even as Asian but as black,' remembered the British academic and journalist Kenan Malik, explaining that one reason for a growing disaffection with left-wing groups was their focus on the class struggle rather than discrimination. Kenan Malik, *From Fatwa to Jihad*, Atlantic, 2009, p. 21. • **6**. In France in the same period, the rise was fivefold, from 136 to 766. Alison Pargeter, *The New Frontiers of Jihad*, I.B. Tauris, 2008, p. 19. • **7**. The conflict in Kashmir drew more than a thousand men from all over the country to fight with extremist, or sometimes less extremist, groups in the brutal, bloody war over the disputed state. • **8**. 'British Muslims take path to jihad', Jeevan Vasagar and Vikram Dodd, *Guardian*, 29 December 2000. • **9**. In 1998, a group of men set out from London to launch attacks on Western targets in Yemen. • **10**. 'Five Britons killed in "jihad brigade"', Paul Harris, Martin Bright and Burhan Wazir, *Observer*, 28 October 2001. • **11**. Others were simply seeking to escape ongoing crackdowns on Islamist activism in countries like Saudi Arabia, Iraq or Syria. • **12**. There he collaborated with then little-known Jordanian-born extremist scholar known as Abu Qutada, running propaganda operations for increasingly savage Algerian militant groups. • **13**. Al-Suri was horrified by the 9/11 attacks. Not through any sympathy for the victims – he argued that bin Laden should have used some kind of weapon of mass destruction that might have laid waste to much of New York and Washington – but because he thought that, by bringing about the end of Taliban rule, they were counter-productive. • **14**. The preferred target was the G8 summit held in Gleneagles, Scotland, at the time but the bombers were put off by security arrangements. An alternative was the London Stock Exchange. This too was rejected. • **15**. Author interview, UK security official, London 2013. Address at the Lord Mayor's Annual Defence and Security Lecture by the Director General of the Security Service, Jonathan Evans, Mansion House, City of London, 25 June 2012. • **16**. Burke, *The 9/11 Wars*, p. 43 • **17**. Author interview, UK security official, London 2006. • **18**. James Smart Lecture by the Director General of the Security Service, Eliza Manningham-Buller, City of London Police Headquarters, 16 October 2003. • **19**. 'Britain stops talk of "war on terror"', Jason Burke, *Observer*, 10 December 2006. • **20**. Author interviews, UK security officials, India and Pakistan 2011. One notable exception was the escape from police custody of Rashid Rauf, a Briton suspected of running both 7/7 and 21/7 conspiracies in 2005. He was killed in 2008 by a drone. • **21**. Others had attended a camp run by another local group, Harkat ul-Mujahideen. 'How "Just Do It" bomb plotters planned attacks as MI5 followed their every move', Tom Whitehead,

Daily Telegraph, 22 February 2013. • **22**. 'UK trial reveals new al Qaeda strategy to hit West', Paul Cruickshank, CNN, 21 February 2013. For a contrasting view of the contacts made by these bombers, see 'British Islamic extremist terrorism: the declining significance of Al-Qaeda and Pakistan', Lewis Herrington, Chatham House, January 2015. • **23**. Pantucci, *'We Love Death'*, p. 276. • **24**. 'UK trial reveals new al Qaeda strategy to hit West', Cruickshank. • **25**. Author interview, London, 2011. • **26**. It was associated particularly with the strategy of 'leaderless resistance' of Louis L. Beam, an American Vietnam veteran and right-wing extremist. The term 'lone wolf' was also used by Alex Curtis, another US right-wing extremist, detained in 2000. In the 1920s and 30s 'lone wolf' was a term for a criminal not associated with a gang. 'The phrase "lone wolf" goes back centuries', Ben Zimmer, *Wall Street Journal*, 19 December 2014. • **27**. 'Suspect's journey from schoolboy football to phone-jacking and jihad', Peter Walker, Shiv Malik, Matthew Taylor, Sandra Laville, Vikram Dodd and Ben Quinn, *Guardian*, 24 May 2013. • **28**. 'Lee Rigby: "E"grade Michael Adebolajo scraped into Greenwich University which was targeted by extremists', Javier Espinoza, *Daily Telegraph*, 12 March 2015. • **29**. Al-Muhajiroun was proscribed under UK terrorist laws in 2010. • **30**. Adebolajo had also been arrested in 2007 under the Firearms Act (for carrying CS spray), and had previous arrests for assault. • **31**. Pantucci, *'We Love Death'*, p. 262. • **32**. Author interview, British security official, London 2009. • **33**. 'Bristol man guilty of suicide bomb plot on shopping centre', *Guardian*, Steven Morris, 17 July 2009. • **34**. Burke, *The 9/11 Wars*, pp. 473–7. • **35**. It was later revealed that Adebowale had called a Yemeni telephone associated with an individual believed to be in contact with AQAP. Report on the intelligence relating to the murder of Fusilier Lee Rigby, p. 94. • **36**. Author interviews, senior police officers, Scotland Yard, July 2014. 'Woolwich: How did Michael Adebolajo become a killer?', BBC, Dominic Casciani, 19 December 2013. • **37**. 'Woolwich suspect was victim of frenzied knife attack aged 16', Ben Ferguson, Vikram Dodd and Matthew Taylor, *Guardian*, 24 May 2013. 'Faridon Alizada murderer gets life', *News Shopper*, Erith, 22 December 2008. • **38**. 'Report on the intelligence relating to the murder of Fusilier Lee Rigby', Intelligence and Security Committee of Parliament, p. 72, 25 November 2014. • **39**. 'Special issue: Lone Mujahid Pocketbook', *Inspire*, issue 10, Spring 2013. • **40**. 'Facebook "could have prevented Lee Rigby murder"', Peter Dominiczak, Tom Whitehead, Martin Evans and Gordon Rayner, *Daily Telegraph*, 26 November 2014. • **41**. All these statistics are drawn from the series of polls conducted by ICM Unlimited for the *Guardian*, the BBC and the *Sunday Telegraph* between 2002 and 2009. Available: http://www.icmunlimited.com/media-centre. Economic issues: 'Muslims in Europe: Economic Worries Top Concerns About Religious and Cultural Identity'. Pew Research Center, July 2006. • **42**. 'The Gallup Coexist Index 2009: A Global Study of Interfaith Relations', May 2009. Author interview, Magali Rheault, Gallup researcher, July 2009. • **43**. And then handed over to their US counterparts and then passed on to the Syrians. • **44**. According to the national census. • **45**. For the reporting to the police, see ICM poll for the BBC, June 2009. • **46**. 'Inside the mind of Lee Rigby's killer Michael Adebolajo', Guy Grandjean, Vikram Dodd and Mustafa Khalili, *Guardian*, 20 December 2013. • **47**. 'Birmingham plot: leader of suicide gang used gyms and charity shop to recruit cell', Duncan Gardham, *Daily Telegraph*, 22 February 2013. • **48**. Author interview, London, July 2014. • **49**. 'Islamic rappers' message of terror', Antony Barnett, *Observer*, 8 February 2004. • **50**. 'Terror videos "found at 21/7 homes"', Adrian Shaw, *Daily Mirror*, 13 February 2007. • **51**. '9 disturbingly good jihadi raps', J. Dana Stuster, *Foreign Policy*, 29 April 2013. Al-Hammami later died in internecine fighting within al-Shabaab. • **52**. 'What Drives Europeans to Syria, and to IS? Insights from the Belgian Case', Rik Coolsaet, Egmont Paper 75, March 2015. • **53**. This was particularly clear in some Scandinavian countries, where a clear nexus between gang violence and organised criminality among immigrant populations and extremism was increasingly evident. Often these involved converts. One fairly spectacular example was Morten Storm, a heavily tattooed former gang member with a history of violent crime who became a Muslim, though hardly a very rigorous one, and eventually both an agent for Western intelligence services and a trusted contact of Anwar al-Awlaki in Yemen. • **54**. Pantucci, *'We Love Death'*, p. 21. Report on the intelligence relating to the murder of Fusilier Lee Rigby, pp. 87–8. • **55**. '[They] are more accurately seen as "self-starting terrorists" rather than "lone actors",' the service told a parliamentary investigation.

CHAPTER 8

1. Jean-Louis Bruguière, the French anti-terrorist judge and unsuccessful politician, has given a figure of 1,100, which seems high. • **2**. 'Interview exclusive d'Abdelghani Merah: "Mon frère se réjouissait de la mort de nos soldats"', *La Depeche*, 14 November 2012. 'Drame Toulouse. Le père de Mohamed Merah parle', Adlène Meddi, *Paris Match*, 3 April 2012. • **3**. Abdelghani Merah, and Mohamed Sifaoui, *Mon frère, ce terroriste*, Calmann-Lévy, 2012, chap. 3. • **4**. The 'peripherique' actually lies on the old lines of the ancient walls that protected the city of Paris until the late nineteenth century. • **5**. 'Neighborhood is torn over a killer's legacy', Scott Sayare, *New York Times*, 19 December 2012. • **6**. He did not, however, drink or touch drugs. Merah and Sifaoui, *Mon frère*, chaps 4, 6. • **7**. 'Exactement je me suis converti le 18 février 2008, et depuis ce jour là j'ai toujours été assidu à mes prières.' 'Transcription des conversations entre Mohamed Merah et les négociateurs',

Libération, 17 July 2012. Merah and Sifaoui, *Mon frère*, chap. 7. • **8**. 'Mohamed Merah. Un étrange touriste', Delphine Byrka, *Paris Match*, 25 March 2013. • **9**. This was also the case in the 1990s, for young British volunteers hoping to fight with militant groups against Indian security forces in Kashmir, and in the following decade. Many of these groups were based in or around Lahore and recruited from parts of Punjab state, as well as the regions along the border with Afghanistan. Most were either Deobandi, the hard-line school associated with the Afghan Taliban, or 'Wahhabi', and their religious outlook contrasted dramatically with the more folksy, Sufi-influenced Islam of most Kashmiris. They were, however, funded, trained and often directed by Pakistan's secret services which for decades had used irregular proxy forces to offset its conventional military disadvantage against its hostile neighbour India. The two nations had fought four wars since achieving their independence from Britain in 1947 and Pakistan had lost all of them. • **10**. This is the Red Mosque, where female students would later declare their support for ISIS. Officials at the mosque have denied seeing Merah, though admit that many foreigners do visit them; however, the young Frenchman repeatedly sent emails from a luxury hotel a few hundred yards from their establishment. • **11**. 'Mohamed Merah, un loup pas si solitaire', Yves Bordenave, *Le Monde*, 23 August 2012. 'How did Mohammed Merah become a jihadist?', Paul Cruickshank and Tim Lister, CNN, 26 March 2012. 'Le tueur présumé de Toulouse aurait fait la guerre avec les Talibans', Jacques Follorou, *Le Monde*, 21 March 2012. 'Au Pakistan, Mohamed Merah à l'école du crime', Patricia Tourancheau and Luc Mathieu, *Libération*, 6 April 2012. • **12**. *Libération*, transcript. • **13**. *Libération*, transcript. • **14**. 'Merah. Les errements de la DGSE', Delphine Byrka, *Paris Match*, 6 February 2013, • **15**. A first statement from the group was incoherent and full of odd inaccuracies. A second statement ten days after the death of Merah gave details of his training which matched those he had described to police negotiators, mentioned the gift of the camera, and displayed a knowledge of his personality and appearance. Author interview, French intelligence official, Paris, July 2014. • **16**. *Libération*, transcript. • **17**. 'Souad Merah, "pilier de la famille" et cauchemar de l'antiterrorisme', Doan Bui et Olivier Toscer, *L'Obs*, 2 November 2011. See Merah and Sifaoui, *Mon frère*. • **18**. Eric Pelletier and Jean-Marie Pontaut, *Affaire Merah: l'enquete*, Michel Lafon, 2012. 'Les lectures glaçantes d'Abdelkadr Merah', *Le Parisien*, 12 April 2013. • **19**. Merah and Sifaoui, *Mon frère*. • **20**. 'Souad Merah', Bui and Toscer, *L'Obs*. • **21**. Merah and Sifaoui, *Mon frère*, chap. 2. • **22**. 'Souad Merah se dit "fière" de son frère', *Le Monde*, 10 November 2012 • **23**. Merah and Sifaoui, *Mon frère*, chap. 13. 'Quel est le vrai visage de Souad Merah?', *Le Point*, 14 November 2012. • **24**. It seems likely that Tamerlan Tsarnaev, though gravely wounded already, was actually killed by injuries sustained when hit by the car being driven by his brother as the latter fled.

See the account in the (fairly cursory) report: 'The road to Boston: Counterterrorism challenges and lessons from the Marathon Bombings', House Homeland Security Committee Report, March 2014. • **25**. A possible exception might be a Lebanese immigrant who opened fire on a van carrying Orthodox Jewish students on Brooklyn Bridge in 1994, though he was not convicted of terrorism offences. • **26**. See Burke, *The 9/11 Wars*, pp. 383, 387. • **27**. According to one study, most of the Islamic extremist terrorist plots uncovered since 11 September 2001 never moved beyond the discussion stage. Only ten had what could be described as an operational plan, and of these, six were FBI stings. Another analysis found that nearly three-quarters were entirely home-grown. Seth Jones, 'Stray Dogs and Virtual Armies: Radicalization and Recruitment to Jihadist Terrorism in the United States Since 9/11', Seth Jones, RAND Corporation, 2011. • **28**. A few appeared more authentically dangerous. Just a month before the Boston bombing, a convert was arrested after he attempted to detonate a (fake) bomb in an SUV outside a bank in California. • **29**. Masha Gessen, *The Brothers: The Road to an American Tragedy*, Riverhead Books, 2015. • **30**. The Caucasus is a region with a history of Islamic militancy dating back to the time when it was incorporated into the expanding Russian empire in the late nineteenth century. As so often, resistance to the invaders was mobilised under a religious flag and using religious networks, bringing disparate local forces together to fight occupiers. Islamic traditions remained moderate, closer to the pluralist, tolerant practices in much of South Asia at the time, then the rigour of the Gulf and the influences of the religious revival of the 1970s and 80s across the Islamic world were partly deflected by Soviet rule. When this ended, and Chechnya and neighbouring Dagestan declared their respective independence in the early 1990s, the changes in the rest of the Muslim world began to have an impact, but the real radicalising force was wars fought by Moscow to retain authority over Chechnya and repel Islamic militants from Dagestan. These were atrociously violent and brutal struggles with widespread human rights abuses by both sides, high civilian casualties and tremendous destruction. But there is no real link between these conflicts and the eventual radicalisation of the Tsarnaevs, or if there is, it is very indirect. • **31**. Quite what prompted this is one of the many parts of their story which remains unclear. They claimed persecution as ethnic Chechens, but experts deem this improbable. Another possibility is that Anzor, who eked a living as a mechanic and by shifting semi-legal goods to and from Russia, had run foul of a gang of violent criminal smugglers who abducted and tortured him. A third is that they simply wanted a better life. See Gessen, *The Brothers*, for the best account. Also 'Fall of the house of Tsarnaev', *Boston Globe*, 15 December 2013. • **32**. 'Jahar's world', Janet Reitman, *Rolling Stone*, 17 July 2013. • **33**. 'Fall of the house of Tsarnaev', *Boston Globe*. • **34**. 'Family matters: Dzhokhar Tsarnaev

and the women in his life', Michele McPhee, *Newsweek*, 16 October 2014.
• **35**. Zubeidat Tsarnaev's refusal to work with men has been widely reported.
Some have challenged it, however. See Gessen, *The Brothers*. 'Fall of the
house of Tsarnaev', *Boston Globe*. • **36**. 'Boy at home in U.S. swayed by one
who wasn't', Erica Goode and Serge F. Kovaleski, *New York Times*, 19 April
2013. • **37**. 'Fall of the house of Tsarnaev', *Boston Globe*. • **38**. 'Turn to religion
split suspects' home', Alan Cullison, Paul Sonne, Anton Troianovski and
David George-Cosh, *Wall Street Journal*, 22 April 2013. • **39**. These relied on
leaks from Russian security services who had warned the FBI in 2011 that
Tamerlan was a security risk after reportedly overhearing his mother mention
her son's readiness to die as a martyr. Shortly afterwards, the Russians told
their counterparts, Zubeidat had urged her son to go to Palestine, though
for what purpose is unclear, and they feared that having failed to fulfil one
maternal order to join 'the jihad', Tamerlan would try to join another. He
and his parents had then been interviewed. US agencies subsequently closed
the investigation, having decided the Russian fears were baseless. • **40**. He
did not, apparently, fit in very well there, seen as a showy and suspicious
foreigner. 'Dagestan Islamists were uneasy about Boston bombing suspect',
Alan Cullison, *Wall Street Journal*, 9 May 2013. Gessen, *The Brothers*. 'Dagestan
and the Tsarnaev brothers: The radicalisation risk', Tim Franks, BBC, 24
June 2013. 'Fall of the house of Tsarnaev', *Boston Globe*. U.S. House of
Representatives Committee on Homeland Security, 'Homeland Security
Committee Releases Report on Boston Marathon Bombings', 26 March 2014.
• **41**. 'Jahar's world', *Rolling Stone*. • **42**. 'Family matters', *Newsweek*. • **43**.
'Boston bombing suspect was steeped in conspiracies', Alan Cullison, *Wall
Street Journal*, 6 August 2013. 'A family terror: The Tsarnaevs and the Boston
bombing', Alan Cullison, *Wall Street Journal*, 13 December 2013. • **44**. United
States of America v. Dzokhar A. Tsarnaev, indictment, US district court,
district of Massachusetts. • **45**. https://twitter.com/Al_firdausiA. • **46**.
https://twitter.com/J_tsar. • **47**. The Tsarnaevs may well have wanted to
kill lots of people but practically speaking their bombs were of limited
destructive power. This choice may have been forced upon them by circumstances but the attack on the Boston Marathon was of a different order from
the attacks in Madrid in 2004 or London in 2005, or indeed planned by many
other US attackers over the previous four or five years. • **48**. This quote
comes from the excellent and entertaining *Carlos the Jackal* by Colin Smith,
Penguin, 2012. Clearly not all Arabs are Muslim, but the point remains a
valid one. • **49**. Statistics from the database of suicide attacks run by the
University of Chicago project on security and terrorism. The surge in the
first half of the decade was in part due to a massive wave of suicide bombing
in Israel. • **50**. *Libération*, transcript. • **51**. Of course, common elements such
as suicide bombings or executions were not always present in conspiracies

or attacks. Despite the spread of these global tropes of violence, much remained locally specific. The vast majority of terrorist operations over the last decade or so have occurred within a couple of miles of the homes of the attackers, or within a short journey, and use local materials and follow local habits that are not necessarily exclusive to Islamic extremists. So, for example, the formal indictment of the Tsarnaevs refers to their bombs as improvised explosive devices, of which, official statistics show, 172 were built and used across the US in the six months before the Boston attacks, largely in pranks, acts of vandalism or other crime. Gordon Lubold, 'IEDs hit the US more than you think', *Foreign Policy*, 17 April 2013. • **52**. As bin Laden himself said in 2010, writing to a senior commander, 'the wide-scale spread of jihadist ideology, especially on the Internet, and the tremendous number of young people who frequent the jihadist websites is a major achievement for jihad'. Harmony Document SOCOM-2012-0000019, pp. 9–10. 'The Abbottabad Documents: The Quiet Ascent of Adam Gadahn', CTC, 22 May 2012. • **53**. The nature of other attacks elsewhere in Europe reinforced the same conclusions. These included one in Hamburg and one in Stockholm. The attacker in the former had suffered periods of mental illness and was heavily influenced by Internet sites. The one in the latter had spent ten years in the UK, where he had been known to be involved with extremists in the city of Luton, and then, like Merah, had been trained somewhere overseas, probably in the Middle East. In both cases, the attacker had some links to a broader network, online in the case of the German, and less virtually for that in Stockholm. • **54**. 'Who is Mehdi Nemmouche, and why did he want to kill Jews?', Marc Weitzmann, *Tablet*, 15 July 2014. 'Jewish museum shooting suspect "is Islamic State torturer"', Kevin Rawlinson, *Guardian*, 6 September 2014. • **55**. 'Foreign fighter total in Syria/Iraq', ICSR blogpost. • **56**. The biggest contingent was French: various estimates of between 800 and 1,500 people living in France had joined the jihadi cause in Syria or Iraq or were planning to. About a hundred French citizens or residents had died in terrorist ranks in Syria and Iraq by May 2015. 'Plus de 100 jihadistes partis de France tués en Syrie et en Irak', *Libération*/AFP, 3 May 2015 • **57**. 'Muslim fundamentalist who was jailed in Britain for saying gays should be stoned to death kills eight in ISIS suicide attack', Lucy Osborne and Paul Bentley, *Daily Mail*, 8 November 2014. • **58**. 'Inside the mind of a British suicide bomber', James Harkin, *Newsweek*, 12 November 2014. • **59**. Most were dead by October 2014. • **60**. 'My brother, the suicide bomber: why British men go to Syria', Randeep Ramesh, *Guardian*, 26 July 2014. • **61**. *Dabiq*, vol. 3, August 2014. • **62**. 'Why the British jihadis fighting in Syria and Iraq are so vicious', Shiraz Maher, *Daily Mail*, 21 August 2014. • **63**. 'Emwazi and the London schoolmates who became militant jihadis', Ian Cobain and Randeep Ramesh, *Guardian*, 27 February 2015. Emwazi has not given any clear indication either way in communications with his family. • **64**. Other rappers too, from other countries, notably Deso Dogg, a rapper from Berlin's Kreuzberg neighbourhood. • **65**. 'Parents of Muslim fanatic who died in Syria after bragging about his "5-star jihad" are released on bail after arrest on suspicion of Syria related terror offences', Steph Cockroft, *Mail* Online, 15 October 2014 • **66**. 'Twin schoolgirls who ran away to Syria named as star pupils', Miranda Prynne, *Daily Telegraph*, 9 July 2014. • **67**. 'Enquête: comment Souad Merah a préparé son départ en Syrie', Thibault Raisse, *Le Parisien*, 13 May 2015. • **68**. 'Kabir Ahmed, the Derby jihadi, claimed he would "sacrifice my children 100 times"', David Barrett and Lyndsey Telford, *Daily Telegraph*, 9 November 2014. 'Briton Ifthekar Jaman "killed fighting in Syria", family says', BBC, 17 December 2013. • **69**. Actually Merah had only killed two, and badly injured a third, though he did not know it. *Libération*, transcript.

CHAPTER 9

1. 'Reflections on terrorism', Walter Laquer, *Foreign Affairs*, 1986. • **2**. Academics talk of the confusion of the normative and the technical meanings of the word. See Peter R. Neumann, *Old & New Terrorism*, Polity Press, 2009, for a useful discussion. • **3**. The total does not include the dead bombers in 2005. • **4**. Max Weber made the now famous argument about the formation of the modern state in a lecture entitled 'Politics as a Vocation' in 1918 in which, analysing a statement by Leon Trotsky that every state is founded on force, he suggested a state is a 'human community that [successfully] claims the monopoly of the legitimate use of physical force within a given territory'. • **5**. For the Assad regime to roll back IS, one essential element would obviously have to be present: the desire to do so. • **6**. Interrogation report of Areeb Majeed, Mumbai, author collection. 'Dynamic Stalemate', Lister, p. 17. • **7**. Rana Abou Zeid, *The Jihad Next Door: The Syrian Roots of Iraq's Newest Civil War*, Politico, 2014. The second caliph, Omar, was known as 'al-Farouq', the just. • **8**. 'Homeward bound?', Daniel Byman and Jeremy Shapiro, *Foreign Affairs*, November/December 2014. • **9**. United Nations Al-Qaida Sanctions Committee report on foreign fighters, May 2015. 'Should I stay or should I go? Explaining variation in Western jihadists' choice between domestic and foreign fighting', Thomas Hegghammer, *American Political Science Review*, vol. 107, No. 1, February 2013. Author interviews with United Nations, British, French, US and Canadian security officials, in London, Paris, Delhi and by telephone, 2014, 2015. The wording of a report by Europol 2014 made it clear quite how difficult judging the threat posed by such men was. 'In the wake of the Syrian conflict, the threat to the EU is *likely* to increase exponentially,' it said, making clear the danger was only a probability, but still far from certain. 'European fighters who travel to conflict zones . . . *may* seek to set up logistical, financial or recruitment cells, and *may* act as role models to individuals within extremist communities. In addition, their resolve is *likely* to have strengthened in the conflict zones, and they *may* have gained the skills and contacts to carry out attacks in the EU.' Excerpt from 'Europol TE-SAT Report 2014', European Police Office (Europol, The Hague), pp. 10–11. (author's italics) • **10**. 'Syria-related terror arrests up sixfold in UK, police say', Press Association, 23 January 2015. • **11**. Dozens according to the FBI, and no more than two hundred according to other internal US estimates. 'FBI Director: Number of Americans traveling to fight in Syria increasing', Sari Horwitz and Adam Goldman, *Washington Post*, 2 May 2014. 'U.S. intelligence officials say global threats persist from Russia, terrorists', Damian Paletta, *Wall Street Journal*, 26 February 2015. • **12**. In 2009, a network of former LeT militants plotted to attack staff of the Danish newspaper which had printed cartoons of the Prophet Mohammed in 2005 • **13**. 'American al-Qaeda spokesman urges attacks in US', Al Arabiya, 23 October 2010. • **14**. Shortly after planes from the US-led coalition began bombing IS positions in Iraq in 2014. 'Isis urges more attacks on Western "disbelievers"', Yaya Bayoumy, *Independent*, 22 September 2014. • **15**. 'ISIS claims responsibility for Muhammad cartoon "contest" shooting', Kevin McSpadden, *Time*, 5 May 2015. • **16**. Burke, *The 9/11 Wars*, p. 290 • **17**. Author interview, London, 2006. • **18**. 'Revealed: how secret papers led to ricin raid', Jason Burke, *Observer*, 17 April 2005. • **19**. 'Defector admits to WMD lies that triggered Iraq war', Martin Chulov, *Guardian*, 15 February 2015. • **20**. Hoffman, *Inside Terrorism*, pp.118–23. • **21**. Though the group took control of a dump of rotting decades-old chemical munitions in the aftermath of the seizure of Mosul, there was no indication that the stockpile had been tampered with when Iraq forces recaptured the site. 'ISIS seizes former chemical weapons plant in Iraq', Associated Press, 9 July 2014; 'ISIS and Assad wage psychological warfare with further threat of chemical weapons', Katarina Montgomery, Syria Deeply, 23 January 2015. • **22**. 'Iraqi Kurds say Islamic State used chlorine gas against them', Isabel Coles, Reuters, 14 March 2015. • **23**. The article included advice such as 'to fill buckets with uranium and swing them through the air "as fast as possible" to become a human centrifuge'. 'U.S. says it halted Qaeda plot to use radioactive bomb', James Risen and Philip Shenon, *New York Times*, 10 June 2002. 'The CIA claimed its interrogation policy foiled a "dirty bomb" plot. But it was too stupid to work', Adam Taylor, *Washington Post*, 9 December 2014 • **24**. 'British ISIS fanatics have built a dirty bomb and boast of the damage it could inflict on London', Nick Dorman and Neil Doyle, *Daily Mirror*, 29 November 2014. • **25**. 'Isis's dirty bomb: Jihadists have seized "enough radioactive material to build their first WMD"', Adam Withnall, *Independent*, 10 June 2015. • **26**. As indeed President Obama recognised in February 2015. The group, and other

Islamic extremist terrorist organisations, can do harm, but they are not 'an existential threat to the United States or the world order', he said. His view was supported by Lt Gen. Vincent Stewart, director of the Pentagon's Defense Intelligence Agency, who said in February 2015 that the greatest potential danger to the United States comes from Russia and China, not terrorist groups such as Islamic State and al-Qaeda which 'can pose us harm', but 'don't pose an existential threat'. David Cameron differs. In May 2013, he spoke of the UK facing 'a large and existential terrorist threat'. 'David Cameron puts Algeria and Mali crises ahead of EU speech', Patrick Wintour, *Guardian*, 18 January 2013. • **27**. The war in Iraq, a consequence of the 9/11 attacks, led to the deaths of between 150,000 and 200,000 people. The wars in Iraq and Afghanistan cost Britain alone £30bn, according to one estimate. '"Costly failures": Wars in Iraq and Afghanistan cost UK taxpayers £30bn', Oliver Wright, *Independent*, 27 May 2014. 'Iraq war costs U.S. more than $2 trillion: study', Daniel Trotta, Reuters, 14 March 2013. • **28**. 'US spending on Islamic State fight totals $2.7bn', BBC, 12 June 2015. • **29**. https://www.mi5. gov.uk/home/about-us/who-we-are/funding.html, https://www.sis.gov.uk/ about-us/legislation-and-accountability/funding-and-financial-controls.html. • **30**. The survey did not include the Muslim population of India, which may have influenced the result significantly, as Indian Muslims are both extremely numerous, and generally more pro-West than their counterparts in the Middle East. Nor were Muslims in the West included. 'What the Muslim world believes, on everything from alcohol to honor killings, in 8 maps, 5 charts', Max Fisher, *Washington Post*, 2 May 2013. 'The World's Muslims: Religion, Politics and Society', Pew, http://www.pewforum.org/files/2013/04/worlds-muslims-religion-politics-society-full-report.pdf. • **31**. With one exception: in Jordan 2 per cent of people said they felt favourably towards Jews, up from 1 per cent. • **32**. 'Muslim Publics Share Concerns about Extremist Groups', Pew Research Center, 10 September 2013. 'Negative Opinions of al Qaeda Prevail', Pew Research Center, 30 June 2014. 'Muslim–Western Tensions Persist', Pew Research Center, 21 July 2011. 'The Great Divide: How Westerners and Muslims View Each Other', Pew Research Center, 22 June 2006. In another Pew survey of Americans, a sample of more than 3,000 was asked to rate different faiths on a 'feeling thermometer' ranging from 0 to 100 – where 0 reflects the coldest, most negative possible rating and 100 the warmest, most positive rating. Muslims averaged 40, the lowest average by a significant margin and one below atheists. http://www.pewforum. org/2014/07/16/how-americans-feel-about-religious-groups/. • **33**. 'American Attitudes Toward Arabs and Muslims', Arab American Institute, poll conducted on 27–29 June 2014, accessible at http://www.aaiusa.org/reports/ american-attitudes-toward-arabs-and-muslims-2014. '13 years after 9/11, anti-Muslim bigotry is worse than ever', Dean Obeidallah, *Daily Beast*. 'Americans' attitudes toward Muslims and Arabs are getting worse, poll finds', Sabrina Siddiqui, *Huffington Post*, 29 July 2014. • **34**. *Dabiq*, vol. 7, February 2015, pp. 55–6. • **35**. 'Un ticket pour le jihad', Patricia Tourancheau, *Libération*, 21 February 2005. 'C'est écrit que c'est bien de mourir en martyr', Patricia Tourancheau, *Libération*, 8 January 2015. Bruce Hoffman and Fernando Reinares, eds, *The Evolution of the Global Terrorist Threat: From 9/11 to Osama bin Laden's Death*, Columbia University Press, 2014. Filiu, *Apocalypse in Islam*. •**36**. 'Les frères Kouachi, Boumeddiene, Coulibaly . . . Comment ils ont basculé', *Journal du Dimanche*, 12 January 2015. • **37**. 'Inside Europe's largest prison', Danny Shaw, BBC, 18 March 2008. • **38**. 'Coulibaly, un voyou devenu jihadiste', Sylvain Mouillard and Willy Le Devin, *Libération*, 27 January 2015; 'Charlie Hedbo attackers: born, raised and radicalised in Paris', Angelique Chrisafis, *Guardian*, 12 January 2015. • **39**. 'La sanglante dérive de la bande islamiste des Buttes-Chaumont', *Le Figaro*, 20 January 2015. • **40**. 'La dérive sanglante d'un couple djihadiste', François Labrouillère and Aurélie Raya, Alfred de Montesquiou, Frédéric Loore and Nathalie Hadj, *Paris Match*, 21 January 2015. • **41**. 'En 2005, les délires antisémites de la bande du XIXe', Angélique Négroni, *Le Figaro*, 20 January 2015. • **42**. 'Chérif Kouachi, de la prison de Meaux-Chauconin à l'attentat de Charlie Hebdo', *La Marne*, 20 January 2015. • **43**. Including at least one to Yemen to study in a well-known Islamic school in 2009 and 2010. With hindsight, this was a mistake as it is almost certain that the contacts established in Yemen on these earlier journeys facilitated the later connection with AQAP. • **44**. 'La longue dérive de Saïd et Chérif Kouachi', Christel De Taddeo and Antoine Malo, *Journal du Dimanche*, 12 January 2015. • **45**. '"On ne tue pas pour un dessin": le témoignage des femmes Kouachi', *Le Figaro*, 20 February 2015. • **46**. See Burke, *The 9/11 Wars*, pp. 229–34. • **47**. His name was Ahmed Merabet, and he was a Muslim. • **48**. 'Amedy Coulibaly: un arsenal découvert à Gentilly', *Le Parisien*, 11 January 2015. • **49**. The Kouachis also had a loaded rocket-propelled grenade launcher, though probably not the knowledge necessary to use it effectively. • **50**. Most were killed by single shots to the head, officials said. • **51**. 'Attentats: ce que les terroristes ont dit à BFMTV', BMFTV, 9 January 2015. • **52**. Poll of 1,000 Muslims in Britain for BBC Radio 4 *Today*, ComRes, 25 February 2015. • **53**. 'Paris shootings: investigation launched into where gunmen got GoPro cameras', Jason Burke, *Guardian*, 12 January 2015. 'Amedy Coulibaly avait une caméra GoPro pendant la prise d'otages', *Le Monde,* 11 January 2015. • **54**. 'Charlie Hebdo killings condemned by Arab states – but hailed online by extremists', Ian Black, *Guardian*, 7 January 2015. • **55**. 'Saudi Arabia deplores Charlie Hebdo continued "mocking of Islam"', Agence France-Presse, 22 January 2015. • **56**. 'Islamophobic attacks rocket by 500% since Charlie Hebdo murders', Chris Harris with Agence France-Presse, Euronews, 16 April 2015. Cambridge-YouGov Survey, March 2015 was online.

INDEX